S0-BRW-948

Stephen Leacock: A Reappraisal

© 1941 Karsh, Ottawa

Stephen Leacock: A Reappraisal

Edited and
with an
Introduction by
David Staines

University of Ottawa Press

REAPPRAISALS
Canadian Writers

LORRAINE McMULLEN
General Editor

Canadian Cataloguing in Publication Data

Main entry under title:
  Stephen Leacock: a reappraisal

(Reappraisals, Canadian writers; 12)
Bibliography: p.
ISBN 0-7766-0180-6 (bound).-
ISBN 0-7766-0146-6 (pbk.)

1. Leacock, Stephen, 1869-1944–Criticism
and interpretation. 2. Leacock, Stephen,
1869-1944–Bibliography. I. Staines, David,
1946- II. Series.

PS8523.E15Z88 1986 C818'.5209 C87-090062-5
PR9199.3.L367Z88 1986

Manuscript facsimiles courtesy of the Stephen
Leacock Memorial Home, Orillia, Ontario
Cover design by Gregory Gregory, Ottawa
Printed and bound in Canada

Contents

Introduction

DAVID STAINES

"**P**ersonally," Stephen Leacock declared in his preface to *Sunshine Sketches of a Little Town* (1912), "I would sooner have written *Alice in Wonderland* than the whole *Encyclopedia Britannica*." Yet the worlds represented by *Alice* and the *Encyclopedia*, seemingly light years apart, are central to an understanding, appreciation, and assessment of the many worlds that commanded the attention of Stephen Butler Leacock (1869-1944).

Humorist and humanist, economist and educator, professor and pundit, Leacock devoted his life to education, first through his classrooms (at Upper Canada College in Toronto and later at McGill University in Montreal), then through his writings on history, economics, and political science, and finally, and perhaps most enduringly, through his volumes of humour. "Humour is essentially a comforter," he maintained, "reconciling us to things as they are in contrast to things as they might be."

In his own time, Leacock was the most famous Canadian author both at home and abroad. Sales of his books of humour, as well as his textbooks, were phenomenal. In 1906, for example, he published *Elements of Political Science*, which was translated into nineteen languages; this single textbook remained its author's greatest moneymaker.

Leacock has been the subject of biographical studies. His niece and secretary, Barbara Nimmo, wrote an affectionate reminiscence of her uncle shortly after his death in 1944, and another niece, Elizabeth Kimball, published her recollections, *The Man in the Panama Hat*

(1970). Allan Anderson continued the tradition of reminiscences with *Remembering Leacock* (1983), an interesting collection of reflections and anecdotes by many of Leacock's relatives, friends, and colleagues.

Ralph L. Curry's *Stephen Leacock: Humorist and Humanist* (1959) offered the first comprehensive biography, focusing, as its title suggests, on Leacock as humorist and humanist. David M. Legate's *Stephen Leacock* (1970) is a more prejudiced account of Leacock's life. Albert and Theresa Moritz's *Leacock: A Biography* (1985) adds little to the earlier biographical studies.

Stephen Leacock: A Reappraisal addresses the multifaceted career of this complex individual. The collection of essays originated in the Leacock Symposium, which was held under the auspices of the Department of English at the University of Ottawa on April 26-27, 1985. The University of Ottawa initiated its symposium series in 1973 as a means of directing attention to Canadian authors meriting reassessment. The Leacock Symposium was designed to approach its subject from the variety of perspectives demanded by his many careers. Although Leacock's lasting fame rests on his humorous writings, the other dimensions of his long and distinguished life are central to an understanding of his place in Canadian history. The following essays begin to sketch a portrait of a remarkable individual who left his distinctive mark in many areas of national and international concern.

Fifteen years ago, Mordecai Richler reflected on the enviable position of Canadian writers:

> Myth-makers are urgently needed; and, furthermore, applicants needn't be unduly inhibited. The young writer, for instance, who is settling down to a novel in the Maritimes, hasn't the ghost of Faulkner peering over his shoulder. Henry James didn't come before. Or Twain. Or Fitzgerald. If the literary house is haunted, it's only by the amiable Leacock, the dispensable de la Roche. For the rest, the tradition has yet to be made. It's virgin land. Up for grabs.

In the opening essays of this collection, three distinguished Canadian writers, Timothy Findley, Erika Ritter, and Guy Vanderhaeghe, look back at the figure of "the amiable Leacock," paying homage, with affection and laughter, to Leacock the humorist. In "Riding Off in All Directions: A Few Wild Words in Search of Stephen Leacock," Findley returns to his years as an actor to examine the theatrical dimensions of Leacock's written language. Wit, parody, and perhaps even flattery, if imitation is indeed a form of flattery, are central to Ritter's

"Leacock and Leahen: The Feminine Influence on Stephen Leacock." And in "Leacock and Understanding Canada," Vanderhaeghe invokes his western Canadian background to explore the *particular* nature of Leacock's fictional universe.

The next four essays turn from Leacock the humorist to other professional commitments that occupied his teaching and his writing. In "Leacock and the Media," Ralph L. Curry describes, through Leacock's own words, the author's involvement in the relatively new media of radio, film, and television. Leacock as an historian of Canada is the focus of Ian Ross Robertson's essay on "The Historical Leacock." Myron J. Frankman studies "Stephen Leacock, Economist: An Owl Among the Parrots," placing him in his historical context and evaluating his influence in the world of economics.

In his literary essays, Leacock could present himself as a Canadian, an American, an Englishman, or even as a combination of two or three of these nationalities. In "Imperial Cosmopolitanism, or the Partly Solved Riddle of Leacock's Multi-National Persona," James Steele investigates the implications of Leacock's multi-national literary persona, which is, he discovers, consistent with Leacock's political and historical doctrine of imperial cosmopolitanism.

The multi-national persona that Steele discusses provides a natural transition to Beverly Rasporich's study of "Stephen Leacock, Humorist: American by Association." Her essay places Leacock's humorous writings in the tradition of American humour, yet concludes that Leacock's humour is British by heredity, American by association, and, at the very least, Canadian by experience.

Among Leacock's many volumes of humour, *Sunshine Sketches of a Little Town* is universally acknowledged to be his masterpiece. The little town of Mariposa has captured the attention, the affection, and the laughter of generations of readers. A trio of essays approach the book from different and differing angles. In "Religion and Romance in Mariposa," Gerald Lynch begins with an examination of Leacock's structural revisions and discovers a more highly organized and complex work than is usually acknowledged; for Lynch, the centre of the book is the opposition between the virtues of romance and love and the failure of the town's institutionalized religion. In "The Roads Back: *Sunshine Sketches of a Little Town* and George Elliott's *The Kissing Man*," Clara Thomas explores Mariposa through a comparison with the later small Ontario town of Elliott's book. And Ed

Jewinski brings the vocabulary and vision of post-structuralism to his reading, "Untestable Inferences: Post-Structuralism and Leacock's Achievement in *Sunshine Sketches of a Little Town.*"

"The Achievement of Stephen Leacock" presents the final reflections of four senior scholars of Canadian literature. Alec Lucas places Leacock in the context of McGill University, while Malcolm Ross suggests Leacock's importance to the New Canadian Library and, as a consequence, to the introduction of Canadian literature courses in schools and colleges. Glenn Clever and R. L. McDougall return to the irony, the laughter, and the humanity that inform Leacock's vision.

Stephen Leacock: A Reappraisal, the first collection of essays devoted to Leacock, closes, appropriately, with Ralph L. Curry's "Stephen Leacock: The Writer and His Writings," the first complete bibliography of Leacock's publications. Its length is a final testimony to the range of Leacock's knowledge and interests.

Riding Off in All Directions: A Few Wild Words in Search of Stephen Leacock

TIMOTHY FINDLEY

You may wonder why it is that I, who am the author of books with titles such as *The Wars* and *Famous Last Words, Not Wanted on the Voyage* and *The Last of the Crazy People*, am writing in celebration of Stephen Leacock. The name of Leacock, after all, is synonymous with laughter, while my name (if I have one) is synonymous with madness, mayhem, and Armageddon. If the connection between Professor Leacock and myself seems somewhat forced—to say the least—perhaps I can explain.

I have been living for the last twenty-one years on a farm just forty miles south of Orillia, where Leacock lived. But that is not the connection. On the other hand, there is some connection in the fact that the farm where I live is barely seventeen miles to the east of Sibbald's Point, where Stephen Leacock is buried. All one needs to know is that the burial site at Sibbald's Point and the homestead site at Orillia face each other on opposite sides of Lake Simcoe.

Now, it just so happens that, back in the days when Leacock was up there alive near Orillia, my *so-called* Grandfather Findley (the *so-called* will be explained when I come to the end of this connection) had his summer residence down near Sibbald's Point. If they had possessed the right kind of telescopes, they could have seen each other fishing. But that is not the connection.

The next thing one needs to know, in order to make the connection between myself and Stephen Leacock, is about the graveyard at Sibbald's Point: the graveyard where Leacock is buried but where my *so-called* Grandfather Findley is *not* buried: *not* buried, because he *refused* to be buried there. Perhaps with good reason, from his point of view—again, as you will see when I come to the end of this.

The connection continues. In the graveyard at Sibbald's Point, where my *so-called* Grandfather Findley refused to be buried, lie not only the remains of Stephen Butler Leacock but also the remains of little Maisie Roach, otherwise known as *Mazo de la Roche*.

Now, what follows is of immense importance. What is it that is wrong with Canadian literary sleuths that they have failed to discover, and therefore have failed to reveal, the story of the love affair between Mazo de la Roche and Stephen Leacock?

Do they think it is by pure and simple chance these two are buried within kissing-distance of one another? Well, let me tell you, it is not by chance.

For anyone who cares to think about it, the *grande affaire* between Stephen Leacock and Mazo de la Roche is as plain as the nose on Cyrano's face. The trouble is—and has been for far too long—that nobody *has* cared to think about it. And, therefore, our great Canadian literary sleuths have missed the multitude of clues that are virtually massed before them, for all to see, in the works of both Leacock and de la Roche.

Consider: *Jalna*, where Mazo's Whiteoaks family lives, and *Mariposa*, where Stephen's best-known characters live, are both on the shores of a lake.

Consider: the year 1912. It was in that year that old Granny Whiteoaks had all her teeth removed. And it was also in that year that Stephen Leacock's pen gave birth to all the citizens of *Mariposa*. I ask you: is this not Cadmus sowing the dragon's teeth in order to create a whole new race of men?

Well, one could go on and on and on. The references are legion . . . .

How many readers are aware that *Jalna* is the word for *butterfly* in an obscure Hindi dialect?

How many readers are aware that *Mariposa* is the word for *butterfly* in Spanish?

How many readers are aware that early in my acting career, I played the role of Peter Pupkin on television, in a weekly series adapted from Stephen Leacock's *Sunshine Sketches of a Little Town*—his tales of *Mariposa*?

How many readers are aware that, later, in the early years of my writing career I adapted Mazo de la Roche's Jalna epic for television?

How many readers are aware that the title of my second novel is *The Butterfly Plague*?

One last question:

How many readers are now aware of why it was my *so-called* Grandfather Findley refused to be buried in the graveyard at Sibbald's Point along with Mazo de la Roche and Stephen Butler Leacock?

This is what I have always suspected. Because the man I knew as Grandfather Findley *refused* to be buried along with Stephen Leacock and Mazo de la Roche, it is my firm belief that he had some connection with their hitherto unknown liaison, and whatever that connection may have been, given all the literary clues, I can only conclude that I am *not* descended from Thomas Findley, but from that unsuspected and illicit union of literary giants. Here before you is none other than the grandson of Stephen Leacock!

* * *

I really did play Peter Pupkin on a television series back in the 1950s, and I thought I might write a few words about that, about what it's like to be inside a Leacock character. Also what it's like to have a Leacockian character inside of you—because it works both ways.

This is true of all good characters, of course. The universal aspects have to be found inside the actor: the touchstones by which he recognizes and understands the person he is going to play. The other part—the pulling on, the getting inside of the character—can only happen once you have made the basic connections between the character and what you know of yourself.

I think that what I understood first about Peter Pupkin was the quality of his shyness. It was a seething kind of shyness that was kindred to my own: an actor's shyness. He could play all kinds of wonders to the audience in his mind—or the audience out in the dark, where he didn't have to see them—but he was absolutely mortified when made to confront real people. He blushed; he stammered; he did everything wrong. He would confess to things he hadn't done, because it was too embarrassing to admit he hadn't done them. He was also a *klutz*. It was typical of Peter that, when he went out to save the people on the stranded pleasure steamer the Mariposa Belle, he found himself in the middle of the lake, with a single oar, in the dark, in a sinking rowboat. This was very *me*. I understood Peter Pupkin at once.

Peter's greatest embarrassment was his father's enormous wealth. This was not, it so happened, a problem of my own, but it was still a problem that was fun to play. The images Leacock provides of Peter's terror that his father will arrive unannounced in Mariposa—chauffeur-driven in a mammoth touring car, trailing truckloads of servants and tossing huge sums of money into the streets—are wonderfully evoked. *Money, money, money*—all it does is get in the way! It gets in the way of your natural sense of decorum. It makes you seem brash and vulgar, as if you could buy your way through life. It also gets in the way of tragic and romantic love affairs. It was this latter aspect of his father's money that troubled Peter the most, since Peter was overwhelmingly in love, both tragically and romantically, with Zena Pepperleigh. If Zena were to discover that Peter had wealth in his background, how could he possibly ask her to marry him? She would only think that he wanted her because of his money. But, with a stroke of genius, Leacock gives Peter Pupkin a job as a bankclerk. He forces him into a situation where he is surrounded by money day and night, because Peter not only works in the Bank, he lives there. Or, rather, he lives in rooms upstairs, above the Bank. Now, the remarkable thing is, that—through this stroke of genius—all that money surrounding Peter Pupkin is not his own. It is money he can regard objectively; money he must protect; and, therefore, money he can regard with greed and parsimony on behalf of others. In this way, he has control, so to speak, of the kind he cannot exert in his father's case, namely, the control over everyone's perfectly natural inclination to take their money out and throw it around the streets as so much humanitarian largesse. Peter worries so about the human race; he hates to see it embarrass itself. But, above all, he hates to see it embarrass him.

* * *

Sunshine Sketches of a Little Town is not noted for its dialogue. The book is narrated by a character, presumably Leacock himself, who knows all and tells all, but who takes no part in the lives and events he describes. In the television series, written by Don Harron, the Narrator's role was played by the late John Drainie. What a pity a film was never made with Drainie playing Leacock and the town of Mariposa spread out around him. Drainie was—and this is not hyperbole, but simple fact—a genius; and according to everyone who ever worked with him, or who saw him work, he was the finest actor of his time in this country. His voice is inextricably mingled with my memories of playing Pupkin. Which brings me back to what I had started to say about Leacock and dialogue.

Leacock did not write much dialogue, and the dialogue he did write was largely unspeakable. His *prose* was speakable, but not the dialogue as such. From an actor's point of view, the dialogue Leacock wrote was inextricably tied to the prose that surrounded it, and the syntax could often be awkward if you tried to lift the words in quotes from the midst of the words that were not to be heard. Of course, as far as Leacock himself was concerned, he had never intended the dialogue for actors.

In the long run, this could not have mattered less. It could not have mattered less, because what he gave you—as an actor—was an absolutely clear-cut, fully rounded, and marvellous character to play. Though the words themselves were rarely provided, the manner in which the characters would speak, including the pitch and tones of their voices and the rhythms of their speech, was always perfectly clear. Speech, in theatrical terms, cannot exist without character. For an actor, to know the *person* is to know precisely how the person speaks.

Given Peter's character—with all the nuance laid out by Leacock on the page—it was easy enough to discern that his speech was probably *breathless*. Consequently, Harron wrote Peter's dialogue in short, very often unconnected sentences. In between the sentences, it was obvious that Peter himself was under the impression he had voiced the missing connective tissue, and he was under this impression because the connective tissue was being voiced in his mind. Thus, under Don Harron's hand, Peter's stammered, staccato sentences were filled with *non sequiturs*.

Consequently, Peter might say to his best friend and roommate, Mallory Tompkins: "Mal. I love her. My father. I'm going to kill myself." As you can imagine, the unspoken parts of these sentences were of some importance to Mallory Tompkins.

However, as Mallory came to know and understand Peter's ways, he also came to know what the missing words might be. "Her" must be Zena Pepperleigh. "My father" must refer to Peter's terror that his father would appear and throw his money between them. Therefore, Peter would "kill himself" in shame.

Peter was always "killing himself" and Mal got used to it, more or less—although, as Leacock wrote of this situation, "I suppose there are few people, outside of lovers, who know what it is to commit suicide four times in five weeks."

This was another reason Peter was always short of breath. Even when you are young, all that climbing onto roofs and steeples, all those wintry hours upon the bridge, poised above the icy waters, all those automobiles in front of which one is constantly preparing to fling oneself, can really take it out of you.

* * *

Leacock was a master at creating scenes: the stuff of scenes and the shape of scenes seemed, very much, to be the basis of how he worked his wonders. How he avoided becoming a playwright, I cannot tell—unless it was that he knew for a certainty the dialogue would elude him. Nonetheless, it hardly matters. The marvels of his comedy are there to be transcribed theatrically, whether the theatre be a stage, a television screen, or merely in the mind. His theatre is on the page and anyone can give it life.

God bless Stephen Leacock. I write that from the heart. With his stories and his books, his people and his insights, he has left a legacy for everyone who reads and—I must add—for everyone who writes. It well may be, indeed, that Stephen Butler Leacock is the grandfather of us all.

Leacock and Leahen: The Feminine Influence on Stephen Leacock

ERIKA RITTER

Stephen Leacock once said: "when I stand up before an audience to deliver my serious thoughts, they begin laughing. I have been advertised to them as funny, and they refuse to accept me as anything else."

I can relate to that. As a supposedly "comic" writer, I find I suffer from a lack of credibility as a serious thinker—especially when coming before an august academic body with a downright grim new appraisal of Leacock's social criticism.

Most especially when the reappraisal is as wildly radical as mine is, to wit: after having read several examples of what is supposedly Stephen Leacock's social criticism, I have come to the inescapable conclusion that these works *were written by a woman.*

But *what* woman? That was the burning question that drove me on through exhausting hours (well, minutes anyway) of research. The startling results of my investigations are presented here for the very first time.

I have incontrovertible proof to support my contention that Stephen Leacock had a twin sister. Her name was Stephanie and she was, coincidentally, born at exactly the same time he was, in 1869, and like her more famous brother, emigrated from England to Canada at an early age.

But while Stephen, the male child, was sent from Sutton, Ontario, to study at Upper Canada College and the University of Toronto, Stephanie was forced to teach herself economics and political theory at home, with the aid of nothing but a Bible, an old Farmer's Almanac, a geometry text, and a battered copy of "More Jokes For the John." But from these unlikely sources came her masterful humour, terse economical style, and astounding acumen.

Early Accomplishments

Chances are, we would never have heard of Stephanie Leacock at all, were it not for the fact that in the early 1900s, she wrote a book entitled

Elements of Political Science, followed by another called *Responsible Government*.

Attempts to get these serious texts published under her own name failed, however. Finally, she gave the manuscripts to her brother, a slow student, who was more than willing to have them issued under his male (and hence credible) name, in 1906 and 1907 respectively.

Growing Disillusionment

Looking on while her brother got credit for the books she had written did something to Stephanie. Her bitterness, anger, and cynicism are subtly reflected in her 1907 essay, "Greater Canada: An Appeal."

Aware that she would not be able to publish this work, either, under her own name, she laced the essay with feminist rhetoric and stinging social criticism. But ironically, so cleverly were the gibes woven into the work, that "Greater Canada," when published under Stephen's name, was read instead as a rallying cry for greater Canadian independence within the Empire.

It was close examination of the essay that led me to the absolute conclusion that it is indeed Stephanie's work. There are references to "ignorant colonial *boys*" (italics mine), as well as this sharp indictment of the male political establishment: "Harsh is the cackle of the little turkey cocks in Ottawa fighting the while as they feather their mean nests of stick and mud high on their river bluff." Stephanie's perspicacious anticipation of the controversies surrounding former Speaker John Bosley's redecoration of Kingsmere is, of course, hard to ignore.

Stephanie's urgent desire to see women achieve the vote, meanwhile, is reflected in such appeals as "the task is yours to solve, gentlemen. Find us a way whereby the burden and power shall fall on all alike."

Those who doubt a woman's authorship here are asked to consider the unequivocally female phrasing of such choices as "a widow's mite" and "how first to unravel the vexed skein of our colonial and imperial relations?"

New Directions

Embittered not only because her essay was misread, but also because her detested brother once again gained the credit for *her* labour, Stephanie soon determined once more to publish under her own name. Between 1908 and 1910, she concentrated on exploiting the gimmick-crazed market of the pre–World War I period by producing a couple of how-to books. Indeed, in some circles, it is believed that Stephanie Leacock may have actually invented the how-to form.

Now living in Orillia, Ontario, she first wrote a book of astrologically based calisthenics for the local inhabitants called *Sun Sign Stretches for a Little Town*. The very next year, her earlier interest in economics revived itself in a textbook that advises wealthy newlyweds on how to utilize investment techniques first employed by the French settlers of the Maritime regions. I refer, of course, to the famous *Acadian Debentures for the Bridal Rich.*

Alas, however, fame and fortune eluded Stephanie once again. The two books saw publication, but the always unscrupulous Stephen marred their selling potential by poaching versions of both titles to adorn humour books he was in the process of writing—a literary variation necessitated by the fact that, without Stephanie to ghost-write his economics texts for him, he was utterly lost.

A Bold Stratagem

Ironically, it was Stephen's unearned success as a humorist that gave Stephanie an idea that would help her own work reach a wider audience. Returning to the subversive form of feminism that characterizes "Greater Canada," Stephanie resolved no longer to fight her twin's success, but to join it.

Therefore, as Stephen continued to churn out books of humour with alliterative titles, Stephanie returned to ghosting books of social criticism for him. A close examination of the essays contained therein reveals the breadth of her dazzling strategy. Social satire, of a revolutionary type, *masquerades* as Stephen Leacock's most conservative, misogynistic, and, in some cases, even racist writings!

This technique, begun back in 1907, finds its apotheosis in the 1915 essay, "The Woman Question." Generally read as Stephen Leacock's lofty dismissal of the rights and abilities of women to earn their own livings, to choose their own politics, or in any important way to run their own lives, this essay is, in fact, Stephanie's merciless satire on fusty male attitudes. Space does not permit a detailed examination of the essay, but interested scholars are directed particularly to the sections of the work that deal with the foolishness of women in business, the futility of universal suffrage, and especially the insistent conclusion that women should be *grateful* for male guidance of their lives, and content with the housewife and mother role. This last area is one in which Stephanie's satirical genius, as well as the eerie predictive powers already alluded to, really shine, for "The Woman Question" anticipates the Total Woman movement of the 1970s so exactly as to be utterly uncanny.

Quiet Revenge

Even though Stephanie had at last found a way to ventriloquize her most radical ideas through her brother's conservative and unsuspecting mouth, she continued to resent him always for the career advantages that merely being male afforded him. Her methods of revenge were quiet but various, including her playful tendency to give his interviews *for* him, setting out to make him look silly in the eyes of his adoring public.

For example, on his inability to write a sustained narrative line, she commented (as Stephen): "I can invent characters quite easily, but I have no notion as to how to make things happen to them. Indeed, I see no reason why anything should. I could write awfully good short stories if it were only permissible merely to introduce some extremely original character and at the end of two pages announce that at this point a brick fell on his head and killed him."

Of course, the real genius of the foregoing resides in the way in which Stephanie, under the guise of whimsicality, is able to make her male chauvinistic brother utter sentiments which, in a woman's mouth, would stand out as glaring examples of so-called feminine illogic.

Even when speaking as herself, Stephanie's view of Stephen was sniffily dismissive. "Stephen was a nice boy," she declared once in a rare interview, "but he grew up to be a complete idiot. He stole the bushy moustache idea from Mark Twain, and I used to catch him practising his merry twinkle in the mirror."

What Became of Stephanie Leacock?

In the late 1920s, once Dorothy Parker had emerged in the United States to make humour writing an acceptable occupation for women, circumstances eased somewhat for Stephanie Leacock.

She was able to publish her hilariously funny send-up of the male-dominated drapery industry, *Gentlemen Prefer Blinds*. In addition, she presided over the famous Square Table lunches at the Mohawk Hotel in Orillia, with such other witty Canadian notables as Ernest Thompson Seton, L. M. Montgomery, R. B. Bennett, and the wickedly funny Dr. Frederick Banting. However, the group disbanded after its first meeting once it became clear nobody knew any quips.

But it was in the 1940s, when most male humorists were at war, that Stephanie really came into her own. Her Morning Chuckle was syndicated in many newspapers, and she is generally credited with the invention of the knock-knock joke. Unfortunately, in the conservative post-war fifties, with men back from military service, Stephanie was forced out of the front ranks of humour, and into writing lighthearted books about housewives in the suburbs coping hilariously.

Stephanie Leacock Today

At the ripe old age of one hundred and seventeen, Stephanie Leacock is still with us. She writes every day, and her lively mind is engaged by many contemporary issues.

She still resides in Orillia. When I visited her recently, she was delighted to welcome me, as the Canadian literature buff who had finally stumbled upon her existence.

Her mind is as clear as ever, and until recently she continued to edit her economics newsletter, *The Calculator*. Last year, it was subsumed by the Orillia *Packet*—and as we know, is now called *The Packet-Calculator*.

When I spoke to her, she was eager and ready to proffer opinions on a variety of contemporary subjects. Of Brian Mulroney and Ronald Reagan, for instance, she said, "They jointly provide the answer to that age-old question of where the snakes went after St. Patrick drove them out of Ireland." And she went on to remark, "How can we trust two leaders who can't even pronounce their own names the way they're spelled?"

Later in the conversation, the old lady spoke movingly of the new technology, particularly the supremacy of digital over dial watches: "Next thing you know, they'll come up with self-tying shoelaces. Then both signal accomplishments of childhood will have been for nothing."

Stephanie Leacock wanted very much to substantiate in person my claims for her existence. But it turned out that VIA Rail schedules simply could not get her here from there. When I broke the bad news to her, she accepted it with typical humorous philosophy. "Stephen's behind it someplace," she averred. "Trust me on that. He gets a symposium in his honour, and as usual, all *I* get is the fuzzy end of the lollipop. I swear that man is still laughing at me beyond the grave."

Perhaps, Stephanie. But at least we're all still laughing. And that was the way you always wanted it.

Leacock and Understanding Canada

GUY VANDERHAEGHE

This essay should begin with an explanation. I came to read Stephen Leacock late, beyond the bounds of a university, and thus without benefit of supervision. Therefore, whatever I write cannot be attributed to bad teaching. Nor can I pretend to be familiar with more than nine or ten of his books. As you may already suspect, this is an apology for what follows.

The first book of Leacock's which I read was *Sunshine Sketches of a Little Town*, easily the best of the ones I know. This, I hope, entitles me to call it his masterpiece. What I discovered in its pages was that strange and exotic place, Mariposa, a town like no other I have encountered in Canadian fiction. Since I have lived all my life in the West, I am driven to wonder if in commenting on the strangeness of Mariposa I might not be raising the spectre of regionalism which so often haunts discussion of our literature, sowing confusion and dismay. Yet I am convinced that what travels under the name of regionalism is really only the result of looking at the same thing, Canada, from different angles. And I would like to suggest that we might learn something by taking a walk around the monument which Stephen Leacock has become and taking a look at him from a slightly different angle too.

In suggesting this I am not attempting to diminish that monument. No one who wants to understand our literature or our nation can disregard or dismiss Leacock. It seems to me that Leacock is central to an appreciation of both our literature and our nation. His prominent position in Canadian letters could be assured on any number of grounds. His virtues as a stylist alone would cause him to be remembered. No other Canadian has written such elegant, lucid, yet intimate prose. But Leacock is a great deal more than a stylist. He is one of the great interpreters of this country.

It was through Leacock that I came to understand a grandfather who had always succeeded in bewildering me. In turn, what I knew of my grandfather made Leacock seem more familiar and less peculiar than he might otherwise have been to someone who had spent his entire life on the prairies.

Growing up in a small town in Saskatchewan I was fortunate enough to have the benefit of the company of both my grandfathers. Each was an immigrant. One came from Belgium, the other from Ontario. It is the grandfather who seemed most foreign to me—the one who came from Ontario—that Leacock has helped me to understand.

What I perceived as his foreignness, his bizarreness, was a result of context. In a town which was almost entirely populated by men and women of Eastern and Central European stock he belonged to a tiny minority group. He had a British name. He was a Protestant. And he was animated and ruled by all the vices and virtues of old Ontario. Amid those representatives of the wretched and huddled masses of Europe, he was the only bona fide refugee from Mariposa.

What made him so odd, even in the eyes of his children and grandchildren, was that he lived by a set of assumptions that were very different from those of his neighbours. In a society which has often been loosely described as "progressive," where politics were inclined to be liberal or radical, and most people had little notion of, or interest in, ancestors and antecedents, my grandfather was one of the few people who was a loyal Tory and proud of a family tree he could trace back to what he felt were distant horizons.

In a political society my grandfather clung to his politics because they distinguished him from his fellow citizens. His politics were the tip of an iceberg of submerged values. They were a way of standing fast to his race, his religion, and everything he had been taught as a child.

Everyone else in my home town seemed to regard the vote as a way of asserting self-interest or expressing gratitude. Most Eastern Europeans supported Liberals because they were grateful for Clifford Sifton's immigration policies, while the more fiery and radical were partisans of the CCF and Social Credit. These people were not burdened by family notions of political tradition or loyalty. After all, they had not been in the habit of voting. They were the kind of citizens Leacock describes as "people whose aim is to be broad-minded and judicious and who vote Liberal or Conservative according to their judgment of the questions of the day. If their judgment of these questions tells them there is something in it for them in voting Liberal, then they do so."

Nevertheless, after reading *Sunshine Sketches* I came away with the distinct impression that the body politic of Mariposa was leavened by voters of sterner principles, those who were, to quote Leacock, "Liberals or Conservatives all their lives and are called dyed-in-the-wool Grits or old-time Tories and things of that sort."

What differentiated my grandfather from so many of his fellow townsmen was that he followed this fine old Ontario tradition of being born with one's politics decided. Any change in allegiance dictated by a consideration of self-interest would have been an apostasy too horrible to be contemplated. His motivation was not really political, but tribal. My other grandfather, my Belgian grandfather, approached voting with an alacrity that stupefied my British grandfather. My Belgian grandfather had been, in rapid succession, a CCFer, a Liberal, and even once a Conservative. When he had run through all the parties he went back to the beginning and started all over again. That is not to say that he did not demonstrate a passionate commitment to whatever party temporarily harboured him, but then it would adopt some misguided policy such as an increase in the tax on pipe tobacco and he would be forced to withdraw his support.

My British grandfather had no difficulties in this respect. He knew he was a Conservative because he had been born a Conservative. He liked things to be settled this way. In his mind it was a noble arrangement which had served well his father, his father's father, his father's father's father, and so on, back into the mists of time that presumably shrouded that neolithic Conservative from whose loins they had all proceeded. Nor was he blind to the defects in this system. He recognized and felt them. Particularly when he didn't agree with the party's policies, or hated the man nominated to carry the colours in his riding, or thought the party leader was an imbecile. But putting those things aside my grandfather was always proud to be a Conservative.

As far as I could see he got nothing from this loyalty, except a sense of who he was. He was like Leacock who wrote, "I belong to the Conservative party, but as yet I have failed entirely in Canadian politics, never having received a contract to build a bridge, or make a wharf, nor to construct even the smallest section of the Transcontinental Railway." At one point in his life such political success appeared to be within his grasp. After a Conservative electoral triumph my grandfather had hopes of obtaining a clerkship in the local Liquor Board store, but the party, swayed by higher considerations, gave the job to somebody's cousin. Thirty years after the fact Grandfather was still grumbling about the injustice of it all. What the poor innocent did not see was that the party knew he was a Mariposan Conservative and, like Judge Pepperleigh, no more capable of switching party allegiances than a leopard is of changing its spots. So why would anyone be dumb enough to buy support that did not need to be bought?

When election time rolled around my grandfather would breathlessly report that the Lawyer Mackenzie and the Doctor Mackenzie had told him they were voting Conservative, as if this news assured a Conservative sweep of the town. What he could not seem to comprehend was that he and my grandmother, the Mackenzies and their wives, the British element as it were, only accounted for six votes. What about all those Liberal Hungarians, Czechs, and Ukrainians? The truth was that my grandfather could not see them. Not really. Or if he did, he assumed they could be appealed to and touched in the ways he was, and of course they could not. They had been shaped by different circumstances.

All of this is, of course, merely a long preamble to the point that what one is capable of seeing depends a good deal on the angle of one's vision. Perhaps reflecting on my grandfather's unique perspective helped me explain something about Leacock that has always puzzled me. I had wondered why it was that a man who had lived as many years as Leacock had in Montreal never, to my knowledge, introduced a French-Canadian into his fiction. And why were there plenty of Anglican rectors and English peers but no Catholics or Jews? Montreal could certainly boast significant numbers of these last two communities.

In raising these points I do not wish to make a criticism of Leacock but to raise a point. I am not saying that we *ought* to find in Leacock's books French-Canadians, Catholics, or Jews, only that we do not. After all, a writer defines his fictional universe as much by what he excludes as by what he includes. It is not an original remark to say that writers who are contemporaries and who share a common citizenship produce very different work. Henry James is one kind of American writer and Mark Twain another. Writing at roughly the same time, these writers produced their finest work when their talents and imagination discovered what, for want of a better word, I will call their subjects. Their masterpieces proclaim to the world a part of what it meant to be American then and, by extension, a part of what it means to be American now.

The same, I think, can be said of Leacock.

What was his subject? Mariposa. And what is Mariposa? I do not think it is what the back cover of the New Canadian Library edition of *Sunshine Sketches of a Little Town* proclaims it to be in announcing that "although Mariposa can be identified as Orillia, Ontario, it is also true that it represents any small town anywhere in Canada." An orthodox opinion, I suspect.

But I don't believe it for a minute. To claim that Leacock's Mariposa *is* the Canadian small town, a generic village that can be plopped down anywhere in the country to do duty like a Hollywood set, is to misrepresent what the rest of English-speaking Canada is and to diminish what Leacock achieved in his portrait. What Leacock drew with such love and conviction is not necessarily common to us all. Leacock's small town is not Alice Munro's small town, nor Margaret Laurence's small town, nor Sinclair Ross's small town. Nor should we expect it to be. To ignore differences is to diminish Mariposa in all its glorious particularity. As Czeslaw Milosz has written in *The Witness of Poetry*, "we apprehend the human condition with pity and terror not in the abstract but always in relation to a given place and time, in one particular province, one particular country."

Mariposa is a small town of a particular time, place, and people. It is important not to forget that this is a picture of a lost world, an Edwardian town basking in a bright sunshine of confidence, peace, and stability; a town that has no inkling that it will soon send its sons to perish in the bloody mud of Flanders. We also ought not to forget that it is an Ontario town and a British town.

In some sense Mariposa is also the closest thing to a utopia that the small "c" conservative who denies the notion of human perfectibility will permit himself to dream. Here is the organic society so much applauded, a society whose members are bound to one another by common values, traditions, a longing for stability, and a belief in a deity. For a writer of Leacock's convictions and temperament this was a subject he both loved and understood. In no other of his works does his gentle humour illuminate human idiosyncrasy with a steadier light, or does the pathos he evokes seem so much a natural outcome of our common human journey.

Of course, perhaps this Mariposa he created was never more than a dream. But Leacock's dream tells me something about my country as Twain's and James's dreams tell me something about America. In *Sunshine Sketches* I am allowed to glimpse what people of a certain time and place wanted life to be. And such dreams, projected by the force of desire, have consequences far into the future.

Yet how can I, an admitted foreigner to Mariposa, offer these speculations, separated from it as I am by time, region, and perhaps even sympathy? I could offer the suggestion that the love and skill with which Leacock writes lead me to perceive these things. But I have recourse to something else. After all, I knew my grandfather. One test of the dream is to imagine him in Mariposa. I have no difficulty in doing so.

I have no doubt that my grandfather would have been completely at home in Jeff Thorpe's barber shop, as he would have been at his ease promenading the deck of the Mariposa Belle. And how gladly he would have raised his voice in a Mariposa church or a glass in Smith's hostelry. Best of all, I see him as a Knight of Pythias. His Eastern European neighbours were not given to joining fraternal organizations. And what pleasure he would have taken in fighting a *real* election, the kind they fought in Missinaba County.

It is in this fictional landscape that my grandfather appears at home to me, rather than the one he inhabited for most of his life. Perhaps this is some kind of testament to the strange reciprocity which exists between Life and Art. If it is, it suggests another way of looking at *Sunshine Sketches*, not as the embodiment of some kind of vague "Canadianism," but as a distinct and local expression. Perhaps even, to press a point, as a regional and ethnic work. Looked at in this way *Sunshine Sketches* can lay claim to being not only a fine, funny, sad book, but also a book which possesses the power to reveal one Canadian to another, even across the daunting gulfs of space and time.

Leacock and the Media

RALPH L. CURRY

Born in 1869, "the middle of Queen Victoria's reign," Stephen Leacock saw nearly all of the modern media introduced before his death in 1944. Even journalism changed to its modern mode, as he noted in more than one instance.[1] But it is the newer media of radio, television, and the cinema that are the focus of this study. Stephen Leacock was much more heavily involved in these endeavours than is generally supposed. As Mark Twain was the first significant author to employ the typewriter, Leacock may well have been the first significant author for whom these media were important.

Radio came to Leacock's attention first. His 1923 book *Over the Footlights* contained an essay entitled "Radio. A New Form of Trouble." In the beginning, like the rest of the world, he wants to know:

What is radio? I shall be only too glad if any reader of this book will write and tell me, simply and in words I can understand, what Radio is.

Let him understand at the outset that it is no use telling me that by means of Radio, I would be able, seated comfortably in my own armchair, to hear the Pittsburgh orchestra. I know it. I don't want to. Nor need he inform me that, seated comfortably in my own armchair, I can hear a speech by W. J. Bryan. I don't need to. I heard one.

Nor do I wish for information involving the use of such words as "receiving circuit," "rheostat," and "Variometer." These words are no help to me. I have tried them out and I don't get them. I have already read a little book called "*Radio for the Beginner*" and it has beaten me. I have sent away for another that is called "*Radio for Infants*" but I have very little hope from it. I know already that it will tell me that any infant nowadays, seated comfortably in his high chair, can hear the Pittsburgh orchestra. And of course it will contain what are called "directions" telling me to "insert my antennae in my ears." But I refuse to. It sounds like insults, that we used to use when I was young.[2]

The narrator here is one of Leacock's favourite poses; he is the same little man who says, "when I go into a bank I get rattled," in his most famous sketch, "My Financial Career." The piece itself clearly acknowledges radio, and five years later in *Short Circuits*, Leacock turned to the content of radio. "If We Had Only Had the Radio Sooner" parodies a broadcast of the Norman Conquest:

> Announcer: Now, folks, this is Senlac Hill, and we're going to put a real battle on the air for you, and it's going to be some battle. The principals are Harold, King of England—lift your helmet, Harold—and William, the Dook, or as some call him, the Duck, of Normandy. Both the boys are much of a size, both trained down to weight, and each has got with him as nice a little bunch of knights and archers as you'd see east of Pittsburgh. Umpires are: for Harold, the Reverend Allbald of the Soft Head, Archbishop of Canterbury; for William, Odo the Ten-Spot, Bishop of Bayeux. Side lines, Shorty Sigismund and Count Felix Marie du Pâté de Foie Gras. Referee, King Swatitoff of Sweden, ex-Champion of the Scandinavian League. Battle called at exactly 10 a.m. They're off. The Norman boys make a rush for the hill. Harold's centre forwards shoot arrows at them. William leads a rush at the right center. Attaboy, William! That's the stuff! Harold's boys block the rush. Two Norman knights ruled off for interference. William hurls his mace. Forward pass. Ten-year penalty. Quarter time.[3]

Leacock's attack is clearly more direct here. He copies the arch enthusiasm of the sportscaster, pointing out that the radio newsman frequently tries to get the same "rah, rah" effect into his broadcast.

Shortly after, Leacock became personally interested in radio. In 1931 he received an inquiry about the cost of using material from *Sunshine Sketches of a Little Town* in adaptations for radio drama.[4] Three months later W. N. DeFoe proposed that Leacock himself do a broadcast. He suggested a half-hour format, the centre of which would be a ten-minute "talk" by Leacock.[5] Interested in the idea, Leacock scribbled on the bottom of the letter, "new flap *Radio*," Leacock's signal to his niece Barbara Ulrichsen to start a new file. His response to DeFoe was a quick affirmative one in which he proposed to do some old material as well as some written particularly for the program.[6] We may only presume that Mr. DeFoe had trouble finding a sponsor, because the show never went on the air.

In 1934, Leacock made what was perhaps his heaviest commitment to radio. Joe McDougall, first befriended by Leacock when he was editor of *Goblin*, had gone into advertising. Putting together a radio show for Pompeian Hand Cream, he approached Leacock about broadcasting his own show. After some bargaining, they finally came to terms.[7] Leacock was to receive thirteen hundred dollars for twenty-six broadcasts, to be done in thirteen weeks. The shows would be done at station CFCF, at his home on Côte des Neiges, or at Old Brewery Bay in Orillia, wherever Leacock chose. Leacock was entitled to have a dinner party and bring his dinner guests as his audience to the broadcast. "I don't like talking to a box on a stick," said Leacock. Beginning on March 27 in Montreal,[8] the

first four broadcasts were done from Montreal; the last twenty-two originated from Orillia.

Joe McDougall remembers that this was not a very happy experience for Leacock or for radio. "Had it been television," said Joe, "and the
audience could have seen Dr. Leacock's genial face as he spoke, he would
have been a great success. As it was, he sounded conceited, like a man
simply laughing at his own jokes." At any rate, at the end of the thirteen
weeks Pompeian Hand Cream and Stephen Leacock were happy to part
company.

Radio, however, still wanted Leacock's services. The next year the
BBC broadcast an adaptation of "Winsome Winnie,"[9] and the following
year Hans Christian Rude negotiated for the rights to translate "Soaked
in Seaweed" for use on Copenhagen radio.[10] Gladstone Murray, formerly
a student of Leacock's and then head of the Canadian Broadcasting
Corporation, urged Leacock:

> I have not abandoned hope that you might change your mind about
> the microphone some day. . . . How would you like to experiment with
> reading some of your own shorter stories and sketches; why not revive
> "Literary Lapses" and "Nonsense Novels"?[11]

Indeed, Leacock had some other offers which he did consider for a short
time. Barbara Whitley, a radio actress, approached him in 1938, and he
wrote radio monologues for her. The manuscript of "Miss Rush Leaps at
Leap Year" has noted on its title page "written for Barbara Whitley."[12] He
commented the same year in a letter to his agent, Paul Reynolds, that the
manuscript which he enclosed, "Mrs. Easy Has Her Fortune Told," was
intended as a monologue for radio.[13] Tommy Tweed corresponded with
Leacock in 1940, arranging permission to adapt *Sunshine Sketches* for
radio drama.[14] And in 1941 Howard Reinheimer signed an agreement to
pay Leacock a hundred dollars per week while his adaptation of *Sunshine
Sketches* was being broadcast.[15]

From the beginning of radio, then, Leacock kept up with what was
going on in the medium, tried to do some broadcasting himself, and was
writing for radio. Less than a year before Leacock died, Jacques Chambrun, another of his agents, was still urging him to write more material
for broadcast.[16]

A more surprising side of Leacock's involvement in broadcasting
is the production of his work on television. There was not, of course,
much television going on during Leacock's lifetime, but in 1937 Clinton-
Baddeley wrote Leacock that his adaptation of "Behind the Beyond" had
been done by BBC television and had been very well received.[17] In the
next year the publishing firm of John Lane, in its semi-annual statement
to Leacock, reported royalties due him of two pounds, twelve shillings
and sixpence for a television performance of "The Raft" and a similar
amount for a broadcast of "Behind the Beyond."[18] World War II, of
course, very shortly stopped any further playing with so expensive a toy
as television.

Leacock's involvement in the motion picture industry was a more active one than the results would indicate. He could never quite seem to make the right connections, but he was early quite interested in movies. Family legend says that Mary Pickford, formerly of Toronto, tried to have Leacock come to Hollywood to write for Pickfair Productions in the twenties. Certainly, earlier than that, in 1915, a communication from John Lane noted, "amount received from Messers. Hughes Massie and Company on a/c against royalties for Dramatic Movie Picture rights of 'Sunshine Sketches' 44 pounds, 16 shillings."[19]

The next year Leacock wrote in "Madeline of the Movies":

In writing this I ought to explain that I am a tottering old man of forty-six. I was born too soon to understand moving pictures. They go too fast. I can't keep up. In my young days we used a magic lantern. It showed Robinson Crusoe in six scenes. It took all evening to show them. When it was done the hall was filled full with black smoke and the audience was quite unstrung with excitement. What I set down here represents my thoughts as I sit in front of a moving picture photoplay and interpret it as best I can.

Flick, flick, flick! I guess it must be going to begin now, but it's queer the people don't stop talking: how can they expect to hear the pictures if they go on talking? Now it's off. PASSED BY THE BOARD OF—. Ah, this looks interesting—passed by the board of—wait till I adjust my spectacles and read what it—

It's gone. Never mind, here's something else, let me see—CAST OF CHARACTERS—Oh, yes—let's see who they are—MADELINE MEADOWLARK, a young something—EDWARD DANGERFIELD, a—a what? Ah, yes, a roo—at least, it's spelt r-o-u-e, that must be a roo all right—but wait till I see what that is that's written across the top— MADELINE MEADOWLARK; OR, ALONE IN A GREAT CITY. I see, that's the title of it. I wonder which of the characters is alone. I guess not Madeline: she'd hardly be alone in a place like that. I imagine it's more likely Edward Dangerous the Roo. A roo would probably be alone a great deal, I should think. Let's see what the other characters are—JOHN HOLDFAST, a something. FARMER MEADOWLARK, MRS. MEADOWLARK, his something—

Pshaw, I missed the others, but never mind; flick, flick, it's beginning—What's this? A bedroom, eh? Looks like a girl's bedroom— pretty poor sort of place. I wish the picture would keep still a minute— in Robinson Crusoe it all stayed still and one could sit and look at it, the blue sea and the green palm trees and the black footprints in the yellow sand—but this blamed thing keeps rippling and flickering all the time—Ha! there's the girl herself—come into her bedroom. My! I hope she doesn't start to undress in it—that would be fearfully uncomfortable with all these people here. No, she's not undressing— she's gone and opened the cupboard. What's that she's doing—taking out a milk jug and a glass—empty, eh? I guess it must be, because she seemed to hold it upside down. Now she's picked up a sugar bowl— empty, too, eh?—and a cake tin, and that's empty—What on earth does she take them all out for if they're empty? Why can't she speak? I think—hullo—who's this coming in? Pretty hard-looking sort of woman—what's she got in her hand?—some sort of paper, I guess—

she looks like a landlady, I shouldn't wonder if—
Flick, flick! Say! Look there on the screen:

"YOU OWE ME
THREE WEEKS' RENT."

Oh, I catch on! That's what the landlady says, eh? Say! That's a mighty smart way to indicate it isn't it? I was on to that in a minute—flick, flick—hullo, the landlady's vanished—what's the girl doing now—say, she's praying! Look at her face! Doesn't she look religious, eh?

Flick, flick!

Oh, look, they've put her face, all by itself, on the screen. My! what a big face she's got when you see it like that.

She's in her room again—she's taking off her jacket—by Gee! She *is* going to bed! Here, stop the machine; it doesn't seem—Flick, flick!

Well, look at that! She's in bed, all in one flick, and fast asleep! Something must have broken in the machine and missed out a chunk. There! She's asleep all right—looks as if she was dreaming. Now it's sort of fading. I wonder how they make it do that? I guess they turn the wick of the lamp down low: that was the way in Robinson Crusoe—Flick, flick![20]

In this piece, as in his introduction to radio, Leacock played the unsophisticated viewer who does not understand movies. But in 1919 he gives us a much more knowing movie treatment of Christopher Columbus:

Let us make the scenario together. First idea to be expressed:

Christopher Columbus was the son of poor but honest parents.

This might seem difficult to a beginner, but to those of us who frequent the movies it is nothing.

The reel spins and we see—a narrow room—(it is always narrow in the movies)—to indicate straitened circumstances—cardboard furniture—high chairs with carved backs—two cardboard beams across the ceiling (all this means the Middle Ages)—a long dinner table—all the little Columbuses seated at it—Teresa Colombo cutting bread at one end of it—gives a slice to each, one slice (that means poverty in the movies)—Teresa rolls her eyes up—all the little children put their hands together and say grace (this registers honesty). The thing is done. Let us turn back to the history book and see what is to be put in next.

". . .*The father of Christopher, Bartolomeo Colombo was a man of no especial talent of whom nothing is recorded.*"

That's easy. First we announce him on the screen:

BARTOLOMEO COLOMBO .... *Mr. Henderson*

Then we stick him on the film on a corner of the room, leaning up against the cardboard clock and looking at the children. This attitude in the movies always indicates a secondary character of no importance. His business is to look at the others and to indicate forgetfulness of self, incompetence, unimportance, vacuity, simplicity. Note how this differs from the attitude of important characters. If a movie character—one of importance—is plotting or scheming, he seats himself at a little round table, drums on it with his fingers, and half closes one eye. If he is being talked to, or having a letter or document or telegram read to him, he stands "facing full" and working his features up and down to indicate emotion sweeping over them. If he is being "exposed" (which is done by pointing fingers at him), he hunches up like a snake in an angle of the room with both eyes half shut and his mouth set as if he had just eaten a lemon. But if he has none of these things to express and is only in the scene as a background for the others, then he goes over and leans in an easy attitude against the tall cardboard clock.

That then is the place for Bartolomeo Colombo. To the clock with him.[21]

Leacock has begun to understand the idiom of film.

Leacock wrote of what was perhaps his first real encounter with a motion picture camera:

> This picture was taken with a high power (for the time) moving picture camera, by a Mr. Alexander, who came to Orillia (1920) to take pictures of me. I said to him, "Let's drive up and fish in the Black River (about fifteen miles away) where there is real scenery." To be sure of having a fish to be photographed in the act of being caught, I bought one at the butcher's store before we left. On the river at first Alexander was very careful of his camera. "This thing," he said, "cost 1000 dollars." Later when he got excited having never fished before, I called out, "Look out for your camera," and he answered, "To hell with it."[22]

In the same year in an interview in the Vancouver *Daily Province*, the interviewer commented that Leacock was modest, and he replied, "if I am modest . . . it's because I realize all too well the many things I cannot do. That keeps me humble. For instance, I cannot write a movie."[23] The production of movies was clearly on his mind. He continued to receive movie offers, and he said to one of his publishers, who passed on a request for rights, that to make a movie of "My Financial Career" all one had to do was "take the text and illustrate it."[24]

In *Over the Footlights* he parodies the captions and jump-cuts of movies,[25] and the *femme fatale* character so frequently portrayed:

> I believe I first noticed her in the moving pictures. In these she wears a shimmering, snaky kind of dress that fits her like an onion peel. Personally I know nothing of dress. In fact, my wife says I never observe it. That is an error. At the right moment, I do. And I must say that onion peel effect commands my warmest approval. The Vampire Woman wears nothing on her arms and shoulders. She doesn't need to. And her dress is generally slit up the side a good deal. This allows her freedom of movement. In my opinion she ought to have it. Freedom of movement is a splendid thing.[26]

In "One Crowded Quarter Second" he makes fun of the way movies handle time:

> The hero, for example, gets sent to the penitentiary for ten years. You see him arrested, you watch the trial (four seconds), the fruitless appeal

to the governor (two seconds), and then you see him put behind the kind of prison bars, the toast rack pattern, that they use in the movies for penitentiary.

A turnkey with a sad face and slow mournful steps (he takes over five seconds) has locked the hero in. Great Heavens! Ten years! to think that his young life—he is only twenty-eight—is to waste away for ten years behind those stone walls; and then, just as you have hardly had time to finish thinking it—he's out! And quite simple the way they do it! Just a legend or title, or whatever they call it, thrown on the screen:

AND SO THIS TRIED SOUL LEARNS IN SORROW A NEW PEACE

Yes, learns it and is out! Clear out of the penitentiary in a quarter of a second. Just by learning peace! I must say if I ever go in, I'll learn pretty quickly.[27]

And in "Done into Movies" he satirizes what happens to stories once the movies get hold of them:

THE STORY OF ADAM AND EVE
Technical Report of Its Adaptation for the Film

We have looked over this MS. with reference to the question of adapting it to a scenario. We find the two principal characters finely and boldly drawn and both well up to the standard of the moving picture. The man Adam—Christian name only given in the MS.— appeals to us very strongly as a primitive but lovable nature. Adam has "pep" and we think that we could give him an act among the animals, involving the very best class of menagerie and trapeze work which would go over big.

But we consider that Adam himself would get over better if he represented a more educated type and we wish therefore to make Adam a college man, preferably from a western university.

We think similarly that the principal female character, Eve, would appeal more directly to the public if it was made clear that she was an independent woman with an avocation of her own. We propose to make her a college teacher of the out-of-door woodland dances now so popular in the leading women's universities.

It is better that Adam and Eve should not be married at the opening of the scenario but at the end after they have first found themselves and then found one another.

We find the "Garden" lonely and the lack of subordinate characters mystifying; we also find the multiplicity of animals difficult to explain without a special setting.

We therefore propose to remove the scene to the Panama Canal Zone, where the animals are being recruited for a circus troupe. This will allow for mass scenes of Panaminos, Mesquito and other Indians, tourists, bootleggers and the United States navy, offering an environment of greater variety and more distinctive character than an empty garden.

The snake we do not like. It is an animal difficult to train and lacking in docility. We propose instead to use a goat.[28]

That Leacock considered movies a serious part of his culture is attested by a public relations brochure put out by the Graduate School of

Economics and Political Science for the 1930-31 term. On the back of the leaflet Leacock wrote, "The department is anxious to enlist the attention of incoming graduate students for the following topics as subjects for thesis work and publication," and one of the topics he mentions is "Moving Pictures in Canada (social, political and legislative aspect)."[29] It was shortly after this, of course, that Leacock tried his own hand at directing silent movies with a home movie camera. Title cards indicate at least three such films were attempted.[30] And there were negotiations for Robert Benchley to play the lead in a movie made from "My Financial Career"[31] as well as an offer, which Leacock found attractive, to write the English sub-titles for a French movie, under the English title of "They Were Nine Bachelors."[32]

But Leacock's closest brush with the movies came in 1942 with his publication of "My Remarkable Uncle." Appearing first in *Reader's Digest*, the flamboyant character of the remarkable uncle, E. P. Leacock, drew great attention from film makers. First Paramount[33] and then Twentieth Century Fox[34] asked for galley proofs of the book so they might be passed on to story editors even before publication. To one of them Leacock replied,

> I am afraid it will not interest you as it is only a piece—not a book. I have always thought the Winnipeg boom of 1880-82 would make a new setting for a book set up with a character like my uncle as a central figure.
> If you thought of expanding the sketch to a story, I could be of use.[35]

In less than a month, Leacock wrote "Boom Times" and submitted it to Dorothy Purdell, who had first approached him from Twentieth Century Fox. She sent the story to Lubitsch[36] and when no interest was expressed, she requested permission to submit it to MGM as a vehicle for Frank Morgan.[37] Still later she had negotiations with another film maker.[38]

Leacock never wasted anything he wrote, and so in 1943 in *Happy Stories*, he went ahead and published "Boom Times," which he introduced as follows:

> Some readers may be kind enough to recall a sketch which I published in a magazine two or three years ago called *My Remarkable Uncle*, which afterwards became the title piece of a book of sketches. I now take the same distinguished actual person and remove him from the cramped environment of truth to the larger company of fiction. After the opening page he parts company with his origin, and the people who surround him are, individually, fiction, although, I hope, living pictures of the time and place.[39]

But in writing to Dodd Mead about the rights, he agreed that the publisher would receive the usual percentage should any pieces be taken for further publication or use in movies. In the cryptic notes for his answer he had written, "But [not] for *Happy Stories*: longest story written specially for movie pictures—has met fine reception at Hollywood—agents say certain sooner or later."[40]

All in all, the Leacock archives contain more than a hundred and fifty letters on the subjects of dramatic rights, movie rights, and radio permissions. Leacock continued to be interested in all of them. Certainly, since his death some splendid use has been made of Leacock materials. Mavor Moore adapted *Sunshine Sketches* into *Sunshine Town* which played the Royal Alexandra Theatre in Toronto and on television. John Drainie in the early fifties did a series from *Sunshine Sketches*, in 1959 starred in "Baron of Brewery Bay" directed by Norman Campbell, and in the sixties did extensive recordings for radio of Leacock stories and the whole of *Sunshine Sketches*. Tommy Tweed did at least two television shows based on *Sunshine Sketches* in 1963 and four shows in 1970. And, of course, there was the Harry Rasky production in 1976 of "Travels Through Life With Leacock," starring Christopher Plummer and done by the CBC. The National Film Board has animated both "My Financial Career" and "The Awful Fate of Melpomenus Jones." There has been then a considerable media involvement in materials using Leacock's words or characters. It is hard to believe that there is a more significant Canadian writer who might be used by the media, and even harder to believe that there is a more significant author who is easier to adapt to radio, television, or film. There is an eminently dramatic quality about Leacock's writings. John Drainie used to say, "Leacock lines are so easy to learn because they are so sayable."

A great many people are still saying them.

The Historical Leacock

IAN ROSS ROBERTSON

The objectives of this paper are to examine the work of Stephen Leacock as an historian of Canada; to define his role in Canadian intellectual history, aside from literary history *per se*; and to suggest the value to both historians and literary scholars of a holistic approach to him as an author and thinker. The examination of Leacock's work as an historical writer will include an indication of its reputation among professional historians in the decades since his death. Several of his historical volumes have been aptly characterized by a literary critic as "very readable summaries of current knowledge and speculation,"[1] and even his best-regarded monograph was highly conventional in interpretation. It will be argued that his weaknesses as an historian should be understood as a product of the pioneering era in which he wrote and the fact that he was always more writer than researcher. Placing Leacock in Canadian intellectual history will involve a survey of what other historians have written about him, particularly his social criticism, his imperialism, and his attitude towards economics as a discipline, and the links between these aspects of his thought and his humorous writing. The case for a holistic interpretation will be advanced primarily on two fronts. There will be an attempt to situate him more precisely than other intellectual historians have done within his contemporary Montreal milieu, with particular emphasis upon his association with *The University Magazine* and the Pen and Pencil Club. Secondly, it will be argued that in *The Unsolved Riddle of Social Justice* (1920) Leacock made a serious contribution to two significant categories of thought in Canada: "red toryism" and, for want of a better term, social philosophy.

The author wishes to thank J. M. Bumsted, J. I. Cooper, A. R. Gillis, and M. Brook Taylor for their comments and suggestions.

Leacock the historian is not as well known as Leacock the political economist, and there are at least two important reasons for this. In the first place, in his academic career he belonged not to the History Department of McGill University, but to its Department of Political Economy, a fact reflected in the treatment accorded his death by the professional journals of the two disciplines in Canada. The *Canadian Historical Review* took no notice, while the *Canadian Journal of Economics and Political Science* devoted fifteen pages to him.[2] Secondly, none of his historical works became a standard book in its field, as did his successful university text, *Elements of Political Science* (1906), which was translated into nineteen languages.[3]

But Leacock did write six books on Canadian history, the first four of which appeared in two pioneering series of Canadian historical studies. In 1907 he published *Baldwin, LaFontaine, Hincks: Responsible Government*, a volume in the "Makers of Canada" series, which was designed to recount Canadian history through the biographies of leading public figures. The theme of his monograph is evident from its subtitle. When the series was reissued in 1926 a revised edition, with William Lyon Mackenzie's name added to the title, was prepared by W.P.M. Kennedy of the University of Toronto.[4] Leacock also contributed to the highly readable "Chronicles of Canada" series, which was aimed at the general public. Of thirty-two volumes he wrote three, entitled, respectively, *Adventurers of the Far North: A Chronicle of the Arctic Seas* (1914), *The Dawn of Canadian History: A Chronicle of Aboriginal Canada* (1914), and *The Mariner of St. Malo: A Chronicle of the Voyages of Jacques Cartier* (1914). Leacock did not present these books as an original contribution to historical scholarship, but they did bear witness to his versatility as an author. In the words of the *Review of Historical Publications Relating to Canada* concerning *The Dawn of Canadian History*: "That a writer whose reputation has been acquired as a humorist and a teacher of political economy should have written a book in which a knowledge of geology, archaeology, ethnology, Scandinavian folk-lore, cartography, and navigation is required, can only be regarded as a *tour de force*."[5] Aside from the revised "Makers of Canada" volume, Leacock did not produce another historical work until the last years of his life. In 1941 he published *Canada: The Foundations of Its Future*, a book perhaps most notable for its illustrations, under the sponsorship of the House of Seagram, which in his Foreword he described as "public-spirited."[6] A year later, on the 300th anniversary of the founding of Ville-Marie by Paul de Chomedey de Maisonneuve, there appeared *Montreal: Seaport and City*. Both volumes were discursive, opinionated, and lacking in new information; not surprisingly, they received damning reviews from professional historians writing in the *Canadian Historical Review*.[7]

Five of Leacock's six historical volumes are popular or general in nature, and did not make any impact on the study or writing of Canadian history by professional historians. Although J.M.S. Careless' landmark historiographical article, which appeared in the *Canadian Historical Re-*

view thirty-two years ago, cited several dozen historians, Leacock was not among them.[8] The index to Carl Berger's award-winning book *The Writing of Canadian History* (1976) contained references to Leacock as humorist, political economist, and general man of letters—yet none to him as historian. When J. M. Bumsted surveyed the genres of historical work in English for *The Oxford Companion to Canadian Literature* (1983), he did not mention Leacock, although he included sections on "the skilled amateur," "the essay," and "popular history."[9] Thus Leacock appears to be regarded by authorities on Canadian historiography as not having been a particularly significant historical writer. The one exception to the eclipse of his reputation as an historian is his "Makers of Canada" volume, *Baldwin, LaFontaine, Hincks*. It is included in the lists of sources for the *Dictionary of Canadian Biography* articles on LaFontaine, Hincks, and Baldwin, which were published in 1976, 1982, and 1985, respectively.[10] Hence, in terms of scholarly impact, it is a significant piece of work.

In the classification of *Baldwin, LaFontaine, Hincks* in terms of interpretative schools of Canadian historical writing, the fact that it is a "Makers of Canada" volume is relevant. The series as a whole is generally considered part of the so-called Whig tradition, which emphasizes political and constitutional questions, portrays history as a story of progress over time, and attributes exceptional merit to the principles of self-government embodied in the British constitution.[11] There is frequently a readiness to make judgements of good and evil, and although there is often an explicit commitment to the values of freedom and individual liberty, adherents of the Whig approach have been known to become impatient or worse with doubters. A graphic example emerged as the "Makers of Canada" set was being put together. William D. LeSueur, the author writing on William Lyon Mackenzie, did not present the rebel as a man of unmitigated virtue, and indeed found merit in those whom the Whigs considered reactionaries. As a consequence, the publisher, G. N. Morang, who was committed to the Whig perspective, and the Mackenzie family, through lobbying and legal action, suppressed the account, which remained unpublished for seventy-one years after completion. Yet it must be noted that LeSueur's manuscript was not a piece of crude invective, for as recently as 1982 an authority on Upper Canadian historiography declared it to be "the most balanced treatment of Mackenzie that we have."[12] Morang reassigned the task to a writer with a more acceptable point of view who was a grandson of the subject, and who simply revised a volume published in 1862 by his own father.[13] In such a context, Leacock's monograph was a relatively scholarly study. Leacock avoids painting the Family Compact in the darkest hues, and concedes that Tories like John Beverley Robinson could be men of integrity and patriotism. But he does share the general characteristics of the Whig approach. Early in the volume he states that in the Canadas during the twenty years after 1815 "the fact that the executive was not under the control of the representatives of the people constituted the main cause of complaint."[14] The primary focus is on the intricacies of parliamentary manoeuvring, with little examination of the linkages between political postures and social and economic forces. The admiration for British principles of self-government is open, and the portrait of Baldwin, LaFontaine, and Hincks as apostles of moderate reform is virtually unblemished; apparent inconsistencies or contradictions among the three reformers are rationalized. While neither definitive nor sophisticated by modern standards, nonetheless, for the period, the volume was a creditable contribution to Canadian historical literature, avoiding the excesses of the series and the school to which it belonged.

Before I leave Leacock the historian, it is worth noting two related points which help to explain his absence from bibliographies and historiographical studies. In the first place, Leacock, like many other historical writers of his day, was doing pioneering work which, with increasing accessibility of sources and more professional training of historians, was bound to be superseded over time. Secondly, he belonged to a generation of intellectual generalists, men who spoke and wrote with confidence on a wide range of subjects. Historian Michiel Horn has observed that "the academic intellectual of the late nineteenth and early twentieth centuries was likely to regard himself as a moral tutor to society, with a duty to state views on the large topics of the age."[15] This was a self-image which meshed well with the non-specialized nature of his research and writing. Perhaps the best example of this phenomenon was Leacock's close friend and colleague at McGill, Andrew Macphail, a professor of the history of medicine who was also editor of *The University Magazine*, a quarterly of high standards whose declared purpose was "to express an educated opinion upon questions immediately concerning Canada; and to treat freely in a literary way all matters which have to do with politics, industry, philosophy, science, and art."[16] In addition to his own field of professional expertise, Macphail wrote on everything from literary criticism to feminism, including Canadian history. He was involved, as a contributor and one of eleven associate editors, in the third major series of historical volumes to be published in the early part of the century, *Canada and Its Provinces: A History of the Canadian People and Their Institutions* (23 vols., 1913-17). Men like Leacock and Macphail were not specialists, and wrote history not because they were historical researchers but because they were writers who recognized few boundaries between academic disciplines. Hence it would be surprising if their historical writings held up after generations of specialized modern scholars had been at work on Canadian history.

So Leacock the historian does not receive much attention from Canadian historians today, either as a source or as a subject of study. What of Leacock in his other guises? If one begins with the most popular textbooks, the results are meagre. He is not mentioned in Donald Creighton's *Dominion of the North* or Arthur Lower's *Colony to Nation*, and he is only in William Morton's *Kingdom of Canada* and Edgar McInnis' *Canada: A Political and Social History* by virtue of *Sunshine Sketches of a Little Town*. But three of these volumes were originally published in the 1940s and one in the early 1960s; of the four authors, three are deceased and the fourth retired in 1959 at the age of seventy. Thus the established textbooks are not reliable indicators of contemporary trends in Canadian historical writing. During the past fifteen to twenty years it has developed in many new directions: labour history, women's history, business history, regional history, ethnic history, and so on. One of the earliest new approaches to understanding our past as a nation was intellectual history, which, in the Canadian field, received its first sustained attention in the 1960s and 1970s. As a consequence, there has been considerable research on Leacock as a commentator on current affairs, as an imperialist, as a social satirist, and as a social critic; there has also been an evident desire to establish connections among the various spheres of his activity. The results of this work may be reflected in major university-level textbooks sometime in the future. Indeed, the most recent one-volume survey, *A Short History of Canada* (1983) by Desmond Morton, departs from the practice of treating Leacock as a humorist or not at all. Morton mentions him as the author of *The Unsolved Riddle of Social Justice*, linking him to the reform impulse which seemed so strong for a brief period at the end of World War I. He brackets Leacock's book with that of a slightly younger man, William Lyon Mackenzie King, *Industry and Humanity* (1918), as part of the contemporary questioning of the *status quo ante bellum*.[17]

The first writer to attempt to tie together the humorous and the non-humorous strands in Leacock's work was Frank Watt, a professor of English literature. In 1960 he published an essay entitled "Critic or Entertainer: Stephen Leacock and the Growth of Materialism." Watt focused on *Sunshine Sketches, Arcadian Adventures with the Idle Rich,* and *The Unsolved Riddle.* He described *Arcadian Adventures* as Leacock's "closest approach to sustained social criticism,"[18] but argued that even in it he gave more attention to "incongruities within the life of the wealthy"[19] than to contrasts between wealth and poverty. In other words, he was more concerned to amuse his readers than to infuse them with a sense of indignation. Watt also argued that *The Unsolved Riddle* constituted "primarily a critique of radical idealism, an attack on the socialist answer to the 'riddle of social justice'."[20] This emphasis on the anti-socialist aspect of Leacock's book may have arisen in part from one of the angles by which Watt approached the subject; his doctoral thesis, completed in 1957 at the University of Toronto, concerned "Radicalism in English-Canadian Literature since Confederation," and it may not be surprising that, viewed from the perspective of the history of radical literature, the message of Leacock's book would seem essentially negative. In any event, his conclusion was categorical: "Stephen Leacock was a part of the prospering materialistic civilization of which he wrote; he was sometimes its critic, but always its entertainer."[21]

A decade later, historian Ramsay Cook contributed an essay on "Stephen Leacock and the Age of Plutocracy, 1903-1921" to a *festschrift* honouring Creighton. Cook asserted the importance of understanding the period in question as a time of rapid economic development and social change; among its features were the large-scale movement of Canadians from country to city, and the amassing of unprecedented private fortunes by members of the economic élite. Referring to *Sunshine Sketches* and *Arcadian Adventures*, he wrote that Leacock "knew what was happening to Canada; he made it the subject of his two finest books."[22] Emphasizing this broad contemporary context and some of Leacock's lesser-known works, Cook virtually turned Watt's interpretation on its ear: "For the most part Canadian intellectuals appear to have rejoiced in this first age of affluence. But there were exceptions, and of these the most notable because of his later eminence as a humorist was Stephen Leacock."[23] He went on to argue that "some consideration of his political attitudes . . . provides an important element in an understanding of Leacock the humorist."[24] Thus he was both assigning a greater role for Leacock as a social critic than Watt had done, and asserting the relevance of Leacock's politics to an appreciation of his humorous writing.

Cook argued that in *Sunshine Sketches* and *Arcadian Adventures* Leacock was describing contemporary Canadian society as he understood it—beset with materialism, parochialism, and unthinking political partisanship. These were also the problems he identified in such non-humorous writings as "Greater Canada: An Appeal," an article which was reprinted from the April 1907 issue of *The University Magazine* and distributed widely. Leacock states that imperialism, which he defines as "the recognition of a wider citizenship,"[25] is a countervailing force against narrowness of vision and preoccupation with self-interest. He declares that "the time has come to be done with this *colonial* business, done with it once and forever."[26] If Canada assumes her full responsibilities within the empire and becomes engaged in imperial government and defence, Canadians will be elevated in spirit. Money, the claims of the provinces, and the interests of the political parties will have less attraction. No one who has read "Greater Canada" can doubt that Leacock's imperialism was of a piece with the viewpoint informing some of his humorous writing, as he makes evident his deep distaste for the same materialism at which he pokes fun in *Sunshine Sketches* and *Arcadian Adventures*. But Cook went further, suggesting that *Sunshine Sketches* has more of a critical edge than is commonly realized. The dominion election of 1911 preceded publication of the book by only a year, and featured what many regarded as prostitution of imperialism for partisan and transparently material ends. Macphail had declared in disgust that "this parade of holy sentiments for party purposes is like using sacramental dishes for the feeding of swine."[27] If the chapter in *Sunshine Sketches* on "The Great Election in Missinaba County" is read as a commentary on popular understanding of issues in 1911, Cook wrote, it "might well be viewed as one of Leacock's most bitter satires, perhaps exceeding anything in *Arcadian Adventures*."[28] Thus he "was more than just a funny man; at least some of the time he was a funny man with a serious purpose."[29] Cook was also convincing in his statement that within the spectrum of middle-class reform in Canada, *The Unsolved Riddle* displayed a "strong reformist tone"[30] for its era. If governments had a right to conscript citizens for wartime military service, Leacock asserted, they also had an obligation to provide those same citizens with opportunity for employment in time of peace.[31] This may not have been socialism, but it was, as Cook observed, a concept of state responsibility much more advanced than anything Canadians would experience in practical terms for a long time.[32] Thus, judged within its context, *The Unsolved Riddle* was a highly progressive book—and probably not considered entertaining by those in power.

One of Cook's themes had been the relevance of Leacock's imperialism to his fiction, and in *The Sense of Power* (1970) Carl Berger gave the ideology of Canadian imperialism its first extended analysis. He linked it with the Canada First movement of the immediate post-Confederation era, arguing that in the years prior to World War I it was a form of Canadian nationalism. Among the imperialist spokesmen he examined was Leacock, and like Cook, he detected "a coincidence between the underlying values in Leacock's serious social commentary, his satire, and the ideas of Canadian imperialism."[33] He also noted Leacock's association with R. B. Bennett's New Deal broadcasts of 1935, which have been described as heralding the first "legislative assault on the corporate elite" of Canada.[34] In a subsequent article in *Canadian Literature*, Berger noted the different faces of Leacock—humorist, political economist, controversialist—and, while maintaining that all were manifestations of the same set of values, gave close attention to the non-humorous side of his work. He carefully dissected Leacock's imperialism, which he declared to be "inextricably intertwined with his social satire and his distaste for the perversions of Canadian politics . . . . For Leacock the imperial ideal meant a determined effort to accept the obligations of nationhood and to fulfill the promise of freedom."[35]

Imperialism represented a continuation of the drive to expand the sphere of self-government of which Leacock had written in *Baldwin, LaFontaine, Hincks*; indeed, in the Preface to that volume he had described responsible government as "the corner-stone of the British imperial system."[36] But although his imperialism was based in part upon a positive commitment to the Whig ideals of "progress and liberty," it was also, Berger pointed out, "rooted in a profound rejection of the country . . . . Imperialism was a means of escape—an escape from the stupefying preoccupation with materialism and the coils of partyism and race and religious wars into the higher uplands of wider activities and concerns."[37] In the mind of Leacock, who distinctly distrusted institutional and organizational remedies, imperialism was a spiritual purgative, and certainly could not be reduced to a political formula. It followed from its almost mystical quality that it could not be discredited in the eyes of adherents by exposure of weaknesses or impracticalities in particular schemes of imperial federation.

In his article in *Canadian Literature* Berger also explored Leacock's attitude towards the discipline of economics. Leacock was not a modern scholar in the sense of being committed to specialized research in particular sub-fields, and he was hostile towards the incursions of statistical methods. He did not conceive of economics as a tool of social engineering to be put in the hands of governments,

> and he remained dubious about economics as a body of solutions . . . Economics, he believed, was not a science; it was the name of a problem, the problem essentially of a socially just distribution of material goods and this was, in a profound sense, a moral and not a technical question . . . many of his stories were vehicles for expressing his social ideas and economic beliefs . . . the line between his so-called humorous stories and his serious work was blurred and indistinct.[38]

So, as an economist, Leacock was a moralist, and a moralist with more than one avenue for diffusing his views.[39] The focus of much of his writing prior to World War I was the dominant materialist ethic. The war formed a turning-point of sorts, prompting him to address the problem of social justice directly.

> For a brief moment, Leacock was inspired by the example of war-time regulation and a genuine humanitarianism, and he stood with many others on the brink of a new era. This enthusiasm and idealism, however, vanished in the early 1920's. By the 1930's he spoke less and less of a progressive movement of social control and more and more of the spectre of socialism and the dangers of restraint and regulation. The connecting link between his rejection of socialism in *The Unsolved Riddle* in 1920 and his writings of the 1930's were those stories, published in the 1920's, in which he made very clear his suspicion of restraint, restriction and regulation.[40]

Thus Berger deepened Cook's analysis by a closer inspection of Leacock's imperialism and his approach to economics. Both historians argued that an examination of his serious writings was relevant to an interpretation of his humorous works. A reasonable inference would be that a complete understanding of his humorous works was impossible without taking into account his writings as a political economist and controversialist.

In the same year that Berger's article appeared, Alan Bowker brought together a collection of writings entitled *The Social Criticism of Stephen Leacock: The Unsolved Riddle of Social Justice and Other Essays* (1973). The additional six essays, initially published between 1907 and 1919, dealt with imperialism ("Greater Canada: An Appeal"), education, feminism, prohibition, and the morality of social Darwinism. In an Introduction concerning Leacock's career and writings, Bowker presented evidence reinforcing the arguments of Cook and Berger about his aversion to materialism, the nature of his imperialism, and the relevance of his social criticism to his best humour. He took issue with any tendency to reduce Leacock to a novelist *manqué*, a potential writer of great fiction seduced by the market-place into producing repetitive pap. "If we really want to understand him we must cease to fantasize about the novelist who might have been and concentrate our attention on the social scientist who was; for it was a social scientist, not an embryo novelist, who wrote Leacock's best humour."[41] Bowker also emphasized the necessity of relating Leacock's work to its time, the importance of his social criticism in itself, and the sincerity underlying it. Referring to *The Unsolved Riddle*, he wrote that it "was not a piece of hackwork for Leacock but a vitally important task which he performed to the best of his ability, and of which he was proud."[42] He traced the roots of its reformism back to the popular textbook, *Elements of Political Science*, which Leacock had published fourteen years earlier, and even to his graduate studies at The University of Chicago. Towards the end of the text, in looking to the future, Leacock had rejected both "Individualism" and "Socialism," and noted with apparent approval the trend in advanced industrial societies towards a strong regulatory state with responsibility for social services—which he would advocate vigorously in *The Unsolved Riddle*.[43]

Upon one significant point Bowker is mistaken. The city in *Arcadian Adventures*, described in his introduction as "wholly fictional,"[44] was inspired by Montreal, whatever Leacock may have indicated to the contrary. To take only one example, but very close to home: the likeness between Plutoria University's President Boomer, a hustling classicist enamoured with his commercial contacts and obsessed with the growth of "physical plant," and McGill's Principal William Peterson, a classicist with somewhat similar predilections, is too great to be entirely coincidental. Given this and other similarities, and painful memories of Orillia's hostile response to being satirized in *Sunshine Sketches* just two years earlier, Leacock was only exercising reasonable prudence in disguising his model. This point would scarcely be worth mentioning had Bowker not claimed that Mariposa's reality and the city's imaginariness demonstrate that Leacock was still hopeful about Canadian society. The nature of and reason for this supposed optimism are not made clear, although it is reasonable to infer that Bowker means that the relatively innocuous "Mariposan" Canadians of the pre–World War I era could still escape the distasteful "Arcadian" future. If, on the other hand, the city is real and Canadian, and if, as Bowker concedes, the values of Mariposans are "fundamentally"[45] the same as those of the city, then the picture changes somewhat, and Leacock's social commentary becomes more intelligible as a totality. Holding conservative values, he was repelled by the materialism and lack of social solidarity in the urban environment where he worked. Yet from his knowledge of Orillia, where he had his summer home, he realized that the small town had adopted the mores of the metropolis and that Mariposans were dreaming the dreams of Arcadians. As Watt has written, "There is nothing admirable, nothing fine, nothing dignified, nothing sacred in Leacock's portrayal of the little town . . . . The only virtues are its sunshine and its littleness, its failure to achieve the larger vices of modern industrial urbanism, hard as it tries to do so."[46] Leacock recognized that it was too late to return to a small-town past, and in *The Unsolved Riddle* he vehemently denounced the "false mediaevalism" which harped upon the virtues of former times.[47] There could be no turning back. Once imperialism was dead—and World War I certainly destroyed Canadian imperialism as a vital force—the only means of regeneration was social reform.[48]

The six essays selected by Bowker to accompany *The Unsolved Riddle* indicate the range of Leacock's non-humorous writing prior to 1920. "Greater Canada: An Appeal," an enthusiastic endorsement of imperialism as a means towards the social and political cleansing of Canada, contains that element of Canadian self-assertion which was an integral part of indigenous imperialist ideology: "We must realize, and the people of England must realize, the inevitable greatness of Canada."[49] Three other essays drawn from *The University Magazine* deal with education, values, and social Darwinism. In one of these Leacock explores the apparent paradox of the dearth of great literature in America, a land where much formal education is going on. He finds part of the explanation in the educational system, which he compares unfavourably with that of Britain, and part in "the distinct bias of our whole American life towards commercialism."[50] So as not to be misunderstood by his readers, he reminds them at the outset that Canada is in America, and states explicitly that his comments on literature and education in the republic apply with at least equal force to the dominion. He associates commercialism with the acceptance of success as the most important criterion of appropriate conduct and with the downgrading of the old scale of absolute values. In American education these tendencies coalesce to result in organization along the lines of industrial mass production, with a corresponding emphasis upon the number rather than the quality of graduates. Perhaps most telling of all, Leacock thinks he discerns a third and deeper cause for the literary sterility of America: "It is possible that . . . literature and progress-happiness-and-equality are antithetical terms."[51] Put another way, the material comforts of early twentieth-century America may have removed the miseries and flagrant inequalities which inspired so much great literature in darker ages. This suggestion reveals an anti-modernist disposition to raise questions about the contemporary all-embracing acceptance of material progress. In the two other essays included in the collection, Leacock assails the reform movements of feminism and prohibition. For him, it is a man's world and he must be allowed his drink. The views articulated in these essays are, in a broad sense, traditionalist; although the writing is sometimes highly rhetorical, the tendency towards heavy-handed didacticism is alleviated to some extent by irony and wit.

It is appropriate that four essays in Bowker's collection were published initially in a periodical edited by Macphail, who, if anything, was more thoroughgoing than Leacock in his traditionalism. Although nominally assisted by an editorial committee drawn from McGill, the University of Toronto, and Dalhousie College, Macphail controlled *The University Magazine* from 1907 until its demise in 1920, excepting four years when he served overseas as a physician in the Canadian army. Many years later, Leacock, who had been a member of the editorial committee for the first two numbers in 1907, would recall:

> The magazine was to be conducted by some sort of board. . . . But it didn't matter, for the 'board' was virtually swept aside by Andrew, as

you brush away the chess pieces of a finished game . . . . After a meeting or two, the magazine became and remained Andrew Macphail. Like all competent men who can do a job and who know it, he had no use for co-operation.[52]

Macphail gave *The University Magazine* a sense of direction by contributing forty-three pieces of political comment and social criticism; in his mind it was an instrument for advancing "correct opinions,"[53] which predicated the importance of moral rather than materialist values, and centred on a Canada that was rural, traditional, imperial in sentiment, and, aside from Quebec, overwhelmingly British in ethnic composition. Macphail and Leacock did not always agree about specific issues and elections, but they were at one in their general attitudes towards imperialism, modern education, materialist values, feminism, and prohibition. Hence *The University Magazine* was a natural forum for Leacock, and it would seem to have been an important one. Armed with a policy of paying contributors an average fee of twenty-five dollars, Macphail attracted the best writers from English-speaking Canada, along with some from elsewhere; the latter included such prestigious figures as Rudyard Kipling and André Siegfried. Archibald MacMechan, a member of the editorial committee, would later describe Macphail's policy of always paying contributors as "revolutionary,"[54] and for purposes of comparison it might be noted that in pre-war Montreal twenty-five dollars was more than double the average weekly wage earned by adult males employed in manufacturing.[55] This put Macphail, an exacting editor, in a position to pick and choose among submissions; after his second number he told MacMechan, "It is not for what I put into the Magazine I take credit, it is for what I kept out. I had a bitter passage with two important personages."[56] Leacock evidently approved of his friend's project, for he played a prominent part in carrying it out; with ten articles, he stood ninth on the list of contributors, ranked according to frequency of appearance between 1907 and 1920.

The appeal and influence of *The University Magazine* extended far beyond university common rooms, and thus it served as an important link for Leacock and other writers with the educated public at large. The combination of high editorial standards and conservative ideology found a significant audience. At a time when the academic population of Canada numbered in the hundreds and the general population was one-third that of today, the magazine attained a circulation of nearly 6,000, a figure no comparable Canadian quarterly has subsequently matched.[57] A unique phenomenon in pre-war Canada by virtue of both its quality and its circulation, the magazine played a role similar to the journals of Goldwin Smith and Henri Bourassa: a non-partisan institution designed to influence public opinion in a particular direction. Macphail set out consciously to reach beyond the academic community, and in a letter soliciting an article from a Canadian businessman on February 1, 1907 he stated that he wished "to demonstrate that there is no gulf between university men and other intelligent men . . . . Our idea is to interest all intelligent men."[58] Although Macphail did not ban dissenting views—even publishing an article advocating female suffrage immediately preceding an attack of his own on feminism[59]—he placed his conservative imprint on *The University Magazine* as decisively as Smith and Bourassa marked *The Week* and *Le Devoir* with their respective agendas and personalities. He was his own most frequent contributor by a wide margin, and others high on the list, like MacMechan, Peterson, Maurice Hutton, and F. P. Walton, fitted in with the conservatism of Macphail and Leacock. Thus the magazine was the vehicle for a particular ideological current, conservative and imperialist.

In addition to contributing ten articles to *The University Magazine*, all between 1907 and 1914, and being a founding member of its editorial committee, Leacock became involved in the editorial management during World War I. He was for a year part of a four-man "local committee" of McGill faculty members formed to assume Macphail's duties after his departure from Canada in 1915. Peterson, the driving force within the McGill group, instituted several changes, among them devoting about fifteen pages of each number to "Topics of the Day," a series of brief commentaries on the war and other contemporary themes by individual editors or friends of the magazine. Leacock contributed several of these commentaries when on the committee, and some had a stridently anti-German tone. The articles he published in *The University Magazine* between 1907 and 1914, aside from the four collected by Bowker, concerned humour, education, and Canadian external relations, broadly defined. One was a humorous piece on the first newspaper in England and the birth of advertising; in another, "The Psychology of American Humour," Leacock examined what he considered to be the one exception to America's record of literary sterility. In the article he attributes this aberration from the norm to the intrinsically inspiring nature of American life and history, which American humour reflects. But he believes the "original impetus" of the genre to be "largely" a spent force, and given the state of education and letters in contemporary America, is pessimistic about the future.[60] In "The University and Business" he attacks what he regards as the attempt to pass off "practical" courses of study as higher education, and affirms the value of a traditional academic program for even an aspiring businessman.[61]

> The young man who has had a sound training in orthodox college studies is far better fitted to enter business than the boy who has been stuffed with the rigmarole of a bogus, commercial course. After all, the great aim of education is the acquirement of capacity,—not the ability to perform a particular mechanical thing in a particular way, but the power of turning upon any intellectual problem the full effort of a trained intelligence. It is just this power which the Arts course of a university ought to develop.[62]

The articles on Canadian external relations concerned Canada and the Monroe doctrine, American neutrality after the commencement of World War I, and the naval question. In a lengthy essay Leacock denounces the supposed protection afforded Canada by the Monroe doctrine as "the purest fiction,"[63] and in a very brief article gives vent to Canadian resentment over American neutrality. Writing about naval policy shortly after the election of 1911, he advocates "a united fleet," in which Canada would participate by providing men and ships.[64] This was consistent with the assertive sentiments expressed in "Greater Canada: An Appeal," and quite distinct from the more cautious policy of financial "contributions" to the British fleet which Prime Minister Robert Borden would soon adopt.

Since *The University Magazine* was an important dimension of Leacock's intellectual life between 1907 and 1915, understanding the people surrounding it helps considerably to place him in his contemporary milieu. The magazine was always strongly linked with English-speaking Montreal, for six of the twelve most frequent contributors resided there. By 1908 six of the nine most frequent male contributors, including one in Kingston and one in Ottawa, belonged to the Pen and Pencil Club of Montreal. The membership and proceedings of that club, together with its *ambiance* as described by Leacock and Macphail, who first met there after Leacock's election to the body in 1901, reveal something about the atmosphere in which Leacock developed as a writer. The group of artists and writers met on alternate Saturday evenings for the purpose of "Social enjoyment and Promotion of the Arts and Letters."[65] Among the members were Maurice Cullen, Robert Harris, William Van Horne, Edmond Dyonnet, John McCrae, Louis Fréchette, and William Henry Drummond. Each was expected to unveil or read an original piece of work for criticism once every month or six weeks. For Macphail it "was a home for the spirit wearied by the week's work,"[66] and Leacock later recalled "the kindly club, drawn up in a horseshoe of armchairs, the room darkened, and apparently getting darker all the time, listening to the measured tones of an essay-writer reading his essay."[67] Despite the occasionally somnolent character of their literary evenings, members of the club provided Macphail's magazine with a valuable nucleus of writers around which to attract others, and from the beginning English-speaking Montreal was a prime source of contributors. If one widens the sample to include the forty-six who published four or more articles or poetry selections in *The University Magazine*, of the thirty-one who could be placed in 1907, the year Macphail took over the periodical, fifteen lived in Montreal. Among these fifteen, it is noteworthy that six belonged to the Pen and Pencil Club by 1911, eleven were members of the faculty or administration of McGill University, and three of the four who did not work at McGill were McGill alumni. Yet these data are not conclusive evidence of a parochialism centred on English-speaking Montreal, for among the fifteen Montreal residents, of the fourteen whose birthplaces can be determined, only four were born in Montreal; the remaining ten had come from other parts of Canada or from Britain. Within the entire group of forty-six, of the thirty-five whose birthplaces are known, only six were Quebec natives. Equally significantly, of the six Montreal residents among the twelve leading contributors, only two had been born in Quebec, and one of these, the philosopher J.W.A. Hickson, had attended three German universities, gaining his doctorate from Halle.

Such institutions as *The University Magazine*, the Pen and Pencil Club, and McGill University, and the associated friendships and sense of common endeavour, played a vital part in shaping Leacock's early career as a writer. This was a time when Montreal, the largest city in the dominion by a significant margin, could still lay claim to being the intellectual metropolis of English Canada as well as French Canada. Like any metropolis, it drew upon hinterland areas to supplement home-grown strengths, attracting to it such persons as Harris, Leacock, McCrae, and Macphail. The sense of Montreal's centrality within Canada contributed to the seriousness with which the group around *The University Magazine* viewed themselves and their work. In an address to the University Club of Montreal, one of Leacock's favourite haunts, Macphail stated that it was the business of university men to "tell the truth" about all current topics.

> We are a class set apart. We have elevated ourselves into the exploiting, the parasite class. . . . But we can justify our existence by telling the truth even about ourselves . . . . It will not do any longer to stand by and declare that we are holy men who would be defiled by coming in contact with the world, preferring to sit in a well and gazing at the stars.[68]

Men like Leacock and Macphail saw before them a world in a state of flux: women leaving their proper station in the family, educators losing sight of the very meaning of education, the American experiment in undisciplined liberty disintegrating, and Canadians, who lacked a clear sense of who they were, following false gods. In such a situation, the duty of the university professor outside the classroom was to continue seeking truth and attempting to replace confusion with a comprehensive understanding. What was to be done in Canada? Perhaps because of his own youthful experience with marginal farming, Leacock was not inclined to advocate a return to the past. His response was more complex, for he oscillated between imperialism, social criticism, and a retreat into satire, the last of which has been characterized as "a form of criticism practised by the impotent who know that they are impotent."[69] Indeed, none of the historians who have examined Leacock's work closely since 1970 has claimed that it reflects a consistent point of view. Cook summed up Leacock's social thought as eclectic, Berger stated that a striking and persistent feature was "the unresolved tensions in his outlook," and Bowker's account of his changing agenda suggested that he was something of a weather vane.[70] Leacock's comment in his obituary to Macphail that "I am certain that he never quite knew what he believed and what he didn't"[71] applied more to himself than to the deceased. Both were caught in a tremendous social upheaval involving the creation of a new industrial order and a basic shift in the balance between town and country. Macphail was remarkably consistent in his opposition to this change, with its attendant specialization of human functions. But Leacock accepted it, and in one important book, *The Unsolved Riddle of Social Justice*, attempted to outline the principles of equity that should underlie the new age.

There is no need to comment at length on *The Unsolved Riddle*, for Watt, Cook, Berger, and Bowker have all dealt with it. But Leacock's objectives and basic perspective should be noted since, despite his conscious effort at popularization, the book places him within a tradition which has always been in a distinct minority in Canadian intellectual history: that of dealing in a philosophical manner with fundamental social questions of one's own time and place.[72] Writing in the wake of World War I and the Winnipeg General Strike, he recognizes the shortcomings of the old individualist ethic and attempts to define a position between it and socialism. His purpose is to frame the outlines rather than the details of the future. He argues that governments should end unemployment, educate children, assist the aged and infirm, and in general prevent injustice through "intrusive social legislation."[73] Special emphasis is placed upon the fate of children: "every child of the nation has the right to be clothed and fed and trained irrespective of its parents' lot."[74] Equality of opportunity is absolutely basic to his vision, and he affirms that if governments start at once with the children, within a generation the results will be dramatic. The means of financing the requisite measures would be the progressive income tax and taxes on profits and inheritances. Yet he does not argue that the state should control industry as a whole, and certainly does not advocate public ownership. Some of his most interesting passages are those in which he suggests a change in public opinion as to the relation between work and character.

> The nineteenth century glorified work . . . . The ideal of society was the cheery artisan and the honest blacksmith, awake and singing with the lark and busy all day long at the loom and the anvil, till the grateful night soothed them into well-earned slumber. This, they were told, was better than the distracted sleep of princes.
>
> The educated world repeated to itself these grotesque fallacies till it lost sight of plain and simple truths. Seven o'clock in the morning is too early for any rational human being to be herded into a factory at the call of a steam whistle. Ten hours a day of mechanical task is too long: nine hours is too long: . . . a working day of eight hours is too long for the full and proper development of human capacity and for the rational enjoyment of life.[75]

In the 1921 edition of *Elements of Political Science* he strengthened his comments on the hours of labour. Noting that prior to the war, governments had tended to restrict their intervention in this respect to female and child labourers, he stated that the time had come to limit the working hours of adult males as well: "the statutory regulation of hours in general is quite within the scope of legislation. The matter is now rather one of expediency than of principle."[76]

The Unsolved Riddle, with its progressive ideas emanating from a notorious conservative, establishes yet another role for Leacock in the longer perspective of Canadian intellectual history. Many writers have asserted that there is common ground between conservatism and socialism; perhaps the most frequently cited similarities are an organic view of society, distrust of pure individualism, and willingness to use the state to assert the rights of society, as distinct from the interests of powerful individuals.[77] When both ideologies have legitimacy within a political culture, a hybrid known as the "red tory" may emerge. An obvious Canadian example is the author of *The Unsolved Riddle*, for while rejecting utopian socialism and *laissez-faire* liberalism, Leacock simultaneously advocated a remarkably comprehensive welfare state. In this respect he was considerably ahead of the political practice of his time: the state was to act as the guarantor of the rights of all, rather than simply the mediator among interests sufficiently powerful to enforce their right to be heard at the bargaining table. The latter concept of the state, combined with a vague sense of responsibility to the community as a whole, was as far as a contemporary liberal reformer, Mackenzie King, would go, even in print. The goals of state intervention in the writings of Leacock and King presented a noteworthy contrast. For King, in *Industry and Humanity*, the objective was the maintenance or restoration of social peace, and presumably, if a group was not sufficiently restive or important to threaten communal tranquillity, it would be left to its own devices.[78] But Leacock's *The Unsolved Riddle* revealed a vision of social solidarity which went beyond neutralizing menacing forces, for such groups as children, the aged, and the infirm could scarcely pose a significant danger to social peace. If examining the concept of the state is a useful means of differentiating between liberal and "red tory" reformers in the early part of this century, then Leacock is certainly in the latter camp and *The Unsolved Riddle* is a classic statement of that point of view.

The writing on Leacock by historians, which was published in the early 1970s, produced a consensus which may be characterized briefly. His historical publications, with one possible exception, are worthy of little attention; his imperialism is important and complex; and both it and his social criticism are relevant to his humour. Over the past twelve years no one has published an historical work focusing on Leacock, and over the past fifteen years at least two graduate students in history have abandoned proposed theses on him.[79]

The only historian since Cook, Berger, and Bowker who has presented new information on Leacock directly relevant to the concerns of this paper is A. B. McKillop, writing in 1977, whose research on LeSueur touched upon the editorial process lying behind *Baldwin, LaFontaine, Hincks*. As one of three editors for the "Makers of Canada" series, LeSueur was assigned Leacock's manuscript. McKillop has revealed that there was substantial conflict, and even some bad feeling, over the proper interpretation of responsible government, with the editor pressing the author to be critical of the received version. LeSueur detected an apparent contradiction between Leacock's conservative politics and his Whiggish approach to responsible government as an historical problem. He privately attributed this to pressure from the Deputy Minister of Labour, Mackenzie King, but the evidence McKillop presents on this point is not conclusive. It is equally likely that Leacock was following his own inclination when he chose "to stick to the beaten track and view the establishment of responsible government as a great triumph in our history."[80] This is consistent with Leacock's generally casual approach to matters of historical accuracy. It is no exaggeration to state that contemporary topics like imperialism were much more important to him than the history of the middle decades of the last century, for he had a thoroughly contemporary mind and was not interested in the past for its own sake. He was a convinced and committed imperialist when he wrote *Baldwin, LaFontaine, Hincks*, and in his view responsible government was a step towards the devolution of political power within the British empire. Indeed, linking responsible government and imperial federation in a positive fashion assisted in legitimizing the latter.[81] Given this perspective, why muddy the waters by casting doubt on the beneficial character of responsible government? But whatever considerations influenced Leacock's treatment of responsible government, the facts remain that history was of secondary interest to him and that his role in Canadian history does not depend upon his record as an historian.

I would suggest, in conclusion, that there is room for an historian to write a monograph on Leacock, building on the consensus established in the early 1970s and placing him in his Montreal milieu and in the longer perspective of Canadian intellectual history. When such a work is written it may enrich the study of both Canadian history and Canadian literature, which have shown thus far in their general works little interest in the insights offered by the writers surveyed here, if one may judge by two important volumes which appeared in 1983. The articles in *The Oxford Companion to Canadian Literature* on "Stephen Leacock" and "*Sunshine Sketches of a Little Town*" display scant appreciation of the nature and relevance of Leacock's imperialism, and the entry on Leacock himself, although treating *The Unsolved Riddle*, does not touch upon its positive reformist message foreshadowing the modern welfare state.[82] Leacock fared no better at the hands of the five professional historians who produced the 440-page *Twentieth Century Canada*: the only reference to him in the index relates to a passage in which he is cited as an example of nativism.[83] Perhaps, in the future, literary critics may examine Leacock's non-humorous works more carefully and integrate their findings into a holistic interpretation of him. Historians at large, for their part, may recognize in him a writer who, as well as achieving an international reputation as a humorist, revealed much about the Canada of his time in his wide-ranging writings and, in *The Unsolved Riddle of Social Justice*, anticipated the development of the social service state which emerged almost a generation later.

Stephen Leacock, Economist: An Owl Among the Parrots

MYRON J. FRANKMAN

Stephen Leacock the economist is a forgotten man. He is not cited by economists. He left no Leacock school, no Leacock theory, no Leacock effect, nor is there even, surprisingly, a catch phrase associated with his name, such as Thorstein Veblen's "conspicuous consumption." What was for many years a virtually final judgement of Leacock's scholarly work was pronounced by Harold Innis in a 1938 lecture at the University of Toronto. That lecture, which was intended to pay tribute to Leacock as one of the founders of Canadian social studies, was eventually published as his obituary in 1944 in the *Canadian Journal of Economics and Political Science*.[1] With but one exception, Innis chose to refer to Leacock as a political scientist rather than as an economist or even a political economist, although Leacock's 1903 Ph.D. degree from The University of Chicago was in political economy. Though Innis drew links between Leacock and other economists such as Thorstein Veblen, Adam Smith, and Jacob Viner, he glossed over Leacock's writings on economic questions in favour of attention to his humour, which he regarded as having suffered from the influences of social science. In the opinion of Innis, Leacock's humour was "destined not to endure" for "it is written in water and reflects too accurately the atmosphere of its period to interest later readers."[2] As for Leacock's academic work, in Innis' view it suffered either from the "imperialistic blight"[3] or from the insufficiency of his preparation in the social sciences.[4] One suspects that Innis masked his own view only thinly when he attributed to "some malicious individual" the question "What is left of Stephen Leacock?",[5] which was said to have been a response to Leacock's "What is left of Adam Smith?"[6]

Special thanks go to Kim Reany for deciphering and typing successive drafts and to Rosalind Boyd-Jeeroburkhan, Chris Green, James R. Mallory, Carman Miller, Tom Naylor, Ian Ross Robertson, and William G. Watson for helpful comments and suggestions.

In the four decades since Leacock's death the only important notice taken of his social science writings was by Alan Bowker, who in 1973 republished *The Unsolved Riddle of Social Justice*, with other essays, under the title of *The Social Criticism of Stephen Leacock*. Bowker's introduction is a useful complement to Innis' evaluation, but we still lack a careful look at Leacock's economic ideas. Bowker shares in part Innis' judgement that Leacock's humour was strengthened at the expense of his writings in the social sciences.[7] For Bowker the turning point is 1920; after that Leacock is said to have seen himself primarily as a humorist, whose economic proposals "were in large part repetitious of his pre-1920 programmes and . . . were increasingly half-baked and badly written."[8] In fact, most of Leacock's economic writings were done after 1920. Moreover, in May 1930 Leacock wrote from Orillia to McGill's principal, Sir Arthur Currie, to advise him, "I have only five more sessions at McGill and I intend [to] raise hell in Canadian economics during the short time left to me."[9] Nor does a man who sees himself primarily as a humorist turn down US$1,000 plus expenses to entertain the American Bankers' Association in New York and offer instead to come at his own expense to speak "on the restoration of the gold standard or some equally important subject."[10]

Intellectual Influences

To understand better Leacock's economic writings and his other writings as well, it is useful to examine the principal intellectual influences on Leacock. For Innis the following explanation sufficed: Leacock's "work has been solidly based on the individualistic approach which characterized a rural background and his interest in humour."[11] Such a representation obscures rather than clarifies. W. A. Mackintosh, in his 1938 lecture on Adam Shortt, refers to the possibility of including in *Who's Who* an intellectual pedigree of scholars, and suggests "Innis, H. A., by Thorstein Veblen out of Adam Shortt."[12] In a like manner I propose "Leacock, S. B., by Veblen out of John Stuart Mill."

The origins of what Innis called the "individualistic approach" can be traced directly to Mill, whose *Principles of Political Economy* was the text used for a number of years in Leacock's course at McGill in "Elements of Political Economy." Leacock was quite unreserved in his praise for Mill, whom he described as "one of the makers of the modern world . . . as noble-minded as he was clear-headed,"[13] and as someone "who grew younger as he got older"[14] and a "human being first and an economist afterwards."[15] For Leacock, Mill's real achievements were *Principles of Political Economy* and *On Liberty* and his having fortified and enlarged Adam Smith's "industrial liberty by building into it the framework of individual freedom."[16]

Leacock's policy views on production (where freedom should reign) and distribution (where state intervention is appropriate) take their inspiration directly from Mill, whose view is contained in the following passage from his *Principles*:

It is only in the backward countries of the world that increased production is still an important object: in those most advanced, what is economically needed is a better distribution . . . . we may suppose this better distribution of property attained, by the joint effect of the prudence and frugality of individuals, and of a system of legislation favouring equality of fortunes, so far as is consistent with the just claim of the individual to the fruits, whether great or small, of his or her own industry.[17]

Leacock's indebtedness to Veblen, with whom he studied at The University of Chicago at the turn of the century, is neither acknowledged nor apparently even recognized. Leacock's handwritten chapter outline dated October 1, 1926 for a volume which was to have been entitled "Chapters in Political Economy: A View of the Rise and Development of Political Economy from Adam Smith Until Today Illustrated by Selections from Leading Economists" contains the names of a number of twentieth-century economists, including Frank Taussig, Gustav Cassel, Norman Angell, and John Maynard Keynes (subsequently crossed out), but not that of Veblen.[18] Indeed Veblen is not even referred to in Leacock's writings until 1937 in *My Discovery of the West*,[19] where Leacock traces the roots of Social Credit in part to Veblen's writings.

Leacock speaks of Veblen's main idea as being "that human industry is not carried on to satisfy human wants but in order to make money."[20] This does not quite capture the essence of Veblen's distinction between making goods and making money. Moreover, this is not Veblen's central point, but rather a derivative one. Key to Veblen's approach is the constant interplay between technology and institutions, perhaps explaining in part why followers of Veblen are called "institutionalists." To one familiar with Veblen, the influence on Leacock's thinking of Veblen's "Why is Economics Not an Evolutionary Science" (1898),[21] "The Cultural Incidence of the Machine Process" (1904),[22] and *The Vested Interests and the Common Man*,[23] *inter alia*, are unmistakable. Influence, of course, does not commence from the date of publication of a work, for as Leacock noted, Veblen gathered ideas from his turn-of-the-century lectures into later books.[24] C. E. Ayres, one of the leading American exponents of Veblen's thought, in his review of Leacock's *The Unsolved Riddle*, observed that Leacock's critique of economic science was "in the spirit of the younger group of 'institutional' economists (who are not mentioned, however); a trained psychic might even sense the presence of the spirit of Mr. Veblen."[25]

Leacock on Public Policy

In his approach to major economic questions, Leacock firmly opposed, and lavished harsh words on, both the *laissez-faire* implications of mainstream economics and socialist alternatives to the capitalist system. Leacock sought a middle course, rejecting both too much government interference[26] and too little. While some of his formal analysis may be flawed, many of his recommendations still have merit, and his 1920 agenda for resolving the riddle of social justice is as timely now as when it was written.

Distribution. Before presenting his program of action in *The Unsolved Riddle of Social Justice* (1920), Leacock felt obliged to demonstrate the limitations of solutions dictated by supply and demand considerations:

> Hitherto we have been hampered at every turn by the supposed obstacle of immutable economic laws. The theory of 'natural' wages and prices of a supposed economic order that could not be disturbed, set up a sort of legislative paralysis. The first thing needed is to get away entirely from all such preconceptions, to recognize that the 'natural' order of society, based on the 'natural' liberty, does not correspond with real justice and real liberty at all, but works injustice at every turn. And at every turn intrusive social legislation must seek to prevent such injustice.[27]

John Stuart Mill had raised the desirability of income redistribution in 1848, Thorstein Veblen had caricatured the excesses of the leisure class in 1899, and World War I had demonstrated the scope for action. As Leacock observed:

> In this respect five years of war have taught us more than a century of peace. It has set in a clear light new forms of social obligation. The war brought with it conscription—not as we used to see it, as the last horror of military tyranny, but as the crowning pride of democracy. . . . But conscription has its other side. The obligation to die must carry with it the right to live. If every citizen owes it to society that he must fight for it in case of need, then society owes to every citizen the opportunity of a livelihood. 'Unemployment', in the case of the willing and able becomes henceforth a social crime. Every democratic government must henceforth take as the starting point of its industrial policy, that there shall be no such thing as able bodied men and women 'out of work', looking for occupation and unable to find it. Work must either be found or must be provided by the state itself.[28]

For Leacock war finance had utilized a "terrific engine of taxation," which equally well could be utilized in peacetime for social betterment.[29] There was no reason why "work and pay for the unemployed, maintenance for the infirm and aged, and education and opportunity for the children" could not be provided.[30] The children, however (Leacock's own son was five at the time), were the focal point for immediate action: "Our feeble beginnings in the direction of housing, sanitation, child welfare and education, should be expanded at whatever cost into something truly national and all embracing."[31] Leacock was emphatic that no child's opportunity in life should be "obliterated by the cruel fortune of the accident of birth."[32]

Those familiar with the enormous socio-economic problems of the less developed countries since World War II will recognize that Leacock's prescription for social justice overlaps considerably with the Basic Needs approach belatedly advocated by the World Bank in the late 1970s.[33] For two decades development economists had focused their attention on the production side, leaving children to share their parents' lot. To Leacock it was self-evident that a child's brain and body are stunted by lack of food and air;[34] today's development economists required scholarly confirmation of this before reconsidering their policy approaches.

Production. The restoration of industrial production and employment levels after World War I involved lengthy delays. This was addressed by Leacock in his speech on the Gold Standard in 1924. Leacock saw the restoration of the Gold Standard as the key to restoring prosperity. Leacock argued against currency depreciation and applauded the British for not having abandoned a possible return to the pre–World War I sterling-dollar exchange rate. Leacock was, of course, by no means alone in recommending what proved to be a serious blunder, but he also offered extremely wise advice, which remains valid:

> There is only one thing that you can do with gold, or at the best only two things—spend it or lend it. . . . The true banking is to find somebody . . . with the industry and the perception and the intelligence to bring back your money ten times over. . . . Lend it to the right man. Don't lend your money to a bunch of collateral that is dead; lend it to a man.
>
> And the money in the United States should be loaned to the world, to each and every part that has potential wealth, to our Northwest, to the oil fields of Mesopotamia, wherever civilization can find new bases upon which to build up all we have lost in Europe. Lending the gold hoards of the United States is one of the most important financial steps to be taken.[35]

Using reserves or hoards to expand credit was thus seen by Leacock as a critical ingredient for economic expansion. Some of Leacock's proposals for restoring output levels during the Great Depression will be dealt with below.

International Trade and Tariffs. Tariffs, according to Leacock, had their place at a certain stage in the development of a nation, as did government interference with individual economic freedom. Leacock did not join mainstream economics in its elevation of free trade to the most desirable goal of public policy:

> People agree to forget that this wonderful freedom of the working child was one part of a "system of natural liberty," of which free trade was another. The two hung together. A convenient forgetfulness has pushed them apart.[36]

Innis appears to have been most offended by what he terms Leacock's "imperialism." Imperialism or, more precisely, co-operation with and integration within the British Empire was for Leacock what economists now call a "second best solution." Given the apparent impossibility of international economic unity, unity within the British Empire was much to be preferred to nationalist excesses, which were treated with scorn by Leacock: he speaks derisively, for example, of Canadian authorship being "encouraged like Canadian cheese and Canadian apples."[37] Even greater scorn was reserved for the excesses of federalism which bid fair already in the 1930s to split both Canada and Australia asunder and in Leacock's view were likely to stand in the way of recovery from the Depression. He spoke of Bennett's program of social legislation, minimum wages, and maximum hours turning "on whether the power of the Dominion extends to wages, etc. The Delphic provision of 'property and civil rights' will block all economic progress."[38]

Leacock viewed Empire unity as the only way that the members of the Empire, including Great Britain, could hope to offset American economic hegemony. The Americans were to be displaced by recourse to their own methods: use of the tariff; standardization of processes, methods, and machines; unification of weights, measures, and money (including, ideally, decimal currency in Britain); and, in general, the combining of British and Dominion manufacture, capital, labour, technique, research, and industrial science.[39] Leacock recommended in particular an Empire super-tariff (he mentions fifteen per cent for purposes of illustration) which would apply to trade outside of the Empire and initially be added to all existing tariff levels.[40] Leacock was essentially proposing for the Empire arrangements comparable in some ways to those which later formed the basis for the European Common Market.

Leacock on Economic Science

Leacock is said to have remarked that if one could teach a parrot to say "supply" and "demand" one would have an economist. This would seem to be one of his milder pronouncements on the discipline. In *Hellements of Hickonomics*, Leacock observed of political economy: "Here is an obstinate and crabbed science, living on facts and figures, untouched by imagination." "Economic scholasticism is drowsing into final oblivion" behind locked doors. The time had come for political economy to "alter or perish."[41] In the Preface to the *Hellements*, Leacock observed:

> I think the whole science is a wreck and has got to be built up again. For our social problems there is about as much light to be found in the older economics as from a glowworm.[42]

The *Hellements* was published the same year as John Maynard Keynes' *The General Theory of Employment Interest and Money*. Keynes was, indeed, trying to rebuild the science so that social problems might be resolved. Leacock might have found a *careful* reading of Keynes quite flattering: some of the central elements of analysis and policy in Leacock's 1933 *Plan to Relieve the Depression* are at the heart of Keynes' *General Theory*. Leacock had observed of the Depression:

> It grows upon what it feeds on. Each time a worker is thrown out of employment, there is a loss of purchasing power; with each loss of purchasing power, another man is thrown out of work. There is no end, no stop.[43]

This might be considered a reasonable approximation to the process described later by Keynes. One might wish only to add a reference to expectations, as well as an explanation as to why employment and income might not continue to fall.[44]

For both Keynes and Leacock, although the elements of their explanations differ markedly, recovery from the Depression can be accomplished through increases in the money supply and public works expenditures. For Leacock a gap between profits and wages would serve as a stimulus to resumption of production and this could be accomplished by inflation produced "by the circulation of great quantities of paper money, beyond all basis of physical value or redemption."[45] For Keynes, increases in the money supply worked on profits through expanding purchasing power rather than through price increases. Had the following passage, which Leacock would have appreciated, been penned by Leacock rather than Keynes, it would have been denounced as half-baked or absurd:

> If the Treasury were to fill old bottles with banknotes, bury them at suitable depths in disused coalmines which are then filled up to the surface with town rubbish, and leave it to private enterprise on well-tried principles of *laissez-faire* to dig the notes up again (the right to do so being obtained, of course, by tendering for leases of the note-bearing territory), there need be no more unemployment and, with the help of the repercussions, the real income of the community, and its capital wealth also, would probably become a good deal greater than it actually is. It would, indeed, be more sensible to build houses and the like; but if there are political and practical difficulties in the way of this, the above would be better than nothing.[46]

Leacock reacted, not to Keynes' ideas, but rather to his mathematical notation, in an unpublished, undated broadside entitled "The Invasion of Human Thought by Mathematical Symbols: A Call to Arms."[47] Leacock does not identify the economist said to be holding one of the most respected chairs in England lest he "should be crushed flat at once under the deadweight of prestige and authority," but he does reproduce exactly Keynes' equation relating the proportional changes in total demand and investment.[48] Leacock refers to mathematical economics as a "racket" and argues that it is:

> no aid in calculating the incalculable. You cannot express the warmth of emotion in calories, the pressure on the market in horse-power, and the buoyancy of credit in specific gravity! Yet this is . . . what the pseudo-mathematicians try to do when they invade the social sciences. The conceptions dealt with in politics and economics and psychology, the ideas of valuation, preference, willingness and unwillingness, antipathy, desires etc., cannot be put into quantitative terms.[49]

He goes on to speculate as to the consequences if the "invasion" were to spread to poetry, and renders "The Charge of the Light Brigade" as follows:[50]

$$\frac{\dfrac{\ell}{2} + \dfrac{\ell}{2} + \dfrac{\ell}{2}}{600} = 600 - N$$

W. H. Dawson in his review of *Economic Prosperity in the British Empire* suggests that "the sympathetic reader will not be likely to discard the good grain because something that looks suspiciously like chaff occasionally lies alongside of it."[51] In Leacock's many writings on economics there is an ever changing relationship between the serious and the apparently frivolous. There is, however, sufficient grain to repay the effort in insights and still timely counsel.

There is, of course, reward in that which "looks suspiciously like chaff" as well. Take, for example, Leacock's musings on the question of the length of the working day:

> If we could in imagination disregard for a moment all question of how the hours of work are to be shortened and how production is to be maintained and ask only what would be the ideal number of the daily hours of compulsory work, for character's sake, few of us would put them at more than four or five. Many of us, as applied to ourselves, at least, would take a chance on character at two.[52]

Leacock wrote to influence public opinion on what he viewed to be major policy issues of his era. He chose to address neither an academic audience, whose formal analyses he held in disdain, nor the policy makers of the day, but rather the common man. He believed this to require "a gay book on political economy for reading in a hammock."[53] Apparently Leacock believed that the very seriousness of the question required the counterweight of levity, if one hoped to make one's point. And yet his point was not made: the very device with which Leacock hoped to gain attention appears to have contributed to his relative neglect. His light-hearted, increasingly superficial treatment of questions of national policy, combined with the public expectation of mere levity from his pen, assured that his works did not stir thought on the great questions of his time.

Imperial Cosmopolitanism, or the Partly Solved Riddle of Leacock's Multi-National Persona

JAMES STEELE

Leacock's peculiar habit of altering the national character of his literary persona may be explained, at least in part, by a consideration of some of his work as a political theorist. On the one hand, his literary essays provide ample evidence that he could present himself as a Canadian, an American, an Englishman, or even as a combination of two or three of these nationalities. On the other hand, his political writings offer an account of the evolution of the state as a political form and an appreciation of the historic role of nations and empires in its development. A significant connection between these two fields of discourse—between Leacock's literary essays and his professional work as a political scientist—has not been established by either Leacock's critics or his biographers. Yet Leacock's multi-national literary persona was consistent with his political and historical doctrine of imperial cosmopolitanism and even shared some of its paradoxical properties.

That Stephen Leacock frequently changed the national identity of his literary voice is a literary fact that cannot be denied. Sometimes he writes as a Canadian, for a Canadian audience, and about a distinctly Canadian community. His best-known work in this voice is *Sunshine Sketches of a Little Town*, which begins with the following words: "I don't know whether you know Mariposa. If not, it is of no consequence, for if you know Canada at all, you are probably well acquainted with a dozen towns just like it."[1] Although Leacock the narrator can easily contrast the width of Mariposa's Main Street with that of Wall Street or Piccadilly, Mariposa remains a distinctly Canadian place. It is situated, to be sure, on Lake Wissanotti in the Third Concession of Tecumseh Township in the county of Missinaba in the Province of Ontario in the Dominion of Canada within the British Empire. Its inhabitants are more or less aware of Canadian history, Canadian politics, and Canadian religion; they also sing "O Canada" at frequent intervals. Their numbers include at least one person of fourth-generation, Loyalist stock—Peter Pupkin—and at least one specimen of a Canadian nationalist—the antiquated Liberal who, in a letter to the Mariposa newspaper protesting Judge Pepperleigh's Conservatively partisan picnic speech, signs himself "Patriotus Canadiensis." Leacock could thus identify himself with the Canadian community from, as it were, the inside.

At other times, Leacock writes just as unequivocally as if he were an American, writing for an American audience from an American point of view. Consider, for example, *Arcadian Adventures with the Idle Rich*. Although this work reflects certain aspects of Montreal and was originally published in serial form in the *Montreal Star*, its urban setting is distinctly American. Its unnamed "City" is situated somewhere east and south of Wisconsin, not far from Lake Erie, near Cohoga County in an unnamed state of the United States. Members of this community refer to American history, American political parties (both Republican and Democratic), American churches (both Presbyterian and Episcopalian), American companies, American cities (including New York, Boston, and Chicago), American benefactors (such as Carnegie), and American institutions. Some of them name their clubs after Jefferson and Washington, and one inhabitant, Mrs. Everleigh-Spillikins, has affairs with men who serve in the United States Navy, the United States Army, and the state militia. Dr. Boomer, as an archaeologist, has a specialist's knowledge of the stone age and bronze age "in America"; and even the slower-witted characters can quote phrases from the American constitution at election time. The author identifies himself explicitly with this community, mentioning Canada only as a remote holiday resort of unsatisfactory quality.

If *Sunshine Sketches* and *Arcadian Adventures* suggest, when taken together, that Leacock must have been a North American with a dual nationality, another collection of essays, *My Discovery of England*, suggests a third national identity. In the Preface to this work, the reader is informed by Sir Owen Seaman that Leacock is "all British, being English by birth and Canadian by residence" and that "England and the Empire are very proud to claim him for their own." Sir Owen goes on to explain that he does not want Leacock's "nationality to be confused with that of his neighbours on the other side," for "English and American humorists have not always seen eye to eye." He further remarks that "Mr. Leacock's humour is British by heredity," but that Leacock has caught something of the spirit of American humour by force of association.[2] Leacock quietly accepts this characterization yet refers in that same work to *our* North American Continent and to the fact that "*we* do things differently over in America." He makes it clear, in fact, that he is as familiar with Youngstown, Ohio, and with Richmond, Virginia, as he is with Peterborough, Ontario, and that he knows as much about Toledo as he does about Toronto. He likewise refers more generally to "the larger culture of our side of the Atlantic," suggesting that it subsumes the educational system of both Canada and the United States. The reader of *My Discovery of England* could thus reasonably infer that Leacock's nationality was not merely double but triple.

All three national voices, or various mixtures of them, can be found in *My Remarkable Uncle, and Other Sketches*. The narrator's persona in the title essay is distinctly Canadian, as his references to Winnipeg, the old Ontario farm, the uncle from abroad, and the settlement of the Canadian West indicate. A similar voice can be heard in about half a dozen other essays in this volume, including "The Old Farm and the New Farm," "The Struggle to Make us Gentlemen," and "The Passing of the Kitchen." Yet what could be more British than the Leacock persona in "The British Soldier," eulogizing England's vanishing professional serviceman as "the nation's defender and the nation's hero"[3] and implicitly identifying himself as a member of that same English nation. The essay entitled "War and Humour" is likewise primarily about how "we" British have regarded war in the past and about the changing fashions of "our" war memoirs, particularly those concerning such Englishmen as Lord Kitchener and General Roberts. In "Cricket for Americans," on the other hand, the voice is British-Canadian, and its professed mission is "to cultivate cordial relations with the United States." Then, again, in "Migration in English Literature: A Study of England and America," the persona is clearly that of an Anglo-American-Canadian. The speaker explicitly identifies himself as one of the "uncounted millions" who served England by settling in one of her new overseas dominions. Yet he also proudly refers to "John Galt, the moving spirit of the Canada Land Company [and] founder of *our* City of Guelph." In a subsequent passage, his possessive "our" also lays claim to works of American literature, particularly *Uncle Tom's Cabin* and the poetry of Longfellow. Leacock's historical thesis in this essay is consistent with his tri-national persona. His argument is that the British emigrants who were initially expelled by Britain as refugees or convicts have re-created the greatness of Britain by establishing colonies and dominions overseas. Literature thus recognizes the "American uncle" as an empire-builder who has in turn helped to re-create the greatness of imperial Britain. As England, Canada, and the United States are thus united not only by a single national origin but also by family ties (both real and metaphorical), a common culture, and shared imperial interests, Leacock can readily identify himself with the peoples of all three states.

Leacock's articulation of this multi-national literary voice cannot be adequately explained on grounds of biographical circumstance. The fact that he was English by birth, Canadian by upbringing, and American by empathy is, of course, not inconsistent with this cosmopolitan habit. Nor is the fact that he was, as a youngster, educated in Ontario yet stamped with the mentality of Victorian England and inspired by the ideal of American democratic republicanism. Leacock, it may be recalled, informs us in *The Boy I Left Behind Me* that after reading Colonel Thomas Wentworth Higginson's *Young Folks' (or People's) History of the United States*, he developed a sense of "the burning injustice of [British] tyranny" and that "forthwith the theory of a republic, and the theory of equality, and the condemnation of hereditary rights seemed obvious and self-evident truths, as clear to me as they were to Thomas Jefferson."[4] Nevertheless, it should be evident that a person with such a heterogeneous background could just as easily have become a nationalist of the Canadian, American, or English variety, or, for that matter, an anti-nationalist or non-nationalist.

Likewise, the fact that he wrote for audiences in these three countries, with syndicated columns in both Canadian and American newspapers and book-publishing contracts with houses in both New York and London, may seem to provide a plausible motive. There is nothing, however, in either Leacock's published writings or in Vishnu Chopra's edition of his letters to suggest that he ever adopted one nationality or another for reasons of financial gain or popular appeal.[5] Even Leacock's professional activities as a political scientist seem to offer contradictory clues about the riddle of his national identity. As Head of McGill's Department of Economics and Political Science, he encouraged his students and colleagues to study Canadian problems and strongly advocated the employment of Canadian scholars. Moreover, several of his popular books on Canadian history and politics, particularly *Canada: The Foundations of its Future* and *All Right, Mr. Roosevelt (Canada and the United States)*, are much concerned with the development and security of this country. Yet Leacock also studied under the American political theorist Thorstein Veblen, earned a Ph.D. degree at The University of Chicago, and served on the executive of the Political Science Association of America. His *Elements of Political Science* was adopted, according to Ralph L. Curry, "as the standard text by thirty-five universities in the United States,"[6] and certain of his polemical writings were admired by Theodore Roosevelt.[7] His links with Britain were likewise maintained not only by his talks at the Royal Colonial Institute and several British universities but also by such books as *Economic Prosperity in the British Empire* (1930) and *Our British Empire: Its Structure, Its History, Its Strength* (1940). (The American edition of the latter work, it can be noted, was published with Leacock's usual shift in voice: *Our British Empire* was re-titled *The British Empire*.) Such biographical facts as these seem to raise more questions than they answer about his attitude towards nationality; they certainly fail to solve the mystery of his multi-national voice.

The solution to this problem may lie in a consideration of certain doctrines of Leacock's political writings, especially his *Elements of Political Science*. In this work, Leacock makes fundamental distinctions between such key terms as "state," "society," "government," and "nation." Specifically, he describes a "state" as an entity having a territory, a population, a governmental organization, and an autonomous unity. "Society" is then defined by Leacock in a much broader way:

> The term society has no reference to territorial occupation; it refers to man alone and not to his environment. But in dealing with man its significance is much wider than that of state. It applies to all human communities, whether organized or unorganized. It suggests not only the political relations by which men are bound together, but the whole range of human relations and collective activities. The study of society

involves the study of man's religion, of domestic institutions, industrial activities, education, crime, etc.

"Government," however, is a term with a much narrower scope:

It refers to the person or group of persons in whose hands the organization of the state places for the time being the function of political control. The word is sometimes used to indicate the persons themselves, sometimes abstractly to indicate the kind and composition of the controlling group. The ordinary citizens of a community are part of the state, but are not part of the government. The term has moreover no reference to territory.[8]

As for "nationality," Leacock makes the following observation:

The term nation, though often loosely used, is properly to be thought of as having a racial or ethnographical significance. It indicates a body of people—the Germans, the French, the Hungarians, etc.—united by common descent and a common language. But such divisions by no means coincide with the political divisions of the civilized world into states. Austria-Hungary constitutes a single state, but its population is made up of members of a great many different races. The political division of the civilized world into states freely intersects with the division into races, although sometimes the political units—as in the case of modern France—are almost coincident with the ethnographic.[9]

Using the term "race" as a synonym for "nation," Leacock then points out (in the present-perfect tense) that "the historical relation between the nationality and the political organization of the state has been a changing one":

In the political thought of classical Greece the conception of the state is limited to a small area occupied by persons of the same race. In the Roman world, the original conception of a city state with a common nationality was transformed by the process of absorption and conquest into the larger conception of a world-wide state and universal sovereignty. Nationality is here lost from sight. The foreign nations occupying the subjugated provinces were recognized by virtue of the Emperor Caracalla's act of general enfranchisement (A.D. 212) as citizens of the universal empire.[10]

Although "such a conception [of empire] long served as a basis of European polity," Leacock argues that it was eventually displaced by feudalism, a system which linked territorial sovereignty to dynastic supremacy regardless of the nationality of the subject peoples. In more recent times, "nationality as the paramount basis of state organization strongly asserted itself."[11] Leacock cites as evidence for this claim not only the American and French revolutions but also the formation of national states by Italy and Germany, and the attempts to form such states by Hungary and Ireland.

In a subsequent section of his text, under the heading "The Ideal State," Leacock observes that "in our own day the national state has served as the embodiment of perfect political organization." Nevertheless, he also insists that a "wider ideal is conceivable in the form of a world state or state universal" and that the establishing of such a political organization was long "the haunting ideal of European policy."

We see . . . [this ideal] reflected in the claims of the Roman emperor, in the less substantial claims of the Eastern emperor at Constantinople after the fall of Rome, in the resuscitation of the empire by Charles the Great (A.D. 800), and in the vague sovereignty of the Holy Roman Emperor from that date until the abolition of the titular dignity (1806) through the power of Napoleon. The same ideal hovers before us as offering the goal of the political organization of the future.[12]

Leacock, in other words, regarded the nation-state, like the feudal domain, as a temporary stage in the realization of a much broader form of world political organization.

It may be inferred from Leacock's remarks on the general direction of mankind's political development that a world organization of this kind would have several distinctive features. It would be based on territory whose bounds would be ever more widely set. While respecting the separation of church and state, it would foster the development of democracy where appropriate. Through an ever widening application of enforceable law, it would also offer its citizens a greater certainty and regularity in civil affairs than could be assured by any single nation-state. A further attribute would be a higher form of world political consciousness among its citizens, a cosmopolitan outlook that could transcend merely national modes of thought.

Leacock believed that the British Empire offered mankind a strong and well-developed basis for advancing towards this state universal. With a population of about five hundred million distributed over some fifty-eight states, the British Empire, he pointed out, comprised a quarter of the world's territory and constituted a great reservoir of human and natural resources.[13] Throughout this domain there prevailed the rule of enforceable law, a *sine qua non* of economic and social development. In the more advanced dominions, the Empire had proven its ability to foster the development of democracy. Its autonomous unity, whether achieved through formal federation or through free association, was already evoking, in his view, a higher form of cosmopolitan consciousness.

Yet Leacock seems to have always assumed that the quest for world dominion was an enterprise to be undertaken jointly by the British Empire and the emerging empire of the United States. As early as 1906, in the first edition of his *Elements of Political Science*, he described the "colonial expansion" of the United States. It included the Hawaiian Islands with their port of Pearl Harbor (annexed in 1898), the Samoan group of islands (annexed in 1899), and the several islands that were acquired from Spain as the "just" result of the Spanish-American War: Puerto Rico, the Philippines, and Guam. In 1909, in an article warning Canada not to rely on the Monroe Doctrine for security, Leacock observed, with some irony, that the United States had become an empire within the "outer empire" of Britain. Its possessions in the Pacific, he argued, had made the United States an "Asiatic power with new lines of interest radiating in all directions across the Pacific." With its control of the strategically placed Virgin Islands and the right to intervene in Cuba, it had also become "the predominant partner in the West Indies, the former battleground of the maritime nations of Europe." In Leacock's eyes, the United States was therefore a "commercial power whose colossal and highly organized industries at home look[ed] to its new possessions as bases for the conquest of the export trade."14 As one of the world's "leading states" it had, like Britain, claimed a share of the "great natural resources of the modern colonial area."15 Leacock always believed, of course, that only a free-enterprise, industrial, capitalist economy could provide an adequate material basis for his expanding world civilization.16

Leacock's discussions of the imperial role of the United States were thus consistent with the "big stick" policy of Theodore Roosevelt and with the imperialist "Corollary" to the Monroe Doctrine enunciated by that same president in 1904. Woodrow Wilson's conduct of foreign policy, on the other hand, was the object of Leacock's scorn. Although Wilson intervened forcefully in Nicaragua, Leacock mocked Wilson's ineffectiveness in using military power against Mexico and the Dominican Republic and ridiculed his inconsistency, indecisiveness, and isolationism in respect of European affairs. Wilson's reluctance to have the United States enter World War I—a conflict which resulted in the re-division of the colonial world—was a source of particular irritation.17

In "Over the Grape Juice; or, The Peacemakers,"18 Leacock likewise scoffed at the proposition that world peace could be achieved by the self-congratulatory idealism of teetotallers and do-gooders. The moral underlying the satiric humour of this story is that true world peace was to be gradually and securely established for everyone's happiness by the forcible expansion of Anglo-American imperial rule. A timely intervention in Haiti was his fictional case in point, an occurrence that had some basis in historical fact.

While maintaining that Anglo-American imperialism was the highest stage of man's political evolution, Leacock also asserted that the development of a world empire was part of the natural order of things. If, as he observed in June 1939, the quest for imperial unity had been inspired "by grandeur and by courage, by meanness and by fear," it had also been guided by "instinct." Because "instinct" is by definition a type of non-conscious behaviour based on biological forms of existence in the process of adapting to an environment, Leacock could further claim that imperial unity was essentially "organic."19 In another context, he argued that the spirit of the free-enterprise system is that "vital principle (the élan vital) which biologists seek to find to explain the life and growth of the animated world."20 Vitalism together with voluntarism subsumed his imperial philosophy.

Even near the end of his life, Leacock's vision of Canada's future was informed by this world view. In 1941, he argued that the British Empire and the United States should combine their forces in the postwar period to "rule" the European world. Canada, he believed, would then have "a higher place and a higher responsibility" than anything the past had seen:

> From its very situation, Canada must be reorganized as the central buttress of imperial power. Wedged, as it were, between Great Britain and the United States, our Dominion becomes the keystone of a new arch of mutual support and common security.[21]

Leacock spelled out exactly what he meant by this role:

> In point of force, then, it is plain that Canada must become, as it were, not exactly a fortified country in the old sense, but a country with a vast capacity, sufficiently developed to expand with ease, for producing armaments and munitions in places so safeguarded by natural obstacles that no war could impede their manufacture. Here is boundless water-power, as willing to run in subterranean channels as above ground; great battlements of rock that can be hollowed out into underground factories against which the largest bomber in the world is as harmless as a dragon-fly. With that is a store of minerals and metals that Pluto himself might envy. All hell can be raised in the bowels of northern Canada.[22]

This goal was articulated by Leacock, it may be noted, just two years before Winston Churchill and F. D. Roosevelt agreed secretly at Quebec City to develop the atomic bomb with Canadian uranium. Although Leacock certainly wanted Canada to be a liberal, democratic, and humane society, the imperial alliance of which it was a part was to form the core of a hegemonic iron fist.[23] Leacock clearly understood that cosmopolitanismal—doctrine which teaches, in the final analysis, the renunciation of patriotism, national sovereignty, and national culture and which calls for the merging of nations by forcible association—would be an appropriate ideological underpinning for such an empire.

Leacock's attitude towards Canadian nationalism was consistent with this world view and therefore ambivalent. Like Thorstein Veblen, he believed that nationalism was useful in time of war for the mustering of patriotic forces.[24] He further argued that the "close of the Great War made Canada not only a nation in its consciousness but even in the acknowledged sense of the term, as a signatory of the Treaty of Versailles and a member of the League of Nations."[25] In times of peace, however, nationalism was a regressive and dangerous movement. He told the Empire Club in 1909 that the goals of nationalism were mean and provincial[26] and that nationalism lacked the power in Canada to compose either the racial feud between English and French or the religious strife between Protestant and Catholic. Only the Empire, as a higher and more powerful organization, could guarantee the security of Canada's confederation as well as offer "the joint greatness of a common destiny."[27] Even as late as 1945, Leacock argued that a breach of unity between Canada and Britain would "disrupt Confederation."[28]

While Leacock observed that the development of international law, particularly since the time of Grotius, was contributing to the construction of an international world order,[29] he always assumed that the strongest bonds that linked the peoples of the British Empire with the people of the United States were of a non-legal, social kind. These ties he described in some detail in such works as *The British Empire: Its Structure, Its Unity, Its Strength* and *All Right, Mr. Roosevelt (Canada and the United States)*. They included, to be sure, links formed by tourism and migration, by trade and commerce, and by an awareness among peoples that they share a kindred descent and common traditions. These bonds were also based on the fellowship fostered by such organizations as the Boy Scouts and Rotarians and on a "union of intercourse and ideas" in such fields as education, the professions, and sport. Still other ties had been created by the use of a common language and by "the community in literature that it brings."[30] Taken together, these social bonds made for a "union of hearts" that constituted the basic strength of the imperial polity. Political and legal forms were their mere shadows.[31]

Leacock thus regarded literature as a basis for one of the bonds of union in an imperial community. In his view, "speech, thought and language [in the Anglophone community] now amalgamate, not diverge."[32] All great literature in English was therefore a powerful intellectual instrument for the formation of the desired supra-national, cosmopolitan consciousness.[33] As the world was being "unified into one" with the increasing "standardization of mankind," even humour, he argued, should be used to create the "kind of world-consciousness that [would] one day replace nationality."[34] While Leacock suggested in "Laughing off our History"[35] that each nation could use humour to exorcise outmoded social behaviour, he also argued, with perfect consistency, that jokes ridiculing national stereotypes are themselves outmoded. To the best of my knowledge, there are no vulgar Americans, parsimonious Scotsmen, or stupid Frenchmen inhabiting the cosmopolitan civilization of Leacock's fiction, although such qualities as vulgarity, parsimony, and stupidity are certainly objects of Leacock's humour. The only exception is the German people, an imperial enemy ridiculed by Leacock in time of war.[36]

His perception of Canadian literature in particular was informed by this world vision. In an essay entitled "The National Literature Problem in Canada," Leacock asserted that he could discern no literature written in Canada that could make a distinctively Canadian contribution to the stock of great literature produced by England and the United States. He doubted, in fact, whether Canadians could ever develop a distinctive way of writing, given the general historical process of cosmopolitan amalgamation.

> The world is changing into an intellectual unity, drawing on all sources. The Canadian may have to remain a mere contributor to the chorus, like the American negro. Nay, the very British and American themselves will more or less amalgamate, under the new encircling influence of common thought. The American revolution is all over.
>
> This, however, in no way circumscribes our efforts and our aims. We don't have to be different.

> There is no reason why we should not be superior. If our thought must run in the common mould of all who use the English language, that does not in any way impede a gifted child of Canada. He need not try to write a Canadian play; let him just write one like those of Shakespeare. He needn't write a Canadian work: anyone as good as Dickens will do nicely.
>
> It seems to me, in short, that the attempt to mark off Canada as a little area all its own, listening to no one but itself, is as silly as it is ineffective. If a Canadian author writes a good book, I'll read it: if not I'll read one written in Kansas or Copenhagen. The conception of the republic of letters is a nobler idea than the wilful attempt at national exclusiveness.[37]

Leacock's idea of a world empire that would incorporate all nations, his understanding of history as a movement towards that goal, and his concept of national literatures as part of a proleptic universal republic of letters all provide implicit rationales for his multi-voiced cosmopolitan persona. The riddle of his multi-national literary identity is therefore partly solved. Leacock himself, however, nowhere comments directly on his own contradictory practice. The prime witness is, so to speak, silent in this case, and all the evidence textually circumstantial. A complete solution to the riddle is therefore wanting.

The mystery is only "partly" solved in another sense as well. In the real world—even the real world of Anglo-American imperialism—a supra-national Leacock could have had no real existence. He would have been stopped and questioned at national borders, as indeed he tells us he was. In the freer world of literary discourse, however, he was at perfect liberty to assume whatever identity his heart and mind desired. Yet Leacock always believed that literature, or at least great literature, is an expression of the individual human spirit—a force that ultimately, in his vitalist and voluntarist philosophy, governs and directs the real world. The paradox involved here is perhaps analogous to the paradox that he attributed to the Empire as a whole when he described it as a spiritual unity of nations that were without formal union. Leacock's cosmopolitan persona was made of the same spiritual stuff. Through the artifice of literary masks, he attempted to realize a cherished ideal: a unity of distinct national voices in the identity of a single spirit—his own. Whatever one may think of these contradictions and their imperialist underpinnings, it should be evident that Leacock's theory and practice of cosmopolitanism were consistent with each other.

Stephen Leacock, Humorist: American by Association

BEVERLY RASPORICH

"Gentlemen," said Mark Twain's contemporary, Artemus Ward, rising at a banquet with his glass held aloft, "I give you Upper Canada!"; *then he added mournfully, "because I don't want it myself."*
STEPHEN LEACOCK, "Mark Twain and Canada," *Queen's Quarterly* 42

The study of humour is a fascinating, complex, truly interdisciplinary pursuit, which engages a great many critical thinkers from various disciplines. The point of view of this essay is necessarily limited, but it is one which Leacock and his early twentieth-century audience would have approved and one which is loosely faithful to the socio-literary approach of some modern writers on humour: their point of intellectual departure being that humour is often an expression of culture or, in nineteenth-century terms, of nation. Just as literary reviewers of Leacock's time liked to speculate about the national biases of his humour, some of the classic studies in American humour, such as Constance Rourke's *American Humor* and Norris Yates' *The American Humorist*, investigate American humorists and their humour as articulations of their society.

The society that Leacock inhabits in his humour is rarely, as a Canadian audience might expect, overtly Canadian. Leacock's Canada was a colonial society; unrealized both psychologically and economically, it afforded him little inspiration or market for his humour. He preferred to define himself as an American writer and humorist in the continental sense. In 1936 he declared that "there is no such thing as Canadian literature today, meaning books written by Canadians in a Canadian way,"[1] just as much earlier, in 1916, he had dissolved the 49th parallel for Canadian authors, insisting that "Canadian literature—as far as there is such a thing—Canadian journalism, and the education and culture of the mass of the people approximates more nearly to the type and standard of Canada than to those of Great Britain."[2] Leacock was able to exploit this common cultural experience in books such as *Moonbeams from the Larger Lunacy* and *Further Foolishness* where his humorous sketches on such timely topics as movies, politics, literature, and education seemed to make him successful in the American market-place.

Leacock's humorous literature did not, of course, spring simply and directly from the American macro-culture he inhabited; his disposition was very much a literary one, which studiously revelled in the artistry of past and contemporary American humorists. For Leacock, American literary humour was a New World wonder, a "not unworthy literary product"[3] which reflected American life and history and invited literary emulation. Not surprisingly, then, Leacock gravitated to the spirit and techniques of humorists south of the border, as his own literary tributes, *The Greatest Pages of American Humour* and *Mark Twain*, would indicate.

Literary critics and humorists in the United States have claimed Leacock as one of their own. Ralph L. Curry's biography of Leacock begins: "Stephen Leacock represented in a way the paradox which is Canada. Born in England, he moved to Canada and wrote American humor,"[4] and Robert Benchley admitted that as a humorist he was greatly indebted to Leacock.

Although Leacock may have considered himself an American humorist, it is impossible to overlook the fact that his own national experience of being a Canadian also distanced him from American culture and its humorous expression. However much he understood, even welcomed, the close social and cultural relations of Canada and the United States, he also demonstrated in his humour that longstanding nervousness about American dominance. "We share the weather," he noted. "If the barometer falls to a new low in Montana we have to watch out. If a farmer is reported frozen in Kansas, we lose a couple near Sudbury. If the Ohio floods the lower section of Cincinnati, it is likely that the Grand River will flood the lower section of Galt, Ontario." "In fact," he continues, "we have to watch the American papers or we might get drowned in our sleep."[5] Claude Bissell's general analysis of Leacock's ambiguous attitudes to things American, as well as his sense of separateness, is well taken:

> Leacock developed in close relationship to American traditions, but his sense of being a Canadian, which was sharply felt and eloquently expressed, gave him a sense of separateness. A study of his relationship to American cultural traditions reveals the pattern that can be expanded indefinitely—pattern of indebtedness and independence, of similarity and differentiation, of sympathy and withdrawal.[6]

This sense of separateness from the American cultural experience is occasionally demonstrated explicitly by the Canadian context of Leacock's humour, as with the Grand River flooding Galt, but most often it is indirect, exercised by the authorial voice. A man of genteel, civilized Upper Canadian sensibilities, Leacock was a member of that time-honoured class in Canadian society that distrusted republican excess. He accepted republicanism but, in his own words, "I stopped short at the Queen, partly I suppose because one touched there on Heaven and Hell and the Church service and on ground which I didn't propose to tread."[7] Leacock's was an Anglo-Canadian voice, conservative, literate, a gentlemanly echo of Susanna Moodie's. Small, but often nimble and ironic when threatened to be shouted down by John Bull and Uncle Sam, it is a voice that is softly audible even as its author happily realizes the comic modes and techniques of nineteenth-century American humour.

As a theorist of humour, Leacock was a civilized Victorian who believed that humour had evolved with society from primitive and destructive forms to a higher, genial stage, and that sentimental humour was the ultimate art. The real artist was the Mark Twain who created *Huckleberry Finn*, a "great book" because "it elevates humor to that high reach, beyond the comic and the accidental, in which our human lot itself invites our tears and our smiles."[8] And he was the Bret Harte whose "serious Western tales are permeated with humor, which at times breaks to the surface and floods the page." The real artists were "the California 'school' of writers—who never went to school. Of these Bret Harte and Mark Twain stand pre-eminent."[9]

As Constance Rourke points out, the California mining camps were a natural milieu for the development of such sentimental humour. She explains that in this frontier circumstance, vast sentimentalism overflowed with hilarity: "The current mood in California was purely native; and it was comic. With all the vicissitudes, the heartbreak, the losses, the abundance of human failure, the comic mood arose irresistibly. Quickly the curve of theatrical interest ran up from romantic tragedy to extravaganza."[10] For Leacock, the hyperbolic mood of the California school was a high achievement in the field of humorous literature. He understood humour as a romantic flight which stressed the joy in expectation, followed by the melancholy of its defeat. The upbeat rhythm of comedy was the grand aspiration and nowhere was it grander than in the mythological frontier climate, west of the Mississippi, and in its Canadian equivalent, west to Winnipeg. Leacock learned of the former through Twain and Harte, and discovered the latter through the experience of his remarkable uncle, E. P. Leacock, who went west to Winnipeg in the early eighties.

In *My Remarkable Uncle*, a personal reminiscence, and "Boom Times," a fictionalized account, Leacock creates a legend in the western odyssey of the enterprising and thieving Britisher, who, reminiscent of Twain's Colonel Sellers, discovered in the boom time of Winnipeg the wonderful expectation of "the promised land" and the "new Eldorado."[11] In *My Remarkable Uncle*, Leacock reveals his own romantic reckoning of the West:

> There is something of magic appeal in the rush and movement of a "boom" town—a Winnipeg of the 80's, a Carson City of the 60's . . . . Life comes to a focus; it is all here and now, all *present*, no past and no outside—just a clatter of hammers and saws, rounds of drinks and rolls of money. In such an atmosphere every man seems a remarkable fellow, a man of exception; individuality separates out and character blossoms like a rose.[12]

Although Leacock's hyperbolic interpretation of his uncle is in the tradition of American frontier humour, his character "so exaggerated already that you couldn't exaggerate it" (p. 3), the character is also remarkable as a genuine Canadian folk type, and a very curious hybrid indeed of gentleman and folk. British by birth but American by experience, Philip Leacock is a flim-flam man of aristocratic caste who confounds the locals in the bar-rooms of Ontario in the Canadian election of 1878 (he picked up the history and politics of Upper Canada in one day) by British pretension:

> "Why let me see"—he would say to some tattered country specimen beside him glass in hand—"surely, if your name is Framley, you must be a relation of my dear old friend General Sir Charles Framley of the Horse Artillery?" "Mebbe," the flattered specimen would answer. "I guess mebbe; I ain't kept track very good of my folks in the old country." "Dear me! I must tell Sir Charles that I've seen you. He'll be so pleased."
> . . . In this way in a fortnight E. P. had conferred honours and distinctions on half the township of Georgina. They lived in a recaptured atmosphere of generals, admirals and earls. Vote? How else could they vote than conservative, men of family like them? (p. 4)

In the boom times of Winnipeg, E. P. comes into his own. With his humble "hail-fellow-well-met" instinct, in combination with his *aristocratic* side, his "activities were wide":

> He was president of a bank (that never opened), head of a brewery (for brewing the Red River) and, above all, secretary-treasurer of the Winnipeg Hudson Bay and Arctic Ocean Railway that had a charter authorizing it to build a road to the Arctic Ocean, when it got ready. They had no track, but they printed stationery and passes, and in return, E. P. received passes over all North America. (p. 6)

Leacock's E. P. is a delightful comic characterization, grandly individualistic in the frontier style, genuinely Canadian in his final definition as the failed British gentry, distinctly North American in his boom-to-bust story, and, in Leacock's melancholy sentimental recollection of him, a perfect representation of sentimental frontier humour:

> If there is a paradise, I am sure he will get in. He will say at the gate—"Peter? Then surely you must be a relative of Lord Peter of Tichfield?"
> But if he fails, then, as the Spaniards say so fittingly, "May the earth lie light upon him." (p. 12)

Through the history of the gold rushes, then, with their atmospheres of hysterical expectations and personal defeats, a comic mythology—a pattern of humour—was developed which Leacock, speaking with a strong Canadian accent in *My Remarkable Uncle*, brought to life in E. P. For Leacock, the boom-to-bust frontier pattern was obviously rooted in the local, in Canadian history, but it was equally, if not more importantly, a North American phenomenon; in fact, he interpreted it as a North American principle of economic life:

> It seems to me also that this alternation of sunshine and shadow, so plainly to be seen in the boom times and bad times of a new Eldorado, characterizes also all the economic side of our collective human life. We

see it in the alternating prosperity and depression of big business of which the "peaks" and "crashes" of the stock exchange are only the outward signs of the tumult within . . . .[13]

This economic principle is also an inspiration to some of Leacock's best humorous narrative: the rags-to-riches-and-rags-again stories of Jefferson Thorpe from *Sunshine Sketches of a Little Town* and Tomlinson of Tomlinson's Creek from *Arcadian Adventures with the Idle Rich*. Leacock creates some fine "frontier" gold rush humour in the exhilarating comedy of the great expectations surrounding these characters. The wonderfully optimistic illusions of grandeur of ordinary men, triggered by Northern Ontario mining booms, by Twin Tamagami, Abbitibbi Development and the Erie Auriferous is also, in the spirit of Harte and Twain, followed by the melancholy humour of their economic defeats.

As well as appreciating the sentimental humour of Harte and Twain, Leacock attempted to reach out towards Twain's revolutionary spirit, an American burlesquing spirit which, Constance Rourke explains, conspired "toward the removal of all alien traditions, out of delight in pure destruction or as preparation for new growth."[14] Leacock favoured Twain's *Innocents Abroad*, a classic of that comic genre where humour depended on criticism of the old country (and which was predated by the Canadian James de Mille's *The Dodge Club* or *Italy in 1869*,[15] and Thomas Chandler Haliburton's *The Attaché; or, Sam Slick in England*). He was very much impressed by the comic method of the frontier "eye of innocence," particularly when, as in *Innocents Abroad*, Twain applied it satirically to European culture: "He [Twain] was able to turn on Europe—on its forms and ceremonies, its monuments and its mummies (dead and living), its hauteur and its humbug—the eye of innocence of the Westerner."[16]

The "eye of innocence," or the persona of the solemn wise fool, is perhaps as old as comedy itself, but prominent in America. Rourke differentiates it as the puritan mask:

> The mask was a portable heirloom handed down by the pioneer. In a primitive world crowded with pitfalls the unchanging, unaverted countenance had been a safeguard, preventing revelations of surprise, anger or dismay. The mask had otherwise become habitual among the older Puritans as their more expressive or risible feelings were sunk beneath the surface.[17]

She recounts Twain's statement that "the humorous story is told gravely; the teller does his best to conceal the fact that he even dimly suspects that there is anything funny about it" (p. 212) as indicative of the mask tradition in American humour and its procession of dull-looking oracles.

One of these dull-looking oracles was Artemus Ward (Charles Farrar Browne), a famous comic lecturer, Twain's western contemporary, and a master of the puritan mask. Leacock championed Ward as a comic genius and was obviously impressed by his method, which he described as "that of solemnity itself. He affected an intense dullness of intelligence. His face was stamped with melancholy. He assumed an air of utter embarrassment, and in this mood, with his assumption of sorrow, he got off the little sayings and epigrams that he called his lectures."[18] Here is Leacock's own report of the opening of Ward's lecture in London, 1866, at Egyptian Hall in Piccadilly:

> You are entirely welcome, ladies and gentlemen, to my little picture-shop.
>
> I couldn't give you a very clear idea of the Mormons—and Utah and the Plains—and the Rocky Mountains—without opening a picture-shop—therefore I open one.
>
> I don't expect to do great things here—but I have thought that if I could make money enough to buy me a passage to New Zealand I should feel that I had not lived in vain.
>
> I don't want to live in vain.—I'd rather live in Margate—or here.
>
> (p. 101)

The manner of the solemn, blunt little sayings conveying an innocent American outlook, symbolic of a continent's genesis, special to Twain as well as to Ward,[19] is incorporated into Leacock's comic style. The British writer C. K. Allan was so convinced that this was Leacock's outstanding feature as a humorist that in 1945 he wrote a parody of Leacock's work, *Oh Mr. Leacock!*, in which this very feature of comic delivery—the short, simple, apparently naive observation—is the heart of the comic imitation. The most pristine example of the puritan delivery in Leacock's work is a short piece in *Literary Lapses*, "A Study in Still-Life—The Country Hotel," which is used with comic success, and not without some perversity, to celebrate drinking:

> The country hotel stands on the sunny side of Main Street. It has three entrances.
>
> There is one in front which leads into the Bar. There is one at the side called the Ladies' Entrance which leads into the Bar from the side. There is also the Main Entrance which leads into the Bar through the Rotunda.
>
> The Rotunda is the space between the floor of the bar-room and the cigar-case. . . .
>
> The walls of the bar-room are perforated in all directions with trap-doors. Through one of these, drinks are passed into the passages. Drinks are also passed through the floor and through the ceiling. Drinks once passed never return. . . . The Proprietor stands in the doorway of the Bar. He weighs two hundred pounds. His face is immovable as putty. He is drunk. He has been drunk for twelve years. It makes no difference to him. . . .
>
> Attached to the bar is a pneumatic beer-pump, by means of which the Bar-tender can flood the Bar with beer. Afterwards he wipes up the beer with a rag. By this means he polishes the Bar. Some of the beer that is pumped up spills into glasses and has to be sold.[20]

While Leacock often aped the puritan delivery, in the bulk of his work he did not wear the puritan mask as easily as this early sketch would suggest. The mask of sober innocence that Ward perfected as a lecturer through platform manner, with its awkward hesitancies, digressions, and innocent truisms was not generally translated by Leacock, as it was by

Twain in his mature writings, into the authorial pose of the innocent dupe, the naive rube, or the innocent child. Unlike Mark Twain and Artemus Ward who fully assumed the guise of a foolish native American as naturally as they did their pseudonyms, Leacock stopped short of being totally absorbed into the popular will. Whereas Twain and Ward satirized America at home and Europe abroad through the eyes and idiom of the average American, to whom they were sympathetic, Leacock often took exception to him, dismissing him, for example, as a "poor shrimp" and a "poor nut" without a chin or opinions of his own, in the preface to *Winnowed Wisdom*.[21]

The deadpan manner applied by Ward and Twain on stage and in literature to convey the effect of the all-American babe-in-the-woods is used by Leacock, but mainly in a careful, occasional way as illustrated by the last sentence of this quotation from "At the Ladies Culture Club" in *Winnowed Wisdom*:

> The day I was there the meeting was held in the ballroom of the new Grand Palaver hotel, because that is a simple place suitable for science. There were no decorations except flowers and no music except a Hungarian orchestra which stopped the moment the lecture began. This is a rule of the club. (p. 120)

The last line is pure Artemus Ward, but of more significance is the real voice of this sketch which keeps his ladies at an ironic and somewhat patronizing distance. I have previously argued that the real voice of Leacock's humour is that of a civilized and literate Canadian gentleman, the persona of the preface to *Winnowed Wisdom*.[22] This Leacock voice may, under the right circumstances, admit or confess to being foolish, but he does not stoop to play the fool at much length or in any genuinely convincing way. He cannot *pretend* to what James Austin points out was a "new point of view" established by Ward and Twain in American frontier humour, that of the self-deprecating, unsophisticated naïve American.[23] Perhaps, as Silver Donald Cameron suggests, Leacock, unlike Mark Twain before him who was buoyed by his nation's self-confidence, was too insecure to be a fool.[24]

Nonetheless, Leacock did applaud the Yankee irreverent comic eye turned towards European culture, and emulating Twain, became his own innocent abroad in the volumes *Behind the Beyond* and *My Discovery of England*. Silver Donald Cameron in *Faces of Leacock* has commented extensively on this very matter, on Leacock's debt to Twain, in these two volumes, as well as on the literary alchemy that occurs as Leacock moves beyond mere imitation into sophisticated and complex postures of what Cameron calls "negative irony." This feature, an ironic undercutting of all that Leacock pens, of both visitor and visited—of the small-town Orillian or the average American traveller (the guise of whom the Canadian professor periodically assumes)—as well as England, as well as America itself, is remarkable for the scope of its playfulness; it is also remarkable for the chameleon-like character of the authorial voice, which, unlike Twain's in *The Innocents*, does not project consistent ironic standards.

However, what Cameron says of *Behind the Beyond* is also true here, that the reader often has the impression that Leacock himself, as author, adheres to another, mature set of values.

Leacock's private voice of Canadian tone and accent is immature in this volume, but his country's national definition of being *in media res*, of being between two cultures, would nonetheless seem to allow a comic advantage. In *My Discovery of England* the multi-faceted point of view and the sophisticated technique of negative irony seem the natural, self-comprehending expression of the archetypal Canadian patriot, introduced earlier to the Leacock reader in *Sunshine Sketches* as the Mariposan who is glad to be an Englishman on St. George's Day and equally glad to be an American on the Fourth of July.

Obviously, Leacock also understood that the innocent eye needed adjustment, that the time had passed when simple satire of the Old World was possible; in effect, New Eden had in its own way become Old World and the American traveller was coming collectively now to Europe invariably projecting his own not-so-innocent cultural absurdities. Delighting in burlesquing the whole spate of what he calls "the balance of trade in impressions"[25] from both sides of the Atlantic, Leacock nonetheless takes an almost wicked delight in cocking America's own innocent eye inwards, ironically, on itself. In the following experience of the innocent abroad, Leacock humorously deflates America for being a somewhat aggressive and ideological country:

> I pass over also the incidents of my landing in Liverpool, except perhaps to comment upon the extraordinary behaviour of the English customs officials. Without wishing in any way to disturb international relations, one cannot help noticing the rough and inquisitorial methods of the English customs men as compared with the gentle and affectionate ways of the American officials at New York. The two trunks that I brought with me were dragged brutally into an open shed, the strap of one of them was rudely unbuckled, while the lid of the other was actually lifted at least four inches. The trunks were then roughly scrawled with chalk, the lids slammed to, and that was all. Not one of the officials seemed to care to look at my things or to have the politeness to pretend to want to. I had arranged my dress suit and my pyjamas so as to make as effective a display as possible: a New York customs officer would have been delighted with it. Here they simply passed it over. "Do open this trunk," I asked one of the officials, "and see my pyjamas." "I don't think it necessary, sir," the man answered. There was a coldness about it that cut me to the quick.
>
> But bad as is the conduct of the English customs men, the immigration officials are even worse. I could not help being struck by the dreadful carelessness with which people are admitted into England. There are, it is true, a group of officials said to be in charge of immigration, but they know nothing of the discriminating care exercised on the other side of the Atlantic.
>
> "Do you want to know," I asked one of them, "whether I am a polygamist?"
>
> "No sir," he said very quietly.

"Would you like me to tell you whether I am fundamentally opposed to any and every system of government?"

The man seemed mystified. "No, sir," he said. "I don't know that I would."

"Don't you care?" I asked.

"Well, not particularly, sir," he answered.

I was determined to arouse him from his lethargy.

"Let me tell you, then," I said, "that I am an anarchistic polygamist, that I am opposed to all forms of government, that I object to any kind of revealed religion, that I regard the state and property and marriage as the mere tyranny of the bourgeoisie, and that I want to see class hatred carried to the point where it forces every one into brotherly love. Now, do I get in?"

The official looked puzzled for a minute. "You are not Irish, are you, sir?" he said.

"No."

"Then I think you can come in all right," he answered. (pp. 12-14)

Interestingly, the persona himself, with his fussy tone, his antipathy towards "the dreadful carelessness" and bad manners of the officials, is suspiciously British. Donald Cameron is right about *My Discovery of England*. It is one of Leacock's best books; in it "negative irony becomes an artistic principle" (p. 93).

Besides the humour of the innocent abroad, the characteristic most typical of frontier humour was exaggeration. As Leacock himself concluded, "Above all the new West, spacious and unlimited . . . helped to bring back into humorous literature the feature of exaggeration which was one of its primitive elements."[26] On the western front, it was Mark Twain who became the master of the tall tale and the big lie, an art which in Leacock's reckoning was a "national" characteristic: "The amazing rapidity of American progress, and the very bigness of our continent, has bred in us a corresponding bigness of speech; the fresh air of the western country, and the joy of living in the open, has inspired us with a sheer exuberant love of lying that has set its mark upon our literature."[27]

In Leacock's humour, the exaggerative mode is not precisely of the same nature as that of Twain's—nor of the American frontier. It is most certainly there, as it is in Twain's work, as a grand comic streak of absurd or overblown metaphor and outrageous anecdote or statement. The clue to Leacock's difference from Twain is in the special literary emphasis of Leacock's exaggerative response. Typical of Twain's humour is a yarn like "Dick Baker's Cat," spun in homely dialect and dependent for its fun on the simple exaggeration of a cat who is a wise miner but who becomes prejudiced against quartz mining when he is partially blown up by dynamite. In contrast, in Leacock's fiction, exaggerative humour is most often rooted in a literary reference, spun out of a literary context, or combined with other subtle techniques of humour such as verbal absurdity or understatement. The purely native sky-breaking physical humour of Twain's western yarns is not typical of the genial and sophisticated Canadian professor.

While Leacock loved the exaggerative method as positive exuberance in Twain, he clearly had his decorous Canadian reservations about the primal quality that was often characteristic of Twain's exaggeration. The Canadian humorist delighted in the outrageous fantasy of Twain's "Cannibalism in the Cars" where a number of Congressmen, snowed in and about to die of hunger, resort to eating one another through full legislative procedure, but he was critical of the savage aspect of the humour. "Crude," "coarse," and "vulgar" were all epithets applied indirectly by Leacock to this piece (p. 101). It would seem that Twain was treading on that radical, republican ground that Leacock rejected and that he (Leacock) feared most about the American exaggerative method, that is when "it passes the bounds of common sense, and becomes mere meaningless criminality" (p. 107).

In the following pieces Leacock is surprisingly like Twain in his use of the primitive exaggerated anecdote, but even in these tall stories the destructive thrust is muted by pathos or genial celebration. "The Retroactive Existence of Mr. Juggins," for example, is a wildly improbable piece in which Mr. Juggins, with his retrospective glance, looking backwards to the roots of his own education and his own memory, thinks himself out of existence. While Twain could have delighted in the man's stupid act of self-destruction, Leacock is melancholy over Mr. Juggins' eventual demise. Similarly, there is an element of pathos in "The Awful Fate of Melpomenus Jones." Here the curate who goes to tea can't make a graceful exit and can only escape by dying; the passing of his spirit, described in the manner of Twain, is "as rapid as a hunted cat passing over a garden fence."28 In "The New Food" disaster occurs when the whole Christmas dinner, concentrated into a modern pill, is accidentally stolen and eaten by the baby. The baby's subsequent explosion is, however, a happy one. Even in his humour based on primitive exaggeration, Leacock, by introducing pathos or geniality, was most often true to his own conception of humour as a civilized and kindly art. The exaggerative feature of Twain's western humour, then, Leacock could claim in a muted way among his own comic talents. It was a talent, too, for an Ontario gentleman, which, in the above anecdotes, came dangerously close to that uncivilized and savage mode of humour which he steadfastly denied.

Leacock's place in the annals of American humour is not only assured by his use of an outrageous principle of exaggeration characteristic of the Old West. The official evaluation of Leacock in the *Literary History of Canada* is that he was very much indebted to humorists such as Artemus Ward, Josh Billings, Bill Nye, Mark Twain, and others for particular literary forms and verbal techniques:

> As they did, he [Leacock] used a multiplicity of forms: the dialogue, the memoir, the letter, the travel sketch, the tall tale, the anecdote, the literary burlesque and parody. He had the same bag of highly developed tricks as they had: the pun, chop-logic, the sudden juxtaposition of levels of speech, the mixed metaphor, the absurd coupling of words, the malapropisms and the apparently witless flow of free association.29

In his linguistic appreciation of such humorists as Bill Nye, Leacock was often even close to plagiarism. Nye's famous comic line, for example, about how an audience had said, "Come again, we should like to see you in broad sword combat with a meridian of longitude,"[30] is close to that famous Leacock line which describes Isolde as "graceful as a meridian of longitude."[31]

Two aspects of Leacock's North American humour, his penchant for literary burlesque and his verbal nonsense, are particularly interesting because, juxtaposed, they illustrate his characteristic pattern of sympathy and withdrawal from the republican comic muse—the tension between democratic revolt and the Upper Canadian restraint that was his Canadian voice and that underlies his humour.

In the tradition of nineteenth-century free-wheeling America, Leacock preferred the fresh, iconoclastic broad sweep of burlesque to the singular and specific art of parody. His parodies, for example, in the volumes *Nonsense Novels, Further Foolishness,* and *Winsome Winnie* are parodies of genres rather than of specific works and do not depend for their appreciation on a knowledgeable literary readership. Because of this ultra-democratic approach, the author is often called to account. Dwight Macdonald, understanding parody as an elitist and classical genre, does not include Leacock in his anthology, reasoning that "Stephen Leacock's many volumes with titles like *Moonbeams from the Larger Lunacy* are so broad as to be equatorial; they illustrate the tendency of parody towards philistinism."[32] As a parodist, Leacock wrote in the "philistine" spirit of Artemus Ward and Bret Harte, who, Leacock points out, knew the value of loose parody and knew it best as an American jest:

> The test of a good parody, or burlesque, is whether it makes good reading without the original. Those of Bret Harte in his *Condensed Novels* certainly do. More than that—and the fact seems to have escaped the literary historians—they represent American Humor in the real sense. Underneath the surface of many of the stories, the basis of amusement lies not only in the verbal parody but also in the ridicule of the thought and institutions of Europe.[33]

There is even something of Harte's New World ridicule underlying such Leacock parodies as "Gertrude the Governess," "Winsome Winnie," and "The Split in the Cabinet"; and most certainly Leacock understood in "Winsome Winnie" as Harte did in "Lothaw" that "nothing was so fatal to England as to be hit in the prestige."[34]

The surface humour, the verbal play in Leacock's parodies, also argues for him writing in an American vein, as he incorporates the kind of verbal nonsense that he learned from Artemus Ward, Mark Twain, Bill Nye, and O. Henry. Leacock appreciated the "dazzling" verbal technique of the absurd combinations of words, which he lauded in such a Twain delight as "the horses are bituminous from long deprivation" from *Roughing It,* or such an O. Henry comic gem as "I tell you Andy [says old Mack Lonsbury in disclaiming all knowledge of women] I never had the least intersection with her dispositions."[35] This kind of inspired verbal humour is itself an inspiration for such famous Leacock verbal nonsense in *Nonsense Novels* as:

> After he had left, Gertrude had found her aunt in a syncope from which she passed into an apostrophe and never recovered. (p. 77)

> At times in her presence he would fall, especially after dinner, into a fit of profound subtraction. (p. 83)

> He was sitting on a thorn bush beneath her, and his upturned face wore an expression of agonized pallor. (p. 84)

And the most often quoted Leacock line:

> Lord Ronald said nothing; he flung himself from the room, flung himself upon his horse and rode madly off in all directions. (p. 73)

With Lord Ronald, Leacock is at his most spontaneous and quixotic nonsensical self, indulging in an apparently witless game of free association that rivals his American company. With Gertrude's aunt, the technique of absurd word combinations is fun enough, but the Leacock choices of "syncope" and "apostrophe" suggest less the frontier fool than a man of letters. Leacock, in fact, was very much the controlled and literate author of verbal nonsense. He admired the pure fun of the verbal and logical absurdities of the likes of Artemus Ward, who with deadpan stage presence lingered over such nonsensical *non sequiturs* as "I once knew a man in New Zealand who hadn't a tooth in his head," then looked reminiscent and continued, "and yet he could beat a base-drum better than any man I ever knew."[36] He himself, however, could not entertain for long playing the utter fool or indulging in utter foolishness. He was never really comfortable with the complete illogic or the nonsense sounds of Yankee-doodle-dandy that jingle throughout American humour. Neither could one have expected him to make comic claim on the playful foolery of the likes of the following, penned by a humorist Leacock admired, John Kendrick Bangs; it belongs both in content and spirit to the United States of America:

> We are Jackies, Jackies, Jackies
> And we smoke the best tobaccys
> You can find from Zanzibar to Honeyloo.
> And we fight for Uncle Sammy,
> Yes indeed we do, for damme
> You can bet your life that that's the thing to do-doodle-do
> You can bet your life that that's the thing to
>   doodle-doodle-doodle-doodle-do.[37]

Verbal nonsense for its own sake—of the doodle-do variety—is rare in Leacock and the Lord Ronalds are infrequent. More typical are the vocabularies of biology, medicine, business, advertising, education, or the classics, studiously *applied* in an incongruous way not only for a nonsensical effect but for satiric purpose. In this example, in the same vein as "How to Live to Be 200" in *Literary Lapses*, Leacock's verbal nonsense is a studied parody of the nutritionist's argot, meant to discredit the man who takes seriously a mechanistic approach to health through diet:

If he is wise he will realize that the food ought to contain a proper quantity of both proteins and amygdaloids, and, while avoiding a nitrogenous breakfast, should see to it that he obtains sufficient of what is albuminous and exogamous to prevent his breakfast from becoming monotonous.[38]

For the most part, Leacock could not beat the republican humorists at their own game of excited and ingenuous nonsense, partly because he was a modern man and partly because he was not a republican. He was not a frontier American inventing American English for the people, high-spiritedly, freely, and with childlike glee playing the inspired idiot and exploding the linguistic conventions of proper John Bull; he was a Canadian professor, trained to be a gentleman, trained in the classics, willing to concede that language was process, like the making of wine, but, at the same time, firmly believing that slang was its scum.[39] Literary, schooled, conservative, Leacock aspired towards the pure pleasure of gratuitous verbal nonsense that he discovered, not only in American humorists but in the British Victorian writers Edmund Lear and Lewis Carroll,[40] but he was too controlled to unleash it. The unconscious free association of totally absurd language invites the primitive, and with it, the potential for emotional and social anarchy—thus Leacock, a restrained Upper Canadian man of letters, predictably stopped short.

Instead, Leacock's preference and his strength was the rational irrationality of misused terms and the misapplication of language. The fun, of course, in Leacock, is often in the pun, in an intellectual understanding of related but incongruous word play, as in such seventies American college jokes as "Immanuel Kant but Kubla Khan," or "Have you heard about Maxim Gorky and his brother, Minimum?" In *Nonsense Novels*, burlesquing chivalry, Leacock gives us a Coat of Arms that shakes the heroine's heart with its heraldic design: "A lion, proper, quartered in a field of gules, and a dog, improper, three-quarters in a field of buckwheat."[41] As a humorist of verbal nonsense, Leacock is definitely, unlike the California school, a man who went to school. American humorist George Ade described him well as "a college professor who can be a quizzical fun-maker without sacrificing his dignity as a member of the Faculty."[42]

When Stephen Leacock gave his first lecture in London, England, he was introduced by a Sir Owen Seaman, who claimed, as many appreciators of Leacock have done and still do, that "Mr. Leacock's humour is British by heredity; but he has caught something of the spirit of American humour by force of association."[43] And so he had. The comic patterning of sentimental gold rush humour, the puritan delivery, the perspective of the innocent eye, the comic method of frontier exaggeration, the form of literary burlesque and the techniques of verbal nonsense were all special to the New Republic—and to Stephen Leacock, a Canadian professor of Northern Attic voice. Ironically, even as Leacock insisted on there being no such thing as Canadian literature or Canadian humour, his own voice began to make a difference. As he withdrew from the edge of the republican abyss with a gentlemanly caution and in respect of his own character, he demonstrated that if his humour was British by heredity and American by association, then, at the very least, it was also Canadian by experience.

Religion and Romance in Mariposa

GERALD LYNCH

Stephen Leacock made three major structural revisions to *Sunshine Sketches of a Little Town* between its serial publication in the *Montreal Star* from February 17, 1912 to June 22, 1912 and its publication in book form later the same year. He added the preface and reorganized the sketches as follows: the first two installments for the *Star*, "Mariposa and its People" and "The Glorious Victory of Mr. Smith," were combined to form the book's opening sketch, "The Hostelry of Mr. Smith"; and the sixth installment for the *Star*, "Mariposa's Whirlwind Campaign," was divided to become the fifth and sixth sketches of the published book, "The Whirlwind Campaign in Mariposa" and "The Beacon on the Hill." The addition of the preface is significant because it, with "L'Envoi: The Train to Mariposa," provides a kind of framing device for the sketches proper. That is, Leacock's preface and "L'Envoi" present the reader with different, though complementary, perspectives on *Sunshine Sketches* and Mariposa, perspectives which differ not only from one another but also from the point of view of the narrator of the sketches proper. All three perspectives—those of the authorial prefacer, the ironically involved narrator, and the distanced, reflective narrator of "L'Envoi"—are necessary to a rounded view of the town and the book. By reorganizing the opening and middle sketches, Leacock gave prominence to the character of Josh Smith and created in the interior sketches—four through nine—two three-sketch sections, of which the first is concerned with Mariposan religion, and the second with Mariposan romance. This symmetrical centre of the *Sketches* opposes three

---

I am grateful to D.M.R. Bentley, David Staines, and J. M. Zezulka for their advice on an earlier version of this paper, especially to D.M.R. Bentley for his contribution to that part of the paper which deals with the satire on High Anglicanism.

sketches on the virtues of Mariposa in matters of romance, love, marriage, and family to three sketches on the failure of Mariposa's institutionalized religion to meet simply the needs of its Anglican parishioners. This structurally contrived, balanced opposition at the centre of *Sunshine Sketches* begins to suggest that Leacock's masterpiece is a more highly organized and complex work than has hitherto been shown.[1] The organization and concerns of sketches four through nine reflect the values of Leacock's humanism and toryism, the tory-humanism that values continuity in human affairs, responsibility and tolerance, organicism, balance and equipoise in all matters, and the community over the individual—a community such as Mariposa, an individual such as Josh Smith.

Since I have dealt elsewhere in detail with the opposition between Mariposa and Mr. Smith,[2] here I will briefly outline the nature of that opposition and proceed to a discussion of the religious and romantic concerns of the book—what may be called the spiritual concerns at the heart of *Sunshine Sketches*.

Josh Smith can be viewed, and has been viewed,[3] as *Sunshine Sketches*' closest approximation of a hero. He runs the hotel which temporarily becomes Mariposa's commercial showpiece; he contracts for eggs with Jeff Thorpe's "woman" and thereby assists financially the bankrupt barber; he saves the Mariposa Belle; he sets fire to Dean Drone's debt-ridden church for the insurance money, then single-handedly prevents the fire from spreading to the town; and he champions the conservative cause of protectionism against liberal reciprocity with the United States, thereby saving, by ironic extension, the British Empire. Smith acts, of course, in every instance for patently selfish reasons. The additions to Smith's Hotel are a temporary ruse for the sake of retrieving the lost liquor licence. The contract with Thorpe merely serves to feed the fully operational "caff's" temporary requirement of more eggs. Smith raises the grounded Mariposa Belle to ensure his own comfort and to win a twenty-five dollar bet with Mullins the banker. And it can be speculated that Smith sets fire to Dean Drone's new church and fights the fire to safeguard, financially and then materially, the town which he exploits for his own aggrandisement. The first sketch, "The Hostelry of Mr. Smith," moves most purposefully towards Smith's realization that the "hotel business formed the natural and proper threshold of the national legislature."[4] This realization transforms Smith's vision of himself. Mr. Smith is a quick study. He is victimized in the opening sketch by the telegram ordering him to close down his hotel; he is the victor with the telegram that he has sent from the city in the last sketch, the telegram that prematurely announces his victory, thereby assuring his victory, as in Mariposa no one wants to vote on the wrong side—the losing side. In short, Josh Smith is a marginally likeable, self-serving individualist and manipulative materialist, one who comes from Canada's timber frontier and insinuates his way into the "inner life" of Mariposa. He exploits the deluded Mariposans, becomes the town's elected representative, and by the last sketch is on his way to "Ottaway." Perhaps we are to imagine that

Smith, the "over-dressed pirate" (p. 10), will help guide the Canadian ship of state as shrewdly as he steered the Mariposa Belle to dock.

Against Smith stands the community of Mariposa, the ironically idyllic, somewhat northern Canadian town that embodies Leacock's qualified ideal of tory community. Smith is the materialist, the individualist, the personification of, and "josh" on, liberal individualism. In opposition to Smith, Mariposa's most obvious virtue is its nature as an interdependent community. "This opposition" (p. 12), as Leacock's narrator describes the relation between Smith and Mariposa, is made clear in the contrasting first two sketches, a contrast between real business as practised by Smith—for his own enrichment—and the illusory business of Jeff Thorpe, whose evanescent fortune was to be used partially for local philanthropic purposes, and whose real business, barbering, provides a meeting place for relaxed communal interchanges. The six middle sketches of *Sunshine Sketches* continue to contrast the material values embodied in the individualist Smith with those communal values of Mariposa, with the added and ominous suggestion in the sketches on religion that some of these Mariposan values are being lost and forgotten. The sketches on religion further point up the problems that arise when metropolitan schemes are assimilated to rural Mariposa by the practically incompetent Mariposans. Here again, Smith figures centrally in the resolution of a Mariposan dilemma (the financially troubled church), which, if not in this instance of his making, is the result of those crassly materialistic values that he has come to personify. In the matter of religion, Leacock's anti-materialism finds expression in his subtle satire on the ecclesiastical trappings of High Anglicanism. Opposed to this negative appraisal of misdirected Mariposan religion are the three sketches on romance and love, wherein Mariposan adherence to appearances serves a communally redeeming purpose. Opposed to Smith's outward movement, the three sketches on love offer the contrary inward movement of Peter Pupkin.

The reader who comes to the *Sketches* by way of the many favourable, sometimes sentimental, critical assessments of the Rev. Mr. Drone will be perplexed upon encountering the numerous faults of the misguided and misguiding pastor. Drone, the Anglican minister of the Church of England church in Mariposa, is introduced sitting in his garden and reading drowsily in Greek. The narrator asks a leading question: "For what better could a man be reading . . . than the Pastorals of Theocritus?" (p. 96). Since Greek would appear to be all that this pastor "reads" (and as his muddled biblical references would further suggest), the reader might well answer, "his Bible." It is unnecessary to recall Leacock's frequent invidious remarks on classical literature to observe that in reading the pastoral poems of Theocritus Dean Drone is wasting his time and neglecting the pastoral duties of an Anglican minister. The prefacer provided the pertinent gloss with his remarks on "languages, living, dead, and half-dead," the acquisition of which left Dean Drone knowing "nothing of the outside world" and "intellectually bankrupt"

(p. viii). As developments reveal, Drone's ill-spent time and mismanagement invite the literal bankruptcy of his Church of England church.

The new church is more than a testimony to Drone's and Mariposa's incipient materialism: it is most damagingly a denial of the past. It has replaced the "little stone church, . . . a quaint little building in red and grey stone" (p. 100). The stone from the old church was, as the narrator notes, "devoutly sold to a building contractor, and, like so much else in life, was forgotten" (p. 105). The plan had been to incorporate the stone from the old church into the new church. The central concern of *Sunshine Sketches* could be neither better nor more artfully put: the worthwhile from the past—from "Mariposa"—must be remembered forward if there is to be any hope for a full and continuous life in the present and the future. In the matter of Mariposan religion, such a re-membering does not prove to be the practice.

Leacock's narrator leaves little reason to question the error of the motives behind the new church's existence. The imposing edifice is "a large church with a great sweep of polished cedar beams inside, for the special glorification of the All Powerful, and with imported tiles on the roof for the greater glory of Heaven and with stained-glass windows for the exaltation of the All Seeing" (p. 102). A moment's reflection should reveal the ludicrous incongruity between mistaken aspiration and vain achievement in Mariposa's new Anglican church. In Leacock's view, strong cedar beams do not glorify the All Powerful, nor do imported tiles reflect greater glory heavenward; and whether or not the All Seeing is exalted by stained-glass windows, it is certain that those who are inside the church, admiring the cedar beams and thinking of the tiles and looking at the windows, will not be able to see into the Book of Nature beyond the comparatively opaque windows. Malcolm Ross has summarized popular reaction to the similar importation of High-Church Anglican architecture into the Maritimes in the late nineteenth century: "To stain a window was perhaps to stain a soul."[5] In Leacock's view, such ostentation takes the Anglican Church away from its roots—astray from the *via media*. More than simple materialism, this is the error of Drone and his congregation. And this original error leads to the commission of others.

Drone's new church is a "high" church even in spatial terms. The first sentence of "The Ministrations" reveals that the church stands "a little *up* the hill from the *heart* of the town" (p. 95, emphasis added). The new church "towered above the maple trees of Mariposa like a beacon on a hill. It stood so high . . ." (p. 106). The pastor of this literally "high" church, Rural Dean Drone, rather than tending to his Christian pastoral duties, sits reading his pagan pastorals of Theocritus at a "rustic table" (pp. 95, 97, 100). But the rustic table—"table" being the designation of the traditional Anglican altar—as little reminds Drone of his religious roots and the error of his ways as did the disposal of the old stone church and the defacement of the cemetery. To some extent, Drone's misplaced faith in such *things* as logarithms and ostentatious churches illustrates what Leacock observed of the failure of economics: "The fault of economics was the assumption that what *can only be done by the Spirit* could be done by material interest."[6] Drone is much lacking in the Spirit. He is unconcerned with *Logos*, the Word of the Bible, which, with the Book of Nature, is the true evidence of the Creator's works. Despite the windy intentions of glorifying God, the narrator makes clear the true inspiration of the new church: "You could see and appreciate *things* from the *height* of the new church,—such as the size and the growing wealth of Mariposa,—that you never could have seen from the little stone church at all" (p. 106, emphasis added). This association of "height" and material affluence suggests an appreciation of things from a realtor's point of view. The new church is a testimony to Mr. Smith's and the city's god— Mammon.

In accordance with the suggestive satire on High Anglicanism, there is subtle and straightforward anti-Catholic satire, which is an apt association because the High-Church movement was accused in nineteenth-century England of "Romish" sympathies.[7] When the Anglican congregation begins to turn against Drone,

> Yodel, the auctioneer, for example, narrated how he had been to the city and had gone into a service of the Roman Catholic Church: I believe, to state it more fairly, he had "dropped in,"—the only recognized means of access to such a service. He claimed that the music that he had heard there was music, and that (outside of his profession) the chanting and intoning could not be touched. (p. 109)

The ritualism of Roman Catholic worship is associated, in so far as Yodel's opinion of Latin hymns is concerned, with an inferior sort of auctioneer's yodelling. Drone's one contribution to the efforts to raise money is a "magic lantern lecture" on "Italy and her Invaders" (p. 116). Even if the "magic lantern" (an early version of the slide projector) is not meant to suggest in a derisive fashion the tabernacle light of the Catholic altar (which testifies to the "Real Presence" of Christ at the altar), there should be no question as to the import of "Italy and her Invaders": not only is Drone actively interested in the things of Italy (Roman Catholicism) but he is also permitting her "Invaders" (High Anglican practices) to establish a position in Mariposa. It can thus be seen that by means of spatial imagery (the location of the church), symbolism (the rustic table), and humorous implication (Yodel, the magic lantern lecture), Leacock indicts Drone for leading his Anglican flock away from the roots of Anglicanism and towards a High-Church Anglicanism that is suggestively associated with Roman Catholicism. It is not, however, the ecclesiastical trappings of High Anglicanism that the Mariposans seek to escape. It is the church's financial debt. As Yodel's remarks reveal, and as the conclusion to "The Beacon" will further emphasize, the Mariposans look for solutions to their problem in the very things that caused their dilemma—in a richer ritualism (Roman Catholicism), in city schemes (the Whirlwind Campaign), and in a bigger church which they build with the insurance money.

When the city-inspired Whirlwind Campaign fails, Drone does penance over his letter of resignation. He sees finally that his remaining, mistaken pride in his facility with language is unfounded: "Then the Dean saw that he was beaten, and he knew that he not only couldn't manage the parish but couldn't say so in proper English, and of the two the last was the bitterer discovery" (p. 138). Appropriately, Drone's obsession with words and literalness—with the Greek language, with the epithet "mugwump," and with his letter of resignation—rather than with the spirit of the Word, is associated with the mismanagement of the church. Drone's taste in church architecture finds here a literary parallel in his "fine taste for words and effects" (p. 136). But when Drone attempts to write in "proper English," in the language of the Church of England, his words become merely "one set of words and then . . . something else" (p. 135). At every turn, Drone is defeated by that which caused his problems: affectation in word and deed.

The gregarious cohesion of the Mariposan community of the Whirlwind Campaign may not completely offset the selfishness that they evidence, yet their behaviour does present them in terms of a human, if ineffectual, community. Although the conditions which they place on their contributions to the Campaign assure their financial security and boosterish vanity, these conditions are nevertheless in pointed contrast to Mr. Smith's conditional donation: "Mr. Smith had given [the campaigners] two hundred dollars in cash conditional on the lunches being held in the caff of his hotel . . . . So Mr. Smith got back his own money, and the crowd began eating into the benefactions" (p. 129). From its realization in the city, the Whirlwind Campaign undergoes, like so much else imported to Mariposa, a transformation to mere appearance, an appearance or illusion that attempts vainly to function as reality. Yet this appearance does serve a real purpose. Unlike the costly appearance of the church, the Campaign serves to call forth feelings of communal purposefulness in contrast to Smith's obsessively individualistic avariciousness. But what the Mariposans really needed to redeem their church was a return to the Anglican *via media*, a retreat from High-Church ostentation, a recovery of the inspiration of *pneuma* and the Word as opposed to the whirlwind. In the progress of events, though, this was never a possibility.

When the metaphoric beacon on the hill breaks "into a very beacon kindled upon a hill" (p. 139), it serves specifically to illuminate the error of High Anglican ostentation and functions generally to highlight the folly of Mariposa's materialistic ambitions. This symbolic illumination of error is presented once again in comparison to the shady dealings of Mr. Smith, who functions in "The Beacon on the Hill" as a sort of *deus ex machina*. The firefighting is described: they "fought it, with the Mariposa engine thumping and panting in the street, itself aglow with fire like a servant demon fighting its own kind" (p. 140). The Mariposans fight furiously because "the fire could leap into the heart of Mariposa" (p. 140). The brigade is led by Mr. Smith, by whom the narrator is suddenly fascinated and to whose actions he wishes especially to direct the reader's attention: "Most of all I wish you could have seen Mr. Smith" (p. 141). Much is transpiring in this scene. As leader of the firefighters Smith is imagined to be fighting the fire with fire, and both "fires" are imaged as "demons." Figuratively, Smith is battling a spiritual pride equal to his own materialistic ambitions. Moreover, this fire which Smith started threatens "the heart of Mariposa," the place where, it will be recalled, Smith's Hotel is located (p. 9). Smith fights the fire, then, to save his own hotel and the material possessions of what he already has determined will become his constituency—his political base.

As has been shown, Leacock's narrator disapproves of the new church and of the Mariposans' discarding and forgetting of the old stone church which, "like so much else in life, was forgotten" (p. 105). The new church must come down, by hook (axe) and by crook (Smith). By employing Smith to burn down the church, Leacock effectively points up the relation between the agent of destruction—Smith—and the motivations behind the beacon's existence—pride, affectation, and materialism. Although the narrator ironically celebrates Smith's actions, exclaiming, "At it, Smith! Down with it!" (p. 141), it would be as mistaken to conclude that he approves of Smith even in this instance as it would be to think that he admires the new church. Smith is useful in the matter of the church for his destructive efficaciousness, a quality which again places him in contrast to the habitually ineffectual Mariposans. Moreover, the scene of Smith's transfiguration on the angled beams of Drone's driving shed can be viewed as a grotesque parody of the Crucifixion.

Smith starts the fire "in April" (p. 140), which is the time of the Crucifixion. He does so with the help of "Gingham's assistant" (p. 146)— the assistant of the Gingham whose Christian name is Golgotha, "the place of the skull" where Christ was crucified (Mark 15:22). When Smith splits the beam of the driving shed, "the beam gapes asunder" (p. 141), a suggestively mock-biblical expression that distantly recalls St. Mark's description of Christ's death: "And the veil of the temple was rent in twain from the top to the bottom" (15:36). The scene of the church's fall is described: "Then when the roof crashed in and the tall steeple tottered and fell, so swift a darkness seemed to come that the grey trees and the frozen lake vanished in a moment as if blotted out of existence" (p. 143). Again, the blotting darkness suggests St. Mark's description of Christ's death: "There was darkness over the whole land" (15:33). It can be argued further that not only is the scene of the fire a parody of the Crucifixion but that Smith functions as a hideous parody of Christ. By His death, Christ ransomed mankind and provided *assurance* of heaven; by burning down the beacon, Smith ransoms the indebted parish by indirectly providing the redemptive *insurance* money. Smith, in league with Golgotha Gingham, is associated with death rather than with life. (Smith is also, in his "huge red helmet" [p. 142], something of a Satanic figure. His "voice . . . dominates the fire itself" [p. 142], a fire that earlier is termed "a great Terror of the Night" [p. 140]. And the name "Smith" is, of course, suggestive of the roaring furnace of a blacksmith's smithy.) In fulfilment of Smith's parodic function, the destruction of the church is followed by further moral inversions: what should be experienced as a catastrophe is felt to be a "luxury of excitement . . . just as good as a holiday" (p. 144); the beacon is worth more when extinguished than when beaming; and "a little faith and effort" (p. 145) resolves into faith in illegality and the efforts of Smith as arsonist and axeman.

It may have been the bleak outlook resulting from the sketches on religion that led Leacock to follow them with the three sketches that portray most positively the virtues of life in Mariposa. Although Leacock does not seem to have possessed faith in the conventionally religious sense (he was by most reports an occasional kind of Anglican), the Pupkin-Pepperleigh romance suggests that he believed in the redemptive "enchantments" of love. Where the Mariposans discard the old and truly spiritual in favour of the new and ostentatiously material, Peter and Zena achieve a kind of fusion of the romantic and the realistic.

In the three sketches dealing with love in Mariposa—"The Extraordinary Entanglement of Mr. Pupkin," "The Fore-Ordained Attachment of Zena Pepperleigh and Peter Pupkin," and "The Mariposa Bank Mystery"—Josh Smith's customary manipulative role is undertaken by an indigenous Mariposan, Judge Pepperleigh, and by an appreciative outsider, Pupkin Senior. Unlike Smith, the outsider who comes to Mariposa only to move out, Peter Pupkin is an outsider moving inwards to a permanent place in the heart of the community. Smith comes from Canada's northern timber frontier, where he learned to manipulate both axe and men, and settles temporarily in Mariposa as the embodiment of all that threatens the community. In contrast, Peter Pupkin, the latest issue of Loyalist stock, moves from the older, longer-settled eastern provinces of Canada and settles permanently in Mariposa to become an example of the best the community has to offer. Although useful in the matter of razing the beacon, Smith, the pseudo-frontiersman, threatens the values of the community. Pupkin, from the longer-civilized Maritime provinces, marries a native Mariposan and with her fortifies the community with an "enchanted baby" (p. 211). Those who help to "fore-ordain" the attachment of Pupkin and Zena—Judge Pepperleigh and Pupkin Senior—are the representatives of law and order and the long-established business community.

The three sketches devoted to Mariposan love present a systematic blurring of the line between illusion (or romance) and reality. The romantic perception that makes of commonplace occurrences "extraordinary entanglements" leads actually to extraordinary love; the romantic notion of a "fore-ordained attachment" results in actuality, for the romance is to some extent fore-ordained by Judge Pepperleigh and Pupkin Senior; and the illusory bank robbery serves a real purpose by bringing about a resolution to Pupkin's romantic dilemma. By blending the romantic and the realistic, sketches seven through nine best illustrate Leacock's credo that "you cannot tell a love story just as it is—because it isn't . . . . When a young man sees in his girl an angel, and a young girl sees in her lover a hero, perhaps they are seeing what is really there."[8] Leacock's narrator is insistently "kindly" towards Mariposan folly in these three sketches on Mariposan love, an attitude which is best appreciated in contrast to the satirical-elegiac narrative stance in the preceding three sketches on Mariposan religion.

The scene of Pupkin's meeting and falling in love with Zena, the scene which concludes "The Extraordinary Entanglement," makes clear the enchanting, transforming quality of love. Not only is "the whole world changed" (p. 165) for Pupkin as a result of meeting Zena, but the narrator, too, undergoes a change. He begins the relation of love's effect on Pupkin by revealing the commonplaceness of the ironic, "most peculiar coincidences" which bring Pupkin and Zena together. But as he moves from Pupkin's perception of the "whole world changed" to Pupkin's view of Mariposa, it becomes apparent that the narrator sympathizes with the sentiments expressed and that he bemusedly, patronizingly, though not condescendingly, condones the workings of this romantic love: "And, for Pupkin, straight away the whole town was irradiated with sunshine, and there was such a singing of the birds, and such a dancing of the rippled waters of the lake, and such a *kindliness* in the faces of all the people, that only those who have lived in Mariposa, and been young there, can know at all what he felt" (p. 165, emphasis added). The irradiation of sunshine offers here a contrast to the "darkness" of "The Beacon" which blotted out the trees and the lake (p. 143). However, Mariposa is "irradiated with sunshine" only when the vision is a lover's; Mariposans all have "kindly" faces only when seen with a lover's eyes—Pupkin's, the prefacer's, the narrator's, those of the narrator of "L'Envoi," and Leacock's. Significantly, the sunshine of these *Sunshine Sketches* is contingent upon "an affection," as the prefacer admitted in his concluding paragraph. And "kindliness," it will be recalled, is the key and controversial word in Leacock's definition of humour: "The essence of humour is human kindliness."[9] For Leacock, love, like humour at its best, transforms reality and allows humanity to be viewed in as kindly a light as human folly will allow.

Complications occur, of course, before the story of Peter and Zena realizes its enchanted resolution. A romance would not be a Leacockian romance without its conventions being parodied as they are simultaneously exploited and elevated. In the second sketch of the three-sketch love story, "The Fore-Ordained Attachment," the complications arise, ironically, from Pupkin's adoption of Zena's romantic perspective. In one of *Sunshine Sketches'* characteristic inversions of the conventional, Pupkin is shown to fear that Zena will not marry him because his family is wealthy rather than heroically poor. This threat from unchivalric affluence is termed "cold reality" (p. 179). And as is often the practice in the *Sketches*, the reality that threatens Mariposa is projected onto "the city." Pupkin feels threatened by a poet "up from the city, probably" (p. 188); Pupkin is driven to his final attempt at suicide because "Zena had danced four times with a visitor from the city" (p. 195); and, after the bank "robbery," Pupkin's new role as hero is threatened by the investigating detectives who "come up from the city" (p. 203).

Yet the narrator has made his view clear with reference to the threat of the city in a passage that contrasts the Mariposan girls with their city rivals:

> The Mariposa girls are all right. You've only to look at them to realize that. You see, you can get in Mariposa a print dress of pale blue or pale pink for a dollar twenty that looks infinitely better than anything you ever see in the city,—especially if you can wear with it a broad straw hat and a background of maple trees and the green grass of a tennis court. (p. 169)

The Mariposan girls are more attractive because they "wear" with their simple dress a more becoming environment than do their urban counterparts. Zena and Peter have little to fear. Their romance is not only invulnerable to the threats of reality and the city, it is indirectly assisted by the extra-Mariposan world. This favourable interdependency is illustrated by the realization of Pupkin's greatest fear—that his wealthy father will visit Mariposa.

Upon his arrival in Mariposa, Pupkin's father demonstrates, however, that his son's apprehension was unfounded. The father smokes a corncob pipe with Judge Pepperleigh, casually passes time in Jeff Thorpe's barber shop, hunts ducks, and, unlike Josh Smith who "stiffs" junior bank tellers in "freezeout poker" (p. 79), plays poker for insignificant stakes (pp. 210-11). Pupkin Senior, unlike the auditor of "L'Envoi," is fully capable of returning to and courteously adapting to life in the little town. And he genuinely enjoys Mariposa, for "they had to send him telegrams enough to fill a satchel to make him come away" (p. 211). Most important, Pupkin Senior has passed on to his son the real heroic virtues which make possible the resolution of the romantic complication. Leacock's narrator is little short of lavish in singing the praises of these real Loyalist virtues—the virtues of loyalty, duty, courage, and self-sacrifice.

When in "The Mariposa Bank Mystery" Pupkin suspects that Missinaba County's harvest money is threatened, he forgets "for the moment all about heroes and love affairs . . . . He only knew that there was sixty thousand dollars in the vault of the bank below, and that he was paid eight hundred dollars a year to look after it" (p. 197). Following this tribute to the virtues of work and duty (those Carlylean-Victorian virtues), the narrator eulogizes Loyalist courage—that which Pupkin Senior has bequeathed to his son: "His [Pupkin's] heart beat like a hammer against his ribs. But behind its beatings was the blood of four generations of Loyalists, and the robber who would take that sixty thousand dollars from the Mariposa bank must take it over the dead body of Peter Pupkin, teller" (p. 198). Such sound Loyalist stock comprises for Leacock—the Canadian tory, the British imperialist, the humanist—the real stuff of heroes, of which even a "teller" may partake. Pupkin's courage turns him into "such a hero as even the Mariposa girls might dream about" (p. 198), thus bringing about his proposal to Zena and her acceptance of him, their life in an "enchanted house" which is surrounded by "enchanted grass," and in which house sleeps an "enchanted baby" (p. 211).

Leacock has written elsewhere that in the real world, as opposed to a fictional world, the enchantments of romantic love are impermanent: "All lovers—silly lovers in their silly stage—attain for a moment this super-self, each as towards the other. Each sees in the other what would be there for all the world to see in each of us, if we could but reach it."[10] The narrative perception which conceives of romantic lovers as living permanently in an enchanted world temporarily abandons itself to the subjective perspective of the lovers. This is the case with Leacock's narrator at the conclusion of the love story. It would be wrong to harm the conclusion by forcing it onto some critical Procrustean bed of distorting irony. Of course there is much ironic parody of romance conventions and romance itself throughout the sketches on Mariposan love: the adventurous hero, the beautiful heroine, the providential coincidence, the happy ending, and so on. But as Jerome H. Buckley has observed of Oscar Wilde's often ironic portrayal of women who evoke pathos, "We may suspect the playwright of deliberately burlesquing the distress of his heroines; but we can hardly assume that he would have us regard his most calculated pathos as completely ironic."[11]

As is often the case in Leacock's writings, the love story presents an instance of extremes being modulated—the realistic tempers the romantic and vice versa. The three-sketch love story has similarly tempered the disheartening conclusions that were drawn from the previous three sketches which portrayed Mariposa as extremely affected, materialistic, and dishonest in matters of religion. Effectively excluding Mr. Smith from the love interest, the sketches on love and marriage reveal the town in its most positive light, functioning as a cohesive community towards commendable goals—love, marriage, and a new Mariposan citizen to help justify the town's habit of inflating its census figures. All of which is to say that Leacock's enchanting love story is also a religious chant of a kind. It is a number of humorously intoned variations on a single theme—romantic love—which are chanted to counter the dispiriting failure of Mariposan religion.

"The Engagement of Mr. Pupkin," *Montreal Star*, April 13, 1912

Sunshine Sketches of a Little Town

IV

The marine Excursion of the Knights of Pythias

Half past six on a July morning! The Mariposa
Belle is lying at the wharf decked in flags,
with steam up ready to start.

Excursion Day!

Half past six on a July morning, and Lake
Wissanotti lying in the morning sun as calm
as glass. The opal colours of the morning
lights are shot from the surface of the
water.

Out on the Lake the last thin threads of
the morning mist are clearing away like flecks
of cotton wool.

The long call of the loon echoes over
the lake. The air is cool and fresh. There
is in it all the new life of the land
of the silent pine and the moving waters,

SC

96

Sunshine Sketches of a Little Town

XII. L' Envoi. The Train to Mariposa.

¶ Leaves the city every day about
five o'clock in the evening, the train
for Mariposa.

Strange that you did not know of
it, though you come from the little town,
, or did, long years ago.

¶ Odd that you never knew in all
these years that the train was
there every afternoon, puffing up
steam in the city station, and that
you might have boarded it any
day and gone home. No, not
home, of course you wouldn't call
it "home" now; "home" means

The Roads Back: *Sunshine Sketches of a Little Town* and George Elliott's *The Kissing Man*

CLARA THOMAS

. . . So it is that each one of them in due time marries an enchanted prince and goes to live in one of the little enchanted houses in the lower part of the town.

STEPHEN LEACOCK, *Sunshine Sketches of a Little Town*

People in town never considered the possibility of a birth-giving without the familiar old figure standing on the walk outside the house. . . . There he'd be: a gnarled, brown old man, his back curved, standing still, his sharpening machine down on the walk in front of him. . . . The grinderman is there, outside the door to a birth-giving so that the father and child can love.

GEORGE ELLIOTT, *The Kissing Man*

Stephen Leacock in *Sunshine Sketches of a Little Town*[1] and George Elliott in *The Kissing Man*[2] both use the microcosmic world of an Ontario small town for an exploration of the mysteries of time and memory. Their attitudes and effects are very different, however. While Leacock preserves the distance of the ironist-raconteur with an occasional excursion into sentimentality, Elliott's narrator moves always on the inside, speaking through first one, then another of his characters. Leacock first takes us on a walkabout tour through Mariposa, then halts our movement to treat us to a series of filmic episodes that sets us up as the spectators we continue to be throughout. Elliott draws us in, past the frames of his pictures, to feel for and with his characters and to identify with their ongoing journeys.

Leacock's narrator begins deprecatingly, as a practised story-teller, blandishing his audience into listening to him, though he is, in fact, as compulsively determined to be heard as the Ancient Mariner himself: "I don't know whether you know Mariposa. If not, it is of no consequence . . ." (*SS*, p. 1). The introductory pages constitute a brilliant setting of place and time, a juxtaposing of long shots and close-ups:

> There it lies in the sunlight, sloping up from the little lake that spreads out at the foot of the hillside on which the town is built. . . . On the Main Street itself are a number of buildings of extraordinary importance—Smith's Hotel and the Continental and Mariposa House, and the two banks (the Commercial and the Exchange), to say nothing of McCarthy's Block (erected in 1878), and Glover's Hardware Store with the Oddfellows' Hall above it (*SS*, pp. 1-2).

Then the narrator extends the reader's field of vision, at the same time establishing his appropriate reception of and response to all the sketches that will follow, by the series of appearance and reality contrasts in which the real is named appearance only and the inflation of comedy makes itself manifest:

> Of course if you come to the place fresh from New York, you are deceived. Your standard of vision is all astray. You do think the place is quiet. You do imagine that Mr. Smith is asleep merely because he closes his eyes as he stands. But live in Mariposa for six months or a year and then you will begin to understand it better; the buildings get higher and higher; the Mariposa House grows more and more luxurious; McCarthy's Block towers to the sky . . . why, after a few months' residence you begin to realize that the place is a mere mad round of gaiety (*SS*, p. 3).

The five final paragraphs of this introduction begin, "Outside of Mariposa there are farms that begin well but get thinner and meaner as you go on," and end, "Thus the year runs its round, moving and changing in Mariposa, much as it does in other places" (*SS*, pp. 4-5). They climax and summarize the appearance/reality play that has just gone on—and to anyone of my generation with small-town experience, they are among the most poignantly funny and true lines in all our literature. When they finish, Leacock's scene is set—and so is the reader's relation to it. The town has been framed, miniaturized into an endearing magic world of its own, an enchanted, static world, where nothing is as it seems and, also, nothing is threatening to the outsider/reader/viewer.

Leacock then leads his readers to ringside seats from which we watch and listen in to a series of episodes, short feature films, more accurately cartoons, whose characters overlap and whose attributes and adventures are completely recognizable as likely, though comically inflated. If we recognize our own peccadilloes, our neighbours', or Canada's, in characters and events, it is with an amused, rueful, but ultimately comfortable sense of enjoyment, not dismay. And always we are comfortably outside the scenes we are watching, not required or invited to feel more than a momentary sentimental sympathy for Dean Drone for the loss of his self-esteem, or Judge Pepperleigh for the loss of his son. At the end, of course, Leacock rounds it all off and gives it all away—we have been especially distanced indeed, in the élite "leather chairs of the Mausoleum Club, talking of the little Town in the Sunshine that once we knew," stopping time for the exercise of affectionate memory, of amused, ironic, worldly wisdom, mixed with a certain measure of condescension.

In nineteenth-century American political parlance the comfortably superior group in the Mausoleum Club would have been called "mugwumps," the term that so bewildered and distressed Dean Drone. Mugwump meant a fence-sitter, one who did not have the nerve to dirty his hands with politics and so was seen as being ineffectual in the real business of life. Leacock's use of the word as a key factor in the episodes centring on Drone and his church points to one of the chief literary sources of *Sunshine Sketches*, a book called *Plunkitt of Tammany Hall: A Series of Very Plain Talks on Very Practical Politics*, by William L. Riordan, published in 1905. We are used to thinking of Leacock in conjunction with Thorstein Veblen, especially the congruities between Veblen's *The Theory of the Leisure Class* and Leacock's *Arcadian Adventures with the Idle Rich*. I would argue that in *Sunshine Sketches* George Washington Plunkitt is the prototype for Josh Smith, the hotel-keeper, and, to a lesser extent, for Jefferson Thorpe, the barber. Plunkitt and his career as Chief Boss of New York's Tammany system, State Senator, Assemblyman, Policy Magistrate, County Supervisor, Alderman and Millionaire, fascinated William Riordan, a New York reporter. He interviewed Plunkitt repeatedly at the place Plunkitt called his office, Graziano's bootblack stand in the old New York County Court House. The substance of the book that ensued is Plunkitt's, but the conception and the writing of it are Riordan's. Arthur Mann, the Smith College historian who introduced the 1963 edition, calls Plunkitt a "lovable rogue," and sums him up this way: "The fairest way to evaluate him is by his own standards. To Riordan he said that, 'if my worst enemy was given the job of writin' my epitaph when I'm gone, he couldn't do more than write: George W. Plunkitt. He Seen His Opportunities and He Took 'Em'."[3]

For us the point is how much the real Plunkitt sounds like one or other of Leacock's creations. Here is Plunkitt speaking in Riordan's chapter called "Honest Graft and Dishonest Graft":

> Everybody is talkin' these days about Tammany men growin' rich on graft, but nobody thinks of drawin' the distinction between honest graft and dishonest graft. . . .
>
> Jest let me explain by examples. My party's in power in the city, and it's goin' to undertake a lot of public improvements. Well, I'm tipped off, say, that they're going to lay out a new park at a certain place.
>
> I see my opportunity and I take it. I go to that place and I buy up all the land I can in the neighborhood. Then the board of this or that makes its plan public, and there is a rush to get my land, which nobody cared particular for before.

> Ain't it perfectly honest to charge a good price and make a profit on my investment and foresight? Of course it is. Well that's honest graft.[4]

On the day of the great election in Missinaba County Josh Smith deployed his boys with an equal cunning, so blatant that it almost seems innocent:

> And it was just at this juncture, with one hour of voting left, that Mr. Smith emerged from his committee rooms and turned his voters on the town, much as the Duke of Wellington sent the whole line to the charge at Waterloo. From every committee room and sub-committee room they poured out in flocks with blue badges fluttering on their coats.
> "Get at it, boys," said Mr. Smith, "vote and keep on voting till they make you quit" (*SS*, pp. 144-45).

There are massive differences in the effects of the two texts, however. While *Plunkitt* is a primer for power-bosses throughout, very funny but breath-taking in its assumptions of manipulative politicians and malleable electorate, Leacock's ameliorating genius softens such effects again and again. Jefferson Thorpe, the foolish, bedazzled, and greedy speculator, dreams of helping the poor and the blind with his loot. After the great crash,

> . . . things are not so bad. You see it was just at this time that Mr. Smith's caff opened, and Mr. Smith came to Jeff's Woman and said he wanted seven dozen eggs a day, and wanted them handy, and so the hens are back, and more of them, and they exult so every morning over the eggs they lay that if you wanted to talk of Rockefeller in the barber shop you couldn't hear his name for the cackling (*SS*, p. 35).

Likewise the story of Dean Drone, the incompetent clergyman, ends with a scene of affectionate pathos:

> So you will understand that the Dean's mind is, if anything, even keener, and his head even clearer than before. And if you want proof of it, notice him there beneath the plum blossoms reading in the Greek: he has told me that he finds that he can read, with the greatest ease, works in the Greek that seemed difficult before, because his head is so clear now.
> And sometimes—when his head is very clear—as he sits there reading beneath the plum blossoms he can hear them singing beyond, and his wife's voice (*SS*, p. 86).

All of Leacock's sketches end with a strongly visualized scene, sometimes of stillness like this one, sometimes full of bustle and noise, like the grand torchlight parade to celebrate Josh Smith's victory or the rescue of the Mariposa Belle. But we are always outside the frame, safely detached from involvement in and responsibility for the action.

> Look at the lights and the crowd! If only the federal census taker could count us now! Hear them calling and shouting back and forward from the deck to the shore! Listen! There is the rattle of the shore

ropes as they get them ready, and there's the Mariposa band—actually forming in a circle on the upper deck just as she docks, and the leader with his baton—one—two—ready now—
"O CAN-A-DA!" (*SS*, p. 54).

Leacock played the enchanter when he wrote *Sunshine Sketches*. He stopped time; he placed his readers comfortably in the armchairs of the Mausoleum Club and he miniaturized Mariposa for his viewers, as he reminds us at the end: "How vivid and plain it all is. Just as it used to be thirty years ago" (*SS*, p. 153). With the broad strokes of his comic wand he trivialized real issues and then dismissed his whole conjuring as a nostalgic exercise: "'Mariposa! Mariposa!' And, as we listen, the cry grows fainter and fainter in our ears and we are sitting here again in the leather chairs of the Mausoleum Club, talking of the little Town in the Sunshine that once we knew" (*SS*, p. 153). However, "we" are the readers and the final implication is clear if we wish to take it: if we do not like the Mariposa revealed to us, we still have to share in responsibility for it, for we have chosen to leave the town and to stay outside, in the comfortable leather chairs of our Mausoleum Clubs.

George Elliott wrote *The Kissing Man*, not to stop time, but to join past, present, and future in an ongoing, nurturing process, supportive of the growth and development of individuals. He took as his epigraph this passage from T. S. Eliot's *Notes towards the Definition of Culture*: "But when I speak of the family, I have in mind a bond which embraces . . . a piety towards the dead, however obscure, and a solicitude for the unborn, however remote." After *Sunshine Sketches, The Kissing Man* is the next landmark in our small-town literature. Like its forerunner it is made up of a linked series of sketches or stories, and it, too, is influenced by an American work, though one very different from Riordan's, Sherwood Anderson's *Winesburg, Ohio* (1919). The technique of Elliott's work is entirely different from Leacock's; Elliott is engaged in pulling his readers into the text, into the action and the issues, not in separating us from these. Most particularly he invites and persuades us into a recognition of kinship, with each other, with men, women, and children of the past, in the present, and on into the future.

Winesburg, Ohio stands, with remarkable solidity, as an ancestor behind *The Kissing Man*. Anderson looked at the small town from an angle of vision very different from Leacock's and he saw a clouded scene. He looked at individual striving and loss and pulled his reader in with him, to identify with the characters, not to sit comfortably entertained outside the field of action. His "Book of the Grotesques," the introduction to *Winesburg, Ohio*, is, in particular, so apt to Elliott's work that it, too, could serve as epigraph:

> That in the beginning when the world was young there were a great many thoughts but no such thing as a truth. Man made the truth himself and each truth was a composite of a great many vague thoughts. All about in the world were the truths and they were all beautiful. The old man had listed hundreds of the truths in his book. I

will not try to tell you all of them. There was the truth of virginity and the truth of passion, the truth of wealth and of poverty, of thrift and of profligacy, of carelessness and abandon. Hundreds and hundreds were the truths and they were all beautiful.

And then the people came along. Each as he appeared snatched up one of the truths and some who were quite strong snatched up a dozen of them.

It was the truths that made the people grotesques . . . the moment one of the people took one of the truths to himself, called it his truth, and tried to live his life by it, he became a grotesque and the truth he embraced became a falsehood.[5]

The Kissing Man was published in 1962, but Elliott worked on its stories for many years before, eventually persuaded by John Gray of Macmillan to collect them into a book. His town is not named, but it is, he told me, a composite southern Ontario town within easy distance of Lake Huron. Its geography is that of Strathroy where Elliott worked on the newspaper, *The Age Dispatch*, right after the war. Many of its names, Geddes' department store, Doc Fletcher, and the Butlers, for instance, are Strathroy names. In fact George Elliott told me that one of the impelling reasons for his writing had been conversations with Doug Geddes, who used to tell him stories of Strathroy in which "he seemed to be trying to tell me more than he could express." Years before Northrop Frye wrote the "Conclusion" to *The Literary History of Canada* Elliott was writing about the "Garrison Mentality" facet of small-town life and its effect on individuals.

But he was also writing about "The Way Back," the title of his final story and the clue he leaves with us to continuing community and kinship. The time centre of *The Kissing Man* and the central explication of his ideal occur in the book's fifth story, "A Room, a Light for Love." At the end of World War I Gerald returns to Allie, his wife. Proprietors of the Queen's Hotel, they begin their married life again. Its centre—and the town's—is the Queen's Hotel drawing-room with its great crystal chandelier, the setting of all the parties they give for the community. The chandelier is Allie's symbol for both individual love and community bonding. As the years pass and the parties dwindle, Allie ritualistically breaks a pendant for every friend who dies. When she herself dies Gerald and Dougie Framingham, who had loved her since boyhood, voice their memories and the story's meaning:

"Don't you remember, Doug? The first party in the drawing-room? Helping us to put up the chandelier?" . . .

"But what's the use of knowing," Gerry said. "Alison is dead and it's over now. It doesn't much matter when it started. It doesn't matter what she meant. She was going against the way the world was and it felt right to me and I helped her all I could, but it doesn't matter now."

"It does matter," Doug said. He felt like the boy-man again, helping to carry handfuls of crystal pendants up the stairs to the drawing-room.

"No, we're growing old and it doesn't matter. We're just making old noises."

"But don't you see? Now we have a right to. It matters to the new ones coming along to hear our noises" (*KM*, pp. 61-62).

Gerry goes downstairs and destroys what is left of the chandelier and all its pendants. Then, "one loving, remembering voice flowed into the other. The chandelier was destroyed, so the thread of memory had been established and the two old men took turns remembering."

Time in *The Kissing Man* stretches back two generations and forward two from the dating of this story—four generations from the marriage of Tessie and Mayhew in story one, "An Act of Piety," to the birth of Dan and Victoria's baby in story eleven, "The Way Back." Throughout, the essence of time is seen to be process, movement, and a continuity whose essence is love. At the end of "An Act of Piety," Honey Salkald remembers his grandmother, proud Tessie, and Mayhew, his grandfather. He knows that "the past was in him, never to be forgotten or ignored. But he didn't know whether he was to forgive. He wanted only to keep what was good and pass it on" (*KM*, p. 12). Proud Tessie had worn a black velvet ribbon around her neck, signifying to herself her apartness from the common Irish who had moved into the neighbourhood, and also her general fear of the unknown "other," explained to herself as a fear of catching the goitre that disfigures her neighbour woman. In the book's context, however, the ribbon signifies a cut-off between heart and head, Tessie's wilful breaking of community with herself and with her neighbours.

Mayhew, her husband, was of a different stamp. When he lay dying he wouldn't see the minister: "Oh, don't bother," you said. "I've got a religion better than what you offer" (*KM*, p. 9). At his funeral "Uncle Dan recited 'Thanatopsis', the way you said he was to," and thus the words of William Cullen Bryant voice Mayhew's belief and the book's benign message about the process of man's life in time:

. . . Thou shalt lie down
With patriarchs of the infant world, with kings,
The powerful of the earth, the wise, the good,
Fair forms, and hoary seers of ages past,
All in one mighty sepulchre. The hills
Rock-ribbed and ancient as the sun, the vales
Stretching in pensive quietness between;
The venerable woods—rivers that move
In majesty, and the complaining brooks
That make the meadows green; and, poured round all,
Old Ocean's gray and melancholy waste,
Are but the solemn decorations all
Of the great tomb of man. . . .
　　So live, that when thy summons comes to join
The innumerable caravan, which moves
To that mysterious realm, where each shall take
His chamber in the silent halls of death,
Thou go not, like the quarry-slave at night,
Scourged to his dungeon, but, sustained and soothed
By an unfaltering trust, approach thy grave,

Like one who wraps the drapery of his couch
About him, and lies down to pleasant dreams.

Many times in *The Kissing Man* the flow of time and the concept of the unity and continuity of all things are reiterated. In "You'll Get the Rest of Him Soon" Froody watches, mystified, as Doc Fletcher buries a tiny bit of pink (obviously a piece of the umbilical cord) in his backyard and hears him mutter, "you'll get the rest of him soon." Honey Salkald spies on the doctor on another, similar occasion:

> There the doctor was, standing up straight with his arms up above his head, looking down into the grass.
> The doctor sounded a lot like an Anglican minister, Honey said later.
> "Seventy years isn't much, the way you keep track of it," the doctor said, "a breathing spell while you wait for the rest of him. You'll feel him growing from now on; a little restless in a few years; then an urgent longing; then the discoveries and finally the contentment. Nourish him the way you do all of us. Be patient with him because you'll get the rest of him soon. *There is no question of reward*" (my italics, *KM*, p. 44).

The characters who are really involved in the process of living and who are *for* life in *The Kissing Man* are not bound by the tough old Calvinistic God of rewards and punishments. Mayhew is one of them, Doc Fletcher is another; the Kissing Man, who compassionately kisses lonely women in Geddes' Department Store, is one, as is the Man Who Lived Out Loud, who lay down and died when his attempts to make people really live finally became too much for him. Johnson Mender, who knows that children might show his son Tom, Mordy Macdonald, and the minister the way back to kinship and community, is another. They are all wise old men in the literary tradition of Tiresias—their prototype goes far back beyond written literature. They are all outsiders to the hidebound little town and they all formulate Elliott's perception of time as a natural process and continuum and of our kinship opportunities and responsibilities as we live our times.

The Kissing Man is like an overlay, a palimpsest on *Sunshine Sketches*. Leacock caught and capsulized his town for us forever, under glass, much like the little buildings and tiny figures which used to sit still within a glass paperweight on my grandmother's parlour table. But if you shook the glass, the snow came down and down, and the scene was blurred and full of movement. Elliott in his time shook the glass, and now we can also see within it the old man fishing under the willow tree, and hear him giving pledges of hope and continuity to the boy, Finn:

> "But the leaves fall into the water in October," Finn whispered.
> "Yes. A leaf of love, a leaf of loneliness, a leaf of regret, a leaf of remorse, a leaf of compassion, a leaf for everything good and forgotten, for everything bad and always here. They fall into the pond and the trout eat them."
> "The trout?"

"Sure. There are trout in the pond, son. Everybody in town thinks the trout have gone, but the big ones are still here in the pond. You've got to be patient to see them. That's all."

"I thought the pond was fished out long ago."

"This pond is never fished out. Look at it. A widening. Holding the water that comes down the creek, holding it back for a few minutes, then letting it through the mill-wheel and down the race and going on. That's what's important. Going on because it must. But here in the widening the pond catches all that falls from the willow and the trout eat it. The fish are there now, taking from what's upstream, staying here at the widening, taking from the tree, avoiding the lures, living, living."

"Do you believe that?" Finn got up to go.

"Believe? I know" (*KM*, p. 78).

Untestable Inferences: Post-Structuralism and Leacock's Achievement in *Sunshine Sketches of a Little Town*

ED JEWINSKI

Numerous critics—Davies, Watt, Bowker, Dooley are just some that come to mind—agree that Leacock's *Sunshine Sketches of a Little Town* is riddled with inconsistencies and confusions. In fact, because flaws in the book continually mar the whole, Dooley speaks for these readers when he claims, "We are not sure what moral perspective we are being asked to adopt"[1] to understand and judge the actions of the work. Regrettably, such readers assume that, despite the ironies they see, the narrative pattern should be straightforward reading. Ignoring that the brightest sunshine casts the darkest shadows (the death of Fizzlechip, for instance),[2] such readers are puzzled not only when the work becomes dark, unclear, imprecise, brooding, but also when the narrative becomes unclear, cloudy, and inconsistent.

Although such readers grant that there is a drastic difference between what is *said* and what is *shown* in this book—in fact they may be credited with accurately describing the problem and its possible ramifications—they fail to accept that this difference is not an accidental characteristic, but a necessary feature of the book. The purpose of this paper is to demonstrate that the very "difference" between showing and telling noted by these critics is the first indication of a significant "differance"—a deferral of meaning (as Derrida puts it), an impossibility of a resolution of a "text."[3]

Jacques Derrida's concern with continual "deferral" of all meaning, whenever language is used, can be of great assistance when attempting to come to terms with Leacock's *Sunshine Sketches*. Derrida's methodical (although not methodological) approach may be used to refute the critical rubrics that a "text" must be determinable, that a narrator must be consistent, that the values and morals of a work must be—even can be—clear and straightforward.

The insistence that "ambiguities" in a "text" must forward and unify and integrate the various elements of a work rests upon the shibboleths of New Criticism. Post-modernist approaches to literature, however, do not accept such assumptions, preferring instead to question what constitutes a "reading." Such an approach seems particularly suited to a "text" whose very title, *Sunshine Sketches*, hints at a design and structure that requires whiteness, blank space, emptiness, to make its impression. That the reader cannot determine the right moral stance merely confirms, as the narrator of the "sketches" insists, that to the "eye of discernment" Mariposa is a "perfect jostle." In other words, unless the phrase "sunshine sketches" is seen as oxymoronic—possibly a kind of reversal of Milton's famous "visible darkness"—the "right" perspective may never be attained. As the narrator of the *Sketches* insists, without the proper perspective, "your *standard* of vision is all astray" (*Sketches*, p. 3, my emphasis).

To attain a better "view" of the "text," then, it might be best to consider the problem of language and how it affects a reader's response to the work. One might begin by noting that a single grammatical pattern (a sentence, for example) can generate any number of meanings; moreover, within this group of "meanings," there can exist two mutually exclusive ones. Paul de Man makes this point quite effectively in his *Allegories of Reading*:

> . . . asked by his wife whether he wants to have his bowling shoes laced over or laced under, Archie Bunker answers with a question: "What's the difference?" Being a reader of sublime simplicity, his wife answers by patiently explaining the difference . . . but provokes only his ire. "What's the difference?" did not ask for difference but means instead "I don't give a damn what the difference is."[4]

De Man's point is that the same statement can offer or produce mutually exclusive "meanings"; in the *All in the Family* episode, the literal meaning asks for an explanation of difference, while the figurative meaning asserts that any explanation of difference is irrelevant.

As long as we are discussing statements made by characters from the mass media, it is not especially difficult to distinguish between the obtuse literalness of an Edith and the unwitting metaphoricity of an Archie. In a work like Leacock's *Sunshine Sketches*, however, the distinction is not nearly so simple. Consider, for example, Leacock's narrator wrestling with the problem of how and why "one of the greatest minds in the hotel business" could ever commit the blunder of locking an important man like Judge Pepperleigh out of his bar:

> How he had come to do so, it passed his imagination to recall. Crime always seems impossible in retrospect. By what sheer madness of the moment could he [Smith] have shut up the bar on the night in question, and shut Judge Pepperleigh . . . outside of it? (p. 7)

Certainly the vaudevillian response to the one-liner made by the Ediths of the world—"How could he do it? By locking the door, of course!"—does not do justice to Leacock's sophisticated satire. Yet is the reader being invited to probe the "text" for an answer, or is he compelled immediately to concede that the "sheer madness" of a moment could never be probed, illuminated, or clarified? Is the reader to seek a subtle, but definite, cause/effect pattern that will throw light upon what seems merely arbitrary and accidental, or has the reader been told not to be an Edith-like ninny offering explanations where none is needed or desired? The solution to this rhetorical problem rests in the understanding of Leacock's narrative method as a series of "untestable inferences" followed by a sequence of *non sequiturs*. Initially, the reader is offered a series of statements which lead him to be indecisive about whether X or Y is the answer. Immediately afterwards, the reader is given a sequence of events which relate to the main issue only tangentially. For example, whether Smith locks out the judge with or without reason is left for the reader to infer; the rest of the narrative merely emphasizes how rapidly and surely and confidently Smith can seem to act. Yet in being awed by Smith's seeming ability to act efficiently, does the reader become, like Edith Bunker, wholly absorbed by the literal level of the "text"? The fact that Smith ultimately retains his licence does not clarify what the character's method of action means *in* and *to* the community of the work, or to the morality of the work as a whole. Is the reader to approve or disapprove, admire or condemn, praise or ridicule Smith's method of retaining his privilege to run a bar? It is on this second level that Leacock's book particularly disrupts, disconcerts, even destroys, the reader's confidence that an appropriate framework of beliefs and morals can be constructed to make sense of the characters' actions. Why, in other words, Smith resorts to elaborate and expensive renovations to regain favour is never directly clarified. Without a larger context (a larger series of explanations), the individual inferences often lack a meaning which may be tested, weighed, judged.

This kind of problem recurs throughout the book, and understanding its presence often helps elucidate why *Sunshine Sketches* regularly eludes critical analysis while it consistently captivates its audience. Let me illustrate my argument, before concluding with a focus upon the narrative method and the problem of "perspective," by analyzing three main inferences that control a large part, although not the whole, of the series of sketches. The first is the previously mentioned Josh Smith's "madness of the moment"; the second is Peter Pupkin's love affair with Zena Pepperleigh; and the third is Dean Drone's sanity (or should I say the lack thereof?). In each case, I plan to clarify the inferences a reader might make, reconsider them, and, finally, suggest why they should be abandoned altogether. By tracing the contradictory possibilities of readings, I intend to show how Jacques Derrida's notions of "difference" contribute to a reader's understanding of the enigmatic quality of Leacock's *Sunshine Sketches*. In other words, my argument forwards the notion that a single so-called "text" may be the interweaving of mutually exclusive "readings," for no unified reading need be necessary to a work of literature.

The passage recording the temporary "madness" which drove Josh Smith to lock out the judge is an excellent example of necessary deferral, for the reader is forced to consider what, if anything, might have motivated Smith to act so rashly. Initially, the reader might have been content with accepting how men like Smith can overcome the haphazard, whimsical, irrational persecution of the dishonest and the intemperate. By sheer contrast, Smith seems less the villain than Pepperleigh, even if only because Smith seems more thorough, exacting, rational, and methodical than the unpredictable judge. However, this very description reminds the reader that Smith is supposed to be far too methodical to be a mere victim of a moment's "madness." Another glance at the key passage reinforces that the act is increasingly unlikely in a man who never allowed "any hands but his own" to lock up. The extended and elaborately complex rhetoric of the passage, with its carefully balanced sentences, suggests neither haste nor clumsiness nor accident. Its repetitive and carefully structured quality insists that a reader's opinion or view should be, somehow, suspended for some reason or alerted to some nuance. The short moment is drawn out, extended, elaborated. The subject matter and the method of telling seem at odds. Some cause/effect pattern seems more and more reasonable and rational because the narrator's worrying word after word in the passage implies that a man like Smith, a man ordinarily so thorough, so exact, so deliberate, and so cautious simply does not err so clumsily:

> Punctually every night at eleven o'clock Mr. Smith strolled from the desk of the "rotunda" to the door of the bar. If it seemed properly full of people and all was bright and cheerful, then he closed it. If not, he kept it open a few minutes longer till he had enough people inside to warrant closing. But never, never unless he was assured that Pepperleigh, the judge of the court, and Macartney, the prosecuting attorney, were both safely in the bar, or the bar parlour, did the proprietor venture to close up. Yet on this fatal night Pepperleigh and Macartney had been shut out—actually left on the street without a drink, and compelled to hammer and beat at the street door of the bar to gain admittance. (p. 7)

The reader obviously knows *what* happened, but he is at a loss to explain *why* it happened. Within this chapter, the reader can only wonder if Smith has merely retaliated for having been fined after donating one hundred dollars to the Liberal Party. Was Smith foolish enough to attempt, in a moment of sheer folly, to avenge himself upon those representatives of the "terrible engine of retributive justice"? Or, has this newcomer (for it must be remembered that Smith has only been in Mariposa for three years) simply blundered so badly because of ignorance? Within the entire context of the book, the reader can only speculate as to whether Smith's decision to act is, somehow, based upon his determination to run for office later. But why he should do so by jeopardizing his liquor licence is even more incomprehensible than the possible desire for revenge. The reader, in other words, is thrust into what Derrida would call a *gap* in the "text," a place from where the individual inferences lack meaning. The reader is offered insights which allow neither clear vision nor precise understanding.

Whatever the reader's "tentative" decision about Smith's motives, the results become increasingly unclear and vague, for the rest of the chapter concentrates on the actions, not the motives, of one of the "greatest minds in the hotel business" matching wits with the townspeople. At the end of the chapter, he ends up paying an inordinate amount to retain his licence. To get his way, Smith adds a "caff" and a "Rats' Cooler" to a building he does not even own. He hires a French Chef, rents all the accessories for a European atmosphere and, finally, arranges the prices so that he loses 75 cents for every 25 cents that he earns.

The "greatest mind" seems to have blundered into one of the most unprofitable forms of business imaginable, especially in a town the size of Mariposa, which boasts no fewer than three hotels. Even though Smith is determined to close up everything the moment he regains his licence, the cost seems tremendously out of proportion to the goal. Smith's ability with basic mathematics is made to seem as weak as Dean Drone's.

Has Smith really mastered and manipulated the townspeople, or have the townspeople forced the newcomer to reveal his own vain desire to belong? Is Smith guilty of attempting to buy acceptance and respectability, no matter what the cost? Have the townspeople, moreover, finally accepted his bribes, his alcohol, and his persistent effort to be on a first-name basis, only after making it clear that it will "cost him" to be part of the "inner life" of the town? It seems more than possible that Smith has fully understood the circumstances, for he never formally closes either the "caff" or the "Rats' Cooler" despite his original plan to do so immediately upon having his licence renewed. The first he retains, although he never uses its grills again, and the second he closes for "repairs" that never seem to get done—a tidy compromise for him, but an enigmatic conclusion for the reader.

Much of the agonizing over Smith's fate, of course, results because of the uncertainty and imprecision in a reader's mind when the language of the "text" appears to be denying the very thing it asserts. One must assume, for example, that Smith is an extremely capable and intelligent being; yet Leacock's prose so scrupulously compels the reader to make continual inferences that any such statement has to be held in abeyance. Smith, as the narrator puts it with such exquisite ambiguity, compels readers to recognize that the "ordinary human countenance" is "as superficial as a puddle in the sunlight" (p. 6) when compared to that of Mr. Smith. But does that mean Smith so perfectly reflects what a viewer wishes to see that the hotel keeper never reveals his motives, or does the statement mean that Smith is so absolutely transparent that he hides no motive whatever? Whether Smith is manipulating others or being manipulated by them depends, in part, on the reader's response to such potentially contradictory statements of seeming directness. But in attempts to come to a definite answer, the reader necessarily discovers only the "text," the language used, and that language remains so unswervingly referential that the reader can go only from one word to another, from one passage to another. There seems no way to get beyond the text.

Throughout the sketches, where readers expect the literal, they find the metaphorical; where they expect realism, they find literary convention; where they expect something to be made definite or conclusive, they find that it is perpetually put off or deferred. The difficulty, furthermore, is that the irony, paradox, and so on do not reconcile the variant readings, but rather encourage and multiply them. Where Smith may be seen, at times, as the master of his circumstances, he equally appears to be their slave. The "saving" of the Mariposa Belle, often cited as an instance of Smith's ability to steer the social state of Mariposa on its proper course, is also the instance of Smith's *hubris* and incompetence. Although Smith descends into the bowels of the boat "to plug the timber seams with mallet and marline" (p. 53), he is also the former captain who has "had a steamer 'sink on him' on Lake Nipissing and a still bigger one . . . sink on him in Lake Abbitibbi" (p. 50). Is it any wonder, then, that the reader is confused when, with Smith's hands at the steering wheel, the Mariposa Belle's arrival at the dock sends people scurrying back and forth? "Hear them calling and shouting back and forward from the deck to the shore! Listen!" (p. 54). The national anthem will strike up again, but is it now a tune of triumph or failure? The Mariposa Belle initially sank as its passengers were singing "O Canada," and the narrator haunts the reader with rhetorical questions that increase one's insecurity about that "grip" on "the steering wheel of the Mariposa Belle":

> Can he take her in? Well, now! Ask a man who has had steamers sink on him in half the lakes from Temiscaming to the Bay, if he can take her in? (p. 54)

The sheer bravado and foolhardiness is underscored when the chapter ends: "—one—two—ready now— 'O CAN-A-DA!'"

The reader's inability to establish whether Smith crashed the Mariposa Belle in the harbour or docked it safely leaves the "text" open and indefinite. The reader is lured into believing that there is the possibility of some ultimate reference point for making final sense of the "text." On the one hand, the narrator suggests that certain inferences are legitimate; on the other, then, he continually undermines the inferences by offering just enough information, description and summary, and just enough evidence, to subvert them. The difficulty is that the evidence rests on an "encyclopedia" of information that can never be fully traced. Each time the reader wishes to collect the "evidence," he must defer the presentation of his reference points to another piece of evidence, and defer that piece of evidence to another piece of evidence. The shifting of this reference point exposes the purely fictive or purely arbitrary nature of lifting one fragment from the "text" to establish a conclusive argument. Ultimately, Leacock's *Sunshine Sketches* is a commentary on its own inability to transcend the interpretive function, and this problem is passed on to the reader. What the work is really about, then, is its *unreadability*, which is to say the reader's struggle to impose his own preferred fictions upon the events and episodes and incidents. The work's achievement is that it neither points to a "reality" nor completes itself as a "unified fiction"—rather it draws us back into its own infinite problematics.[5]

Smith's comment about the kerosene used to burn down the church might illustrate this point best. Smith denies starting the fire by insisting that he "had not carried a can of kerosene up the street" on the night of the fire, "and anyway it was the rottenest kind of kerosene he had ever seen and no more use than so much molasses" (p. 86). The *non sequitur*, it appears, gives the game away—the reader infers that Smith did it. Yet, is the reader to examine the statement literally or metaphorically? Literally, Smith need not have carried the can of kerosene up the street, for he had Mr. Gingham's assistant with him, and this second man could have carried the liquid. But if Smith is literally accurate in the first half of the statement, why can he not be so in the second half? The kerosene may have been of little or no use in getting the building to burn. Although the reader is never told exactly how the fire was started, his instinctive recognition of Smith as the culprit makes him forget one thing: the mere fact that Smith did it establishes neither a clear motive nor an insight into the problem of Smith's role in the sketches. Starvation for facts, by this time in the book, blinds the reader to all other concerns.

Is Smith the manipulator or the manipulated? Is he now, unlike his portrayal in the earlier sections of the work, part of the ruling group of Mariposa? Since Mullins "belonged away down the lake" during the fishing season (p. 60), Smith, Mullins, and Nivens could easily have conspired to rid the town of the expensive church. Furthermore, since Mullins continually convinces Drone to "change" (p. 60) the figures which itemize the expenses incurred for the building, they could easily have conspired to defraud the insurance company. Most importantly, they could easily have planned to create enough of a hullabaloo on the night of the fire to mislead the narrator into believing that their actions as firemen were to "save" the town:

> They fought the fire, not to save the church, for that was doomed from the first outbreak of the flames, but to stop the spread of it and save the town. (p. 82)

Yet, as the narrator notices, even this is not quite right, for "most of all they fought to save the wooden driving shed behind the church, from which the fire could leap into the heart of Mariposa." Their method of saving it, of course, is to have Smith cut through the main beam so that they could destroy the shed by hauling it down.

The emphasis upon the actions makes the reader forget both the motives and the reasons for those actions. In part, Smith seems to have been right: the kerosene *was* "useless"; the men had to create the diversion of pulling down the shed to "save" the town only to ensure that the church would burn completely and that all the insurance could be collected. The need for time explains why Smith was made "the head and chief of the Mariposa fire brigade that night" (p. 83).

The skill and strategy employed by Smith and Mullins prepare the reader for Smith's final *coup*: his election to office through bribery and deception. However, the reader is now left in the greatest dilemma of all. Either Smith is the supreme manipulator or he is the supreme victim. He can leave Mariposa to do as he will, but like the dishonest Bagshaw before him, he is fully at the mercy of the townspeople's whims, stupidities, and corruptions. In a sense, the reader has gone full circle. If Pepperleigh is one of the characters who initiates Smith's rise to power, Pepperleigh is also one of the characters who has a final comment upon Smith's "success":

> Judge Pepperleigh spoke and said that there was no need to dwell on the victory that they had achieved, because it was history; there was no occasion to speak of what part he himself had played, within the limits of his official position, because what he had done was henceforth a matter of history. (p. 146)

Has Pepperleigh, the book's seeming prime representative of irrational justice, underscored the shenanigans of a "little" town determined to have a "yes-man" in office? If such a possibility exists, the ironies of the last sentence are too multiple to resolve:

> Mr. Smith, of course, said nothing. He didn't have to—not for four years—and he knew it. (p. 147)

"He knew" could mean that he understood what was expected of him. He might see himself as free—the narrative method never allows for entrance into Smith's mind—or he might see himself as the spokesman for the town's wishes, for four years later he would have to speak, particularly when it came time to account for himself and his actions to a town determined to vote only at the last second, "not wanting to make any error in their vote" (p. 145).

The social "reality" of these sketches is far from solid and determinate; in fact, it is a kind of "text" that persistently eludes a single interpretation. Provisional, not final, readings are possible, but they are readings that a minute's thought will reverse. More interestingly, the readings are mutually exclusive, for Smith may be either the victim or the victimizer, depending on which particular items a reader selects from his "encyclopedia" of information concerning the actions of the work. The book, in other words, is built upon what one might call dialectical contradictions. Many of the narrator's comments offer a choice of readings based not on the ambiguities of descriptive terms alone, but on the evasive syntax of the sentences. As the choices thus generate proliferations of meanings, the possible number of "meanings" conveyed by them multiplies. By the end of the book, the result is a large number of incompatible affirmations, and the notion of assertion itself becomes problematic.

The strategically effective method of narration provided by Leacock works, in part, on the system of compelling the reader to temporarily accept a binary opposition, an opposition that is gradually shown to be an illusion. Initially, the reader must accept that Smith is dishonest, for he keeps the bar open after legal drinking hours. Since this is a minor "sin," cultural relativity may be invoked, for, after all, the people who drink in the bar include the lawyers, prosecutors, and judges. The logic seems to be that if the representatives of justice break the law, one should not judge Smith too harshly. When Pepperleigh seems completely irrational for imposing the technically legal point of late hours to remove Smith's licence, one sees Smith as a victim. The result is a "dishonest victim." Pepperleigh is presented in the same manner. He represents both justice and the legal system, although he breaks the law and abuses it. In effect, he becomes a "legal criminal." The opposites that clash here are not two *characters* but two *readings*. Such mutually exclusive qualities explode the very "binary difference" between one character and the other; it is not a quarrel between a man who breaks a law and one who upholds it, nor between a man who takes the law into his own hands and one who does not. The reader is forced into "differance," for the "general notions" of justice and injustice collapse when the reader must stop to decide where justice begins and where it ends. Such questions, however, are not answered by the "text," and the reader is caught in a web of incompatible strategies of comprehension. To respond to the "text," he is lulled, initially, into believing that one character has more "right" than the other, only to have that notion subverted, for if the reader sides with Smith as the victim, "prudent" manipulation of others is the morality that must be accepted as "necessary," all "human" action being in response to the hypocrisies of a society steeped in moral relativity. If one sides with Smith as the victimizer, then the reader must embrace the notion that society is nothing more than a morass of moral unpredictability. Both readings plunge the reader into the "gap" of the text; he is left only with the "trace" that justice exists somewhere and somehow, for how else could he have perceived the "unfairness" of Pepperleigh's form of "retributive justice"? Some kind of Platonic notion must be invoked here: either the text is so mimetic that it reflects man's inability to link adequately man's nature and his actions, or the "text" is hopelessly incapable of resolution. Since the question of justice in the world is rhetorical, the reader is forced to contemplate the provisional and fictive constructs which link the various parts of his reading of the text.

Since this discussion has become "philosophical," showing that links are made on constructs which precede a "text," and since these constructs are often unverifiable notions that must be examined in themselves, it is important to stress that while New Criticism attempts to bring such ambiguities to a single point which unifies and integrates the various elements of a text, post-structuralist readings tend to remind readers of how a text remains a "collection of irresolvables." Leacock's book, in particular, is amazing in its impenetrability, for one is constantly barraged with incompatible strategies of reading. The ambiguities force readers to acknowledge that "texts" are, at best, seen as instances of "textuality." Let me illustrate the point by turning to the role of Peter Pupkin in the *Sketches*.

Initially the reader is forced to conjecture, at least to some degree, upon the nature and intelligence and quality of mind of the lover Pupkin.

The reader, on this account, is told directly that this lover has been victimized by the education process: "Peter was kept out of the law by the fool system of examinations devised since his father's time" (p. 107). A close reader of the text might never get past this sentence, if he were ever foolish enough to give the statement full thought. A gap has opened here, for what is education, and how can it be measured, and is that "fool system" worth anything when it eliminates individuals like Pupkin? In part, of course, I am toying here with the notions I elaborated earlier: statements in this book simultaneously assert and deny.

The issue of "intelligence" is crucial in assessing what appears to happen to Pupkin. In part, for example, the narrator would have the reader believe that Pupkin is putting his full mind to the issue of keeping his rich family a secret. Yet if that is the case, why would he play the rich man's game, tennis, nearly every day and buy "a white waist-coat and a walking stick with a gold top, a lot of new neckties and a pair of patent leather boots" (p. 102)? Such ostentatious dress does little to suggest that he has accepted his role as a banker's clerk, despite his father's efforts (if one believes the narrator) to "tan [luxury] out of him" and to get it "thumped out of him" and to get it "knocked out of him" (p. 107).

Pupkin's attitudes puzzle the reader. Is Pupkin sensitive about his father's wealth, or does he reveal his own snobbishness and false glorification of wealth and privilege when he considers that it would be foolish to have his father come to Mariposa and meet Jim Eliot and treat him "like a druggist merely because he ran a drug store! or speaking to Jefferson Thorpe as if he were a barber simply because he shaved for money! Why, a man like that could ruin young Pupkin" (p. 105)? But the father, who finally does come to visit and returns home only after being sent "telegrams enough to fill a satchel," enjoys himself with both Eliot and Thorpe, "as if he had never lived any other life in all his days" (p. 123). Sympathy for Pupkin is either gradually eroded as the story continues (for he is revealed as cold, stupid, snobbish, spoiled, and egotistical), or arrested by the reader's inability to decide whether Pupkin is truly none of these, but rather a naive simpleton who neither understands the implications of his actions nor recognizes his own dimwittedness—he believes, for example, that his love was sealed the moment he recognized that, by "the strangest coincidence in the world" (p. 100), his handwriting was exactly like Zena's.

If one reads at the simplest levels of the two mutually exclusive "meanings" of the text, one's effort to reconcile the problems seems impossible. One level denies and subverts the other in Edith-like fashion. Even describing the mere details resembles the difference between lacing over and lacing under.

Pupkin's encounter in the bank with the so-called robber also becomes a self-evident sham of mutually exclusive readings. Money is not enough for Peter Pupkin, nor is social rank, social privilege, or social status. At the moment he senses the robber, he is simply a man, a man of duty, without any secondary motive. In fact, the narrator insists that

Pupkin has even "forgotten" heroism. Yet the following passage, with its reiteration of the same phrase, clarifies that the narrator either protests too much or has lost control of his own presentation of the character:

> I think, as Peter Pupkin stood, revolver in hand, in the office of the bank, he had forgotten all about the maudlin purpose of his first coming. He had forgotten for the moment all about heroes and love affairs, and his whole mind was focused, sharp and alert, with the intensity of the nighttime, on the sounds that he heard in the vault and on the back-stairway of the bank.
> Straight away, Pupkin knew what it meant as plainly as if it were written in print. He had forgotten, I say, about being a hero and he only knew that there was sixty thousand dollars in the vault of the bank below, and he was paid eight hundred dollars a year to look after it. (p. 115)

The repetend subverts any notion of forgetting; it impresses the same point on the mind, leaving it as a phrase that echoes and reverberates. Pupkin may now be seen as either staging the scene—pretending to the heroism that he thinks Zena dreams of—or acting on motives of duty and devotion to the bank. The "reading" that will "determine" the "text" depends upon what the reader accepts as Pupkin's "intelligence." The difficulty is, once again, the problem of which "reading" the reader will determine as he selects from the "encyclopedia" of information available. The selection, however, is dependent upon the socio-cultural values which form the particular blend of inferences determined by the reader. The ambiguities, in other words, do not forward a reading to a single unified reading; rather they thrust the reader into the *gap* between what is read and how that reading is determined. The values imposed, and the construct derived therefrom, indicate the fictions the reader will use to bridge the difference between what is said and what is implied. The "text" remains silent, and the reader is caught in the web of "textuality," the various ideologies that may influence his "reading."

In setting up any series of "legitimate" propositions, we, as readers, select those features which we consider compatible with the "context" and suppress those which are not—or, at least, those which we *suppose* are not. In this way, we write as much as read the fiction before us. Postmodernism can nevertheless help us feel comfortable with recognizing those textual elements which we continually suppress. By granting that our criterion for *appropriacy* in interpretation is often bound by what we consider culturally significant (more militant post-modernists would insist *ideologically* significant), we also limit, guide, control, and suppress the direction of our cultural discourse and self-reflection. To ignore the incompatible qualities of the *character*-istics of Pupkin is to ignore how literature subverts, rather than enhances, the notion of a "unified, consistent" individual. The theory of consistent characterization, in other words, is a cultural imposition upon fiction, a cultural value desired, but a cultural "value" denied by Leacock's *Sketches*. At each stage where Pupkin's character eludes analysis, the reader should be examining which cultural values he has imposed in his efforts to bring the character "together."

A concluding consideration of Dean Drone's role in the *Sketches* might help us see what happens when a "text" is recognized as an enigmatic problem of "textuality." In the narrative, the presentation of Dean Drone's plight probably evokes the most powerful emotions in the reader, for in this section the narrator uses such powerfully equivocal statements that it is extremely difficult to simplify how they deny what they affirm. The statements assuring the reader that Drone did not go mad or insane after his church burned to the ground illustrate the point:

> Dean Drone? Did he get well again? Why, what makes you ask that? You mean, was his head at all affected after the stroke? No, it was not. Absolutely not. It was not affected in the least, *though how anybody who knows him now in Mariposa could have the faintest idea that his mind was in any way impaired by the stroke is more than I can tell.* (p. 86)

The clause I have emphasized seems particularly irresolvable. Does it mean that the people of Mariposa are too insensitive to understand what happened? Does it simply mean the present generation never "knew" him, for most of those who knew him are now dead? Does it mean that, in fact, all the "people" are really characters in a story, and so could not know anyway? Why they cannot know is never made clear.

Yet are readers any more capable of knowing than the people of Mariposa itself?

To determine if Drone got "well," of course, the reader must, at some point, decide what "illness" and "health" are. In a literal sense, the narrator is right: Drone gets over the stroke, and the minister's body does recuperate. At the same time, however, his mind seems damaged, at least to us, because he now has visions:

> So you will understand that the Dean's mind is, if anything, even keener, and his head even clearer than before . . . he has told me that he finds that he can read, with the greatest ease, works in the Greek that seemed difficult before, because his head is so clear now.
>
> And sometimes—when his head is very clear—as he sits there reading beneath the plum blossoms he can hear them singing beyond, and his wife's voice. (p. 86)

The narrative asks us, in short, to consider the two stages of Drone. Before the stroke, he is wholly absorbed with worldly things— his church, his prestige, his vanity—no matter how excessive the burden on his congregation. He has, in effect, a vision of the glory of man that ignores all practical and "down-to-earth" problems. After the stroke, he is not particularly different: he is no nearer the "real world" of social activity than he ever was. From childish desires for material goods, he has moved into literal childishness and infantilism. The history of Dean Drone's life ranges from "ideal" materialism to "naive" spiritualism, a span achieved without any contact with the "human" world in between (assuming that petty matters of bills and payments and parishioners interested in neither can be equated with the "real" world).

But to probe the problem of Drone's values, a reader tends to draw on an all-too-simple series of explanatory bifurcations: sickness and health, sanity and insanity, and so on. In my own account, I have based my division on an unstated "paradigm"—the interplay of wisdom and ignorance in the form of the wisdom of folly and the folly of wisdom. And I have imposed unstated ethical values onto the text which are based on a perception of oversimplified "readings" of the social and religious problems of the "text." In other words, I am *literally* not sure what Leacock ever had to say about Drone, but I do know that my effort to explain his role has forced me to examine the archaeology, my cultural and social presuppositions and assumptions, underlying my notion of what Drone is as a "religious" figure in relation to a "faith" satirized. The difficulty remains: can the "madness of a moment" (Smith) be related to what one might call the "madness of a lifetime" (Drone), so that the "text" has a unified, rather than fragmented, structure? One can only suggest that if no conclusive commentary can be made about the "values" to be invoked, the "text" is to be seen as *jouissance*—unending verbal play that promises closure but never grants it. The narrator of the work, in other words, must be read on the literal and the metaphorical levels simultaneously, for he is perfectly correct when he insists that Mariposa is a "perfect jostle." To the small-town person, Mariposa may be a "perfect hive of activity" and to the person from "New York," it may be a sleepy town. To the Mariposan, it may be a place of great events, and to the city-dweller it may be a place of no consequence. Such a bifurcation is possible only for those who ignore that the division between city and small town is, itself, an illusory binary opposition that only perpetuates the deception, as the closing chapter "L'Envoi. The Train to Mariposa" reveals. Just as a reader cannot determine exactly where the city ends and the town begins, except in some illusory sense of seeming "difference," so the conflicting forces of signification in a "text" cannot be resolved. The reader who accepts that "six months or a year" in Mariposa will cure his "standard of vision" has forgotten the power of human susceptibility to unacknowledged relativity, for "there never was such a place for changing its character with the season" (p. 4).

Creating a narrator who so consistently appeals to a reader's desire to find an encompassing framework for irresolvable details marks Leacock's greatest achievement. Unwilling to recognize that he has been repeatedly thrust into the *gaps* of the "text," the reader who desires the "unified vision" may fault the very artistry that defies the conventions. The desire to find the limits and "margins" of a text must not become so all-encompassing that it begins to deny and devalue as "marred" the very literature that opens the question of what *is* a reading. Man's impulse to "tidy up" his readings must be resisted if the interrelationship of human experience and the representation of that experience are to be kept vital, interesting, alive, and vibrant. Leacock's narrative method—based on the use of a narrator blind to his own incompatible levels of literal and metaphorical speech—should not be condemned, but applauded. If the work fails to be an integrated work, it is only so because it is a supreme achievement of fragmentation, incompleteness, and inconclusiveness.

The Achievement of Stephen Leacock

Alec Lucas

I would like to address the subject of Stephen Leacock and McGill University, my long-time home university, where Leacock spent thirty-five years. I used to tell my students proudly that my office was once Leacock's until some wretch informed me that my office was only next to Leacock's. All the same, I retained my longstanding interest in Leacock and, for the present purpose, began to telephone those who, I was certain, had known Leacock personally at McGill. One easily forgets, however, that Leacock left McGill fifty years ago. His generation is almost gone. All who remember him at McGill were young when he was there, and their memories of him, I have found, are like those recorded in Allan Anderson's *Remembering Leacock* (1983), centring on anecdotes, manner of dress, way of lecturing, or professorial behaviour. But to return to those whom I phoned. One was off somewhere in Greece; another, somewhere in Europe and would not be back until June. (He apparently wished to avoid the Montreal winter, but counted on a mild spell in July and August.)

Finally I reached Senator Carl Goldenberg, who, of all those who knew Leacock at McGill, is probably the best informed. He had Leacock as his graduate thesis director and later, for four years, shared an office with him when Goldenberg himself was on staff at McGill. Goldenberg has already appeared in Collard's *The McGill You Knew* (1975) and in Anderson's collection, and had little to add to what he has already said in these books about his former mentor and colleague. In general, he recalls Leacock as an affable, learned, and eccentric man. Specifically, however, he did emphasize the fact that Leacock liked to drink at the "violet hour," and he gave the lie to those who suggest that Leacock drank to excess and that this habit, along with his frequent lecture tours, detracted much from his work as a teacher, thus probably having some influence on his forced retirement from McGill in 1936.

Senator Goldenberg was specific on two other points. First, he had met George Leacock, Stephen's brother, and learned from him that Stephen much exaggerated the debt, regarding his work as a humorist, that he owed George. Second, like all I consulted, Goldenberg referred to Leacock's desire to make money.

In the introduction to *The Bodley Head Leacock* (1957), J. B. Priestley places Leacock among the finest humorists, but finds him of little significance otherwise, and, in general, Robertson Davies agrees with Priestley. Stevie, Leacock's son, I am told by those who knew him, said, however, that his father never sought greatness; he simply wished to have his say and found that humour helped to increase the size of his audience. True as that may be, Leacock, caught up in the success of *Literary Lapses* (1910), *Nonsense Novels* (1911), and *Sunshine Sketches of a Little Town* (1912), finally tired of this approach. "Do not," he wrote, "ever try to be funny, for it is a terrible curse. Here is a world going to pieces and I am worried. Yet when I stand up before an audience to deliver my serious thoughts, they begin laughing. I have been advertised to them as funny, and they refuse to accept me as anything else."

Priestley and Davies are partly right. Leacock owes his national and international reputation to his humour. The Leacock Symposium, however, has revealed him as a man of wide knowledge and perspicacious mind. It has been most satisfying to see him in a wider context than that in which he usually appears, clearly revealed now as not only a humorist but as a man who had important things to say about Canadian social and cultural matters. In this regard, aside from the pleasure of hearing Leacock discussed by specialists in various disciplines, I was taken with the paper, "The Roads Back: Stephen Leacock's *Sunshine Sketches of a Little Town* and George Elliott's *The Kissing Man*." Here Leacock appears as usual as a writer positioned halfway between those who praise and those who deride village life. On the road from romanticism to realism, he stands, through irony, on both sides simultaneously. He also appeared in a new orientation as a foil for Elliott's psychological analysis of village life. What, in revolt against the pastoral tradition, Leacock mocks in large part, Elliott treats with compassionate perspicacity and moves the pastoral on to new ground.

There is much yet to do in order to discover the boy Leacock left behind him and the man he became. We have many needs. We need a fully annotated scholarly text of *Sunshine Sketches of a Little Town*. Fortunately, we now have Ralph L. Curry's complete bibliography of Leacock's writings, and ECW Press will soon publish Curry's annotated bibliography. McGill recently secured a veritable treasure-house of Leacockiana, a fifty-six-page manuscript notebook covering in detail the dates and other details of Leacock's publications and addresses from 1901 until 1925. Several pages are blank, but all in all it is an invaluable record of twenty-five years in Leacock's literary career. It names and dates some 225 articles (fifty-three in his favourite, *Vanity Fair*) and commentaries that Leacock contributed to sixty-seven publications during that period.

It lists at least (the writing is not always legible) 143 public addresses and readings, along with dates and places, thus enabling one to trace Leacock's lecture tours precisely. Poems are also listed, and these entries contain two tantalizing comments: "Aug. 1910—poems 'Today in History': one each day for a month. Pub. Press Synd." The second entry reads simply: "1913—*verses* (pub. 1914)." There is also a cryptic note for December 1911: "Canada (London) autobiography." If any proof of the industrious Leacock were needed, there are the entries for 1914 when he was simultaneously writing *Arcadian Adventures with the Idle Rich* and a series of five long articles on "My Club."

The notebook is entirely a compilation of titles, dates, and similar details, except for one very specific personal note regarding the birth of Stevie, which is given very precisely as August 19, 1915, 2:45 p.m. It is perhaps noteworthy in this context that he never mentions the death of his wife in 1925. Her death, however, may explain the termination of the notebook in that year. Again in this context, Senator Goldenberg has told me that Leacock was very much moved when leaving in 1925 to take his sick wife to England. When he spoke to Goldenberg, his voice broke and his eyes brimmed with tears.

Leacock's letters have never been edited, so there is no evidence to support Davies' comment that "we need expect no more substantial discoveries about his work from his letters or occasional pieces." In 1975 Vishna Chopra presented an edition of seventy of Leacock's letters as his doctoral dissertation at McGill. "This edition of Stephen Leacock's correspondence," Chopra writes, "reveals his personality in his various occupations: educator, public lecturer, and professional man of letters." Though limited, this selection does indeed disclose some fresh and interesting facets of Leacock's life. This dissertation, however, is only a start; unfortunately, no one has followed Chopra's lead.

Admittedly, simply collecting Leacock's letters would be difficult. As Barbara Nimmo writes, "They alone to his many friends, students, and business acquaintances could fill volumes," or, as Chopra comments, "Leacock's manuscripts are rather widely scattered throughout this continent." Even aside from their numbers (the Stephen Leacock Memorial Home in Orillia holds at least 7,000 items of correspondence), wide distribution, and, perhaps, family reservations, they might still be hard to collect, since they can command high prices. One Montreal lady, for example, hoped to be able to put her son through university from the sale of two letters that were merely notes. Yet Leacock's letters must be collected and edited for Leacock's sake and that of Canadian literature.

An edition of Leacock's letters would surely lead to a more comprehensive biography of the man than we now have. At the time (1959), Ralph L. Curry's biography of Leacock, the first, filled a very great need most adequately. Since then, however, Legate, Kimball, and Anderson have written of Leacock's life, but largely, except perhaps Kimball, again in terms of Leacock's public image. Albert and Theresa Moritz's recent biography has broadened, but not deepened, our knowledge of the man.

We need to look at Leacock's private life, at his dark side, as it were. We want to know more of the inner man, of the influences that moulded him, of his reactions to more than the nation's social, economic, and political affairs.

To illustrate the point: what, for example, motivated his drive for money? All who knew him admit that he wanted to make a lot of money. An old Leacock acquaintance at McGill knows from Leacock himself that he turned down an opportunity to write the history of his beloved McGill because there was "no money in it." Again, it is said at McGill that Leacock sought money in the name of cancer research after the death of his wife from that dread disease. Others assert that Leacock gave his concern for Stevie's future well-being as his motive. (Perhaps, of course, both desires influenced Leacock.) It has been suggested that he wanted to avoid the poverty of his childhood and youth, but what of a poverty that could afford a housemaid, a hired man, private tutoring, and secondary schooling at Upper Canada College?

What were Leacock's relationships with his wife and his son? With his own father? Davies notes that Leacock conceals his deepest feelings, yet neither he nor any other Leacock scholar has done much to get behind Leacock's mask regarding family matters. Almost all, for example, refer to Leacock's terrible threat, allegedly made when he was seventeen, to kill his father, if the latter should ever return to the farm, and, except for an expression of moral indignation over a mother abused, they leave the matter there. (There are two versions of the event. One sets it in winter; the other, in summer, a fact that changes its impact, for the winter version pictures Peter Leacock driving his wife from her home on a cold night to find shelter in a snow bank, a dramatic setting not possible, even in Canada, in August.) We need to know more about that father, Peter Leacock. Did Stephen inherit his wit and exuberance from him? Was his behaviour at the root of the son's cynicism and stoicism? Did Stephen turn from the study of literature to protect his emotional being? Did he turn to humour for the same reason? These are difficult questions. But since 1979 there has been available Elsie Tolson's *The Captain, The Colonel and me*, a history of Bedford, Nova Scotia, which throws at least a little new light on Leacock's father. It contains a photograph of a kindly-looking old man, Captain Lewis (1849-1940), to use Peter Leacock's pseudonym, and some interesting observations:

> It is Stephen Leacock's father who should be explained and the most truthful way to do it is to quote what was told me by people who knew him in Bedford.
> "He was a dandy nice man, and so was his wife. Every day in summer he sailed his 18-foot boat with the two sails, to Webster's point; and every day he went to the graveyard to tend his boy's grave. He had two hogsheads there to catch rain-water and he planted roses and made a garden of the corner lot in the Anglican cemetery."
> (Capt. and Mrs. Lewis had one son, Walter Harold, who died at age 17 and it broke their hearts.)
> "He wouldn't let the undertakers in for a long time."

(Their first home was at the corner of Rutledge and Pleasant Streets, afterwards owned by Dr. Alan Cunningham.)

"Some college boys one summer rented the Fisher house near Canfield's. They used to dive from Lewis' boat and the Captain would race down the hill yelling at them."

(Then Capt. and Mrs. Lewis moved down to the shore property in Isleview.)

"I wondered what he was captain of"? continued the man who had known him, "he had two boats and a dinghy but he wasn't that good a sailor. One day Charlie Boutilier said to him that it was a good day for a sail and you know what good sailors the Boutiliers were. Suddenly out beyond the island one of those Basin storms broke. Boutilier was used to sudden changes but Lewis was nervous. 'Lard thundering Jasus,' yelled Charlie, 'let me at that tiller!'"

A woman who knew the Captain well when she was young said, "Capt. Lewis was so kind to us when we were young. He taught us all how to swim and he was so good to children. He was cranky, sort of, but he never drank and he never was cross with us. He fixed up his boathouse for the girls to change and stood guard outside. We girls practically lived there."

Such was the father, whom Leacock never saw again after their parting in 1887, and such is the portrait of a man that suggests a reassessment of the marital relationship of Leacock's parents, if nothing else. Any future biography must surely take Captain Lewis of Bedford into consideration, as it must, too, draw on the essays that originated at the Leacock Symposium.

Malcolm Ross

Back in the twenties, my family took the *Montreal Standard,* and there was a Leacock piece in nearly every issue. We used to take turns reading Leacock aloud. I remember once, after getting halfway through a piece called "Indoor Football, or Football Without a Ball," breaking down in uncontrollable laughter. My father took over but failed to get beyond the next paragraph as laughter got the best of him too. We managed to finish the piece together in gasping, sputtering silence, our shoulders heaving and tears streaming down our faces. I can remember waking at night in laughter at that little piece by Leacock. It never occurred to me to wonder why I had laughed, and I have never tried to dissect Leacock and put him under a critical microscope. I simply continued to laugh with him down the years.

It was not until the late fifties that Leacock became important to me in a different way, that is, as the saviour of the New Canadian Library.

In the fall of 1956, I approached Jack McClelland with a proposal to publish a series of Canadian novels in paperback. I was teaching then at Queen's University and was anxious to prepare a full course on Canadian literature. We were teaching some Canadian literature from anthologies at the tag-end of a course on American literature. But you cannot teach a novel with only a chapter in an anthology to go by. The older novels were out of print, and the recent ones too expensive for classroom use.

When I saw Jack in Toronto, he expressed interest but feared there was no university market. Canadian literature in most universities was restricted to small graduate courses and thesis writing. I was able to persuade Jack that the availability of texts would *create* the market, and he decided to gamble. We finally got underway in 1958, and McClelland and Stewart announced a new series—the New Canadian Library.

The first two volumes were Morley Callaghan's *Such Is My Beloved* and Frederick Philip Grove's *Over Prairie Trails*. Several newspapers applauded the venture, although doubts were expressed about the chances of a merely Canadian series surviving for more than a couple of years. The bookstore sales were weak, and Jack took a substantial loss. But he went ahead with two more books, one of them being Leacock's *Literary Lapses*. To our surprise this book sold like hot cakes and had to be reprinted. Said Jack, "We'll keep going. But you must put a Leacock in every batch!"

So for the next five or six years, sometimes twice in one year, a Leacock book came out in the New Canadian Library. I must confess that I began to chafe under Jack's directive. One of my colleagues quipped, "Why don't you change the series title to LCL—Leacock's Canadian Library?"

When five years were done, I wrote Jack, imploring him to release me from the burden of my pledge. "Not yet," he said. "We still need him."

By this time there were very few of the humorous books left, and several months after my last desperate plea, I tried again. "Jack, am I to assume that if we are to stay alive we'll have to start reprinting Leacock's books on economics and his history of Montreal?"

He phoned. "We're off the hook. We're making a profit—and not just on Leacock."

Not only had sales in the bookstores mounted. Adoptions were flooding in as university after university introduced courses on Canadian literature. Leacock had not only saved the New Canadian Library, he had advanced, probably by some years, the introduction of full Canadian literature courses in many of our schools and colleges.

Grateful as I was to Leacock, by the time we had published the last of his volumes I had become just a little jaded, even perhaps jaundiced, in my feeling for some of his work. I do not think I read a line of Leacock again for about ten years. Then, under some inner compulsion, I began taking him with me on planes and trains. I still thought that some of his parody and burlesque were contrived and derivative, some of the punning mechanical and done to formula. But in his finest humour (and supremely in *Sunshine Sketches of a Little Town*) there is a tone and a magic utterly and uniquely his own. To be sure, he owed a great deal to Mark Twain and the American tradition of humour. But he did find his own unmistakable and inimitable voice.

The reflections of Guy Vanderhaeghe and Timothy Findley are most illuminating. Vanderhaeghe writes of the marvellous particularity of person and place in the *Sketches*, a particularity so vivid, so intense that it becomes a universality in which we can see ourselves and each other. And Findley stresses the importance of scene in these *Sketches*, of the tight congeries of situation, setting, and event in which people relate dramatically to one another.

Leacock was a conservative and an imperialist. He was also the compassionate friend of the poor and the oppressed. The *personae* of his stories are sometimes American, sometimes British, sometimes Canadian—or a mix of all three. His authorial voice, often heard over the voice of the *personae*, is perhaps multi-national and his toryism (even if sometimes "red") is audible enough.

But there is a Leacock voice which encircles these other voices like a heard halo. It is the voice in which irony, wisdom, and an iron compassion are fused in a golden humanity. This voice is not the breath of Leacock's mixed "national" postures or of his political and social convictions. It is a voice out of the very marrow of the man's inner life and sensibility. Hark and you can hear it—soaring above all that he has made in the image of any political allegiance, any nationality, any literary precedent.

There is in the highest art a purifying fire. Surely there is also a purifying laughter. For me, at least, Leacock's humour, at its highest, has always been therapeutic and, therefore, life-enhancing.

Glenn Clever

I would like to consider two aspects of Leacock: first, his historical place in the development of Canadian literature; and second, his place as a humorist.

I see Leacock as essentially a part of the Confederation period. He was born in 1868, very few years later than that group of writers— Scott, Roberts, Lampman, Carman, Campbell . . .—who, by general consensus, comprise the "Confederation School" of Canadian writers; Confederation because they came to maturity with the new Dominion of Canada—how curiously old-fashioned even the term sounds today! Writers are everywhere much the same in the kinds of worlds they create; once they emerge from the derivative phase of aping their models, they look back for their own idiosyncratic material and, consequently, forms; their major works reflect the decades of their own growing up to maturity and the immediately preceding years fleshed in by parental mythologies. The writer's world is, so to speak, that stretch of years of the parents' maturity and the writer's nonage. So Leacock's world embraces those years from about 1850 to 1900: this is his Mariposan fictional Dominion.

Leacock's world is rather an old-fashioned world, one of class awareness peculiar to the pre–World War I era, of a scorn for encroaching socialism, of automatically accepted male superiority, of nationalism but in the watercolour mode of late nineteenth-century Canada, like Bartlett paintings, not the explosive blood-colour of American Revolution, repeated in the Civil War of the 1860s, nor even Canada's own bloodletting of 1914-1918, and, of course, the imperialist ideal. That Leacock's fiction peaked in popularity between 1910 and 1925 reaffirms that essentially he belongs not to the post-war world of the 1920s but to the Confederation world then closing its doors.

As to his humour, Leacock, it seems to me, considered humour as being of two kinds: divisive or unifying. Divisive being demonical laughter *at* others, the childish regression of delight in demolishing things, the kind of laughter that threatens civilized social behaviour. Unifying humour, to the contrary, being shared laughter *with* others, the adult laughter of the realization of the oneness of all things, the kind that contributes to civilized social behaviour. In Leacock's own work, for example, we can all feel with his comic figures who are nonplussed by new experience, as in "My Financial Career"; by the social unease of the Mr. Melpomenuses of this world; or by the indecision of the Mr. Jugginses.

Leacock's primary mode of humour is that of irony, of which he is the superb master, and where he perhaps most differs from Thomas Chandler Haliburton, the direct satirist. Through Leacock's ironic eye we see late nineteenth-century Canadians in relation to their most reverential myths: of royalty, business, high society, romantic notions, organized religion, politics, education, the booming West, our always gullible selves, even his own public-speaker figure—the irony always functioning to show his deep concern that socialism, technology, and commercialism would deny human individuality and dignity.

It is interesting to compare Leacock as a humorist with Haliburton. Haliburton's colonial world of eighteenth-century, Addison/Steele satiric models sharply differs from Leacock's. Haliburton aims to satirize; consequently, his tales tend to be fable-like in form, with their morals tacked on, often awkwardly. Usually Haliburton gives the text of the day as introduction, then the amplifying example as the body of the story, then the tart moral to close. And his is a totally regional, squirearchical world, curiously remote from the realities of pioneer life, and those parts of his world that he does present Haliburton pictures at arms' length for us to view in their frame. Leacock's stories, being shaped by the principle of irony, habitually extend a situation to its ironical if often absurd extreme so that it *is* whatever moral it *has*; and because his habitual mode is unifying and not divisive, we find ourselves chuckling not at the cut-ups of a Sam Slick secondary world but with characters from *our* primary world, in which we recognize often that there but for the grace of God go we, for we are a part of the world depicted in a way we never are with Haliburton's.

Another of Leacock's achievements, in my view, is that his own deep concern for people shows through enough to indicate that the laughter sometimes borders on tears, as in sections of *Arcadian Adventures with the Idle Rich*. Leacock, superb raconteur though he was, is more than a glib comic, his humour balanced by an awareness of the deliberate evil of much human motive and act. The self-interest and focus on money and power evince a sympathy for the dispossessed, the deprived, the lonely, and the victimized of the age that he saw slowly encroaching on Mariposa.

So, a "Confederation" writer, one whose major fiction was written before World War I, with all the latent colonial regionalism, the Nature with a capital N, that "Confederation" implies? I think so, even though his "nature" was archetypical provincial small-town, for his fictional world is essentially limited to the Upper/Lower Canada pre-existing the new Dominion, without even Duncan Campbell Scott's imaginative extension into the north and west of the new land. And Leacock peopled his world with outscapes of people in typical nineteenth-century mode. The dramatization of the inscapes of characters, comic or serious, of Canadian cities, prairies, Pacific coast, Maritimes, and northern reaches of the postwar era would be done by others whose formative years were later in time.

R. L. McDougall

The upside of the record of Stephen Leacock's achievement is unassailable. I mean the humour at its best. To have made an Englishman (was it J. B. Priestley?) laugh out loud in an English railway carriage is surely a great achievement. It is a mark of Leacock's achievement that the best of his work is still in print and is likely to remain so as long as books are made. In the last few weeks I have pulled Leacock from my shelves for my own refreshment. I too have laughed out loud. Behold Lord Nosh (spelt Knotacent) confronting Gertrude the Governess: "Where had he seen those lineaments? Where was it? At the races? or the theatre? on a bus? No. Some subtler thread of memory was stirring in his mind. He strode hastily to the sideboard, drained a dipper and a half of brandy, and became again the perfect English gentleman." Or Dr. McTeague, confronted with the unlooked-for and unanswerable question from his class, mouth open like a stranded fish, toppling slowly forward over his desk, paralyzed. More moderately, I have admired again the superb control of the opening paragraphs of *Arcadian Adventures*, where expensive birds sing in the trees above Plutoria Avenue, while baby heirs to commercial fortunes roll back and forth in their perambulators, waving their fifty-dollar rattles in an inarticulate greeting to one another.

To classify and to assign influences in the face of humour as intensely creative as this is not usually a rewarding procedure. In the sixties, it was said, in response to the Socratic statement that the unexamined life was not worth living, that the trouble was we had examined the hell out of it. But Beverly Rasporich has done a good job in this area, and we must be grateful to her for a well-reasoned and informative essay. The question of the "American" Leacock has been raised also in James Steele's provocative paper on the "multi-national persona," and our judgement on it may well affect our final tally on Leacock's achievement. Was Leacock, for example, just playing games for money when he slipped into one or other of his American guises? I venture only two pieces of evidence about the nature of Leacockian humour, neither of them new, but both worth recalling. Leacock had two little stories that he loved to tell. One was about an old lady facing a painful terminal illness in hospital who wrote to thank him for the light and joy he had brought to her in her valley of the shadow. She had been blessed by the laughter that, as Leacock said elsewhere, touches universals and unites rather than divides the human family. This was the laughter of release and reconciliation, and Leacock was right in seeing it as no small gift in a world where man was born to sorrow as the sparks fly upward. The second story was about the great clown Grimaldi. A man came to see a doctor who had been recommended by a friend. He was depressed and so utterly weary of life that he had thought of committing suicide. After some talk, the doctor said: "I'll tell you what to do. Buy a ticket for a performance of the great Grimaldi; he will cheer you up." "But," the man said, "I am Grimaldi." Both stories carry bright proud banners of human dignity, and both drift towards the sad end of the spectrum of human experience. My mother-in-law, who is very old now and very wise, knew Leacock reasonably well in his later years at McGill, and when I asked her a few weeks ago what she thought of him, she said simply: "I thought he was a very sad man."

If it is true that the man that suffers is separate from the man that creates, it is true also that a single spirit encompasses them both. Leacock, it seems to me, was very much a whole man; and the whole Leacock— husband and father, academic and teacher, performer and humorist— may be seen as in itself a kind of transcendent achievement. We are indebted to Ian Ross Robertson for placing Leacock in the intellectual milieu of his times. That has been done in part before, but now it is done conclusively. Although these turn-of-the-century years were years of great flux in ideas and values, the flux was contained and disciplined by a remarkable consensus that was being swept on into the new century from the heyday of high colonialism which Roy Daniells has described so well in the *Literary History*. Leacock, together with Lighthall and Macphail and others of an idealistic persuasion, bobbed about a bit in the flux, but each found within the surviving consensus the support they needed to shape a package that made some sense of the world they lived in. The point is that Leacock knew exactly where he stood on most of the major issues of his day. How else could he have implanted those bits of steel that are the satiric dazzle beneath the surface of his best work? Yet the character of the man (I don't know if the word will convey my meaning) remained important. On the question of social justice, for example, Leacock was eclectic, but the cornerstone of his response was his basically tragic view of the human situation—what he called "the appalling inequalities of our human lot." I remember reading a passage from *The Unsolved Riddle of Social Justice* when I was a student at the University of Toronto and being very moved. Having listed some of life's many injustices (and how acutely he must have thought of his malformed son), Leacock went on to say:

> The human mind, lost in a maze of inequalities that it cannot explain and evils that it cannot, singly, remedy, must adapt itself as best it can. An acquired indifference to the ills of others is the price at which we live. A certain dole of sympathy, a casual mite of personal relief is the mere drop that any of us alone can cast into the vast ocean of human misery. Beyond that we must harden ourselves lest we too perish. We feed while others starve. We make fast the doors of our lighted house against the indigent and the hungry. What else can we do? If we shelter one, what is that? And if we try to shelter all, we are ourselves shelterless.

In the fervour of my youth, I thought this at first a shameful cop-out. But I came to think otherwise, for out of his dark vision Leacock articulated, surprisingly for his tory colouring, a rationale for something like the welfare state; and into "the vast ocean of human misery" he cast the sweet potion of his laughter. So it is on these terms, and others, that I think Leacock acquitted himself well as a human being. He wrote lightly, but he took all his work seriously. Rereading his books on Dickens, Mark Twain, the Arctic, and Canada at war, I am impressed, not perhaps by their scholarship, but simply by how well they are written and with what diligence and integrity each task has been carried out. The same qualities, by all accounts, were in his teaching.

Did Leacock prostitute his great gift for humour? Did he allow the talent to grow tawdry in servile response to an audience he knew would lap up anything he wrote, fresh or stale, and pay him well for it? Did he, as Robertson Davies has suggested, betray his talent by failing to accept the challenge of the novel's more exacting forms? This is the area of the downside in Leacock's achievement. I have no time for it now, and not much inclination if I had. I rest my case here.

Stephen Leacock: The Writer and His Writings

Compiled by RALPH L. CURRY

1887

"The Vision of Mirza (New Edition)." *College Times* [Upper Canada College], 6 (April 7, 1887), 75-76.

1890

"(The) Sanctum Philosopher." *The Varsity*, 10 (October 7, 1890), 8-9; (October 14, 1890), 20; (November 4, 1890), 56; (November 11, 1890), 68; (December 2, 1890), 104.

"The Decay of Fiction." *The Varsity*, 10 (October 21, 1890), 28-29.

"A Lost Work [by the Sanctum Philosopher]." *The Varsity*, 10 (November 18, 1890), 76-77.

"The Philosophy of Love." *The Varsity*, 10 (December 9, 1890), 112-13.

1891

"Imogene: A Legend of the Days of Chivalry." *The Varsity*, 11 (October 6, 1891), 2-3.

1894

"That Ridiculous War in the East." *Grip*, 42 (October 6, 1894), 107.

1895

"My Financial Career." *Life*, 25 (April 11, 1895), 238-39.
"An Experiment With Policeman Hogan." *Truth*, 14 (June 29, 1895), 10-11.
"The Puppet Shop." *Truth*, 14 (August 3, 1895), 10-11.
"Home Again." *Truth*, 14 (October 2, 1895), 4.
"The Force of Statistics." *Truth*, 14 (December 21, 1895), 14.
"A Model Dialogue, in Which Is Shown How the Drawing-Room Juggler May Be Permanently Cured of His Card Trick." *Truth*, 14 (December 21, 1895), 9.
"Telling His Faults." *Truth*, 14 (December 28, 1895), 15.

1896

"The New Food." *Truth*, 15 (January 4, 1896), 7.
"The Awful Fate of Melpomenus Jones." *Truth*, 15 (January 18, 1896), 10.
"The Conjurer's Revenge." *Truth*, 15 (February 8, 1896), 10.
"Hints to Travellers." *Truth*, 15 (February 22, 1896), 10.
"How Gorillas Talk." *Truth*, 15 (April 18, 1896), 17.
"The Prize Fight of the Future: A Forecast." *Our Monthly* (May 1896), 23-25.
"A Manual of Education." *Truth*, 15 (November 7, 1896), 6.
"Reflections on Riding." *Truth*, 15 (November 14, 1896), 7.
"On the Old Homestead." *Truth*, 15 (December 12, 1896), 12.

1897

"Saloonio." *Truth*, 16 (January 1, 1897), 10.
"Self-made Men." *Truth*, 16 (January 28, 1897), 11.
"Getting the Thread of It." *Truth*, 16 (February 18, 1897), 11.
"New Winter Game." *Truth*, 16 (March 25, 1897), 11.
"Boarding-house Geometry." *Truth*, 16 (April 15, 1897), 3.
"Borrowing a Match." *Truth*, 16 (April 22, 1897), 6.
"Helping the Armenians." *Truth*, 16 (May 13, 1897), 10.
"On Collecting Things." *Truth*, 16 (August 14, 1897), 3.

1901

"Children's Corner." *McGill University Magazine*, 1 (December 1901), 80-84.

1904

"Looking After Brown." *Old McGill*, 8 (1904), 226-28.

1906

Elements of Political Science. Boston and New York: Houghton, Mifflin, 1906.
"The Imperial Crisis." *Proceedings of the Canadian Club, Toronto For the Year 1905-1906*, 3 (1905-1906), 114-18.
"The Passing of the Poet." *Canadian Magazine*, 27 (May 1906), 71-73.
"A Rehabilitation of Charles II." *McGill University Magazine*, 5 (May 1906), 266-81.

1907

Baldwin, Lafontaine, Hincks: Responsible Government. Toronto: Morang, 1907.
Greater Canada, An Appeal. Let Us No Longer Be A Colony. Montreal: The Montreal News Company, [1907].
"The Psychology of American Humour." *University Magazine* [McGill], 6 (February 1907), 55-75.
"Greater Canada: An Appeal." *University Magazine* [McGill], 6 (April 1907), 132-41.
"Responsible Government in the British Colonial System." *American Political Science Review*, 1 (May 1907), 355-92.
"Discussion." *Proceedings of the Royal Colonial Institute*, 38 (1906-1907), 304-306.

1908

"College Journalism." *McGill Martlet*, 1 (November 5, 1908), 36-37.
"The Limitations of Federal Government." *American Political Science Association Proceedings*, 5 (1908), 37-52.

1909

"Sir Wilfrid Laurier's Victory." *National Review* (London), 52 (January 1909), 826-33.
"Literature and Education in America." *University Magazine* [McGill], 8 (February 1909), 3-17.
"Canada and the Monroe Doctrine." *University Magazine* [McGill], 8 (October 1909), 351-74.

1910

Literary Lapses: A Book of Sketches. Montreal: Gazette Printing Company, 1910.

Literary Lapses. New York and London: John Lane [1910].

Trade and Commerce [by] Simon Litman, Stephen Leacock [and others]. Chicago: Lasalle Extension University, 1910.

"The Apology of a Professor." *University Magazine* [McGill], 9 (April 1910), 176-91.

"Practical Political Economy I. The Theory of Value." *Saturday Night,* November 12, 1910, 15.

"Practical Political Economy II. Monopoly Prices and the Trust Problem." *Saturday Night,* November 19, 1910, 21.

"Practical Political Economy III. Railroad Rates and Railroad Legislation." *Saturday Night,* November 26, 1910, 4.

"Price Monopoly Problem of Today." *Plaindealer* (Strathcona, Alberta), November 29, 1910.

"The Union of South Africa." *American Political Science Review,* 4 (November 1910), 498-507.

"Practical Political Economy IV. The Theory of Money." *Saturday Night,* December 3, 1910, 12.

"Practical Political Economy V. Bi-metallism." *Saturday Night,* December 10, 1910, 23.

"Practical Political Economy VI. Paper Money." *Saturday Night,* December 17, 1910, 21-22.

"Practical Political Economy VII. The Movement of Prices and the Rise in the Cost of Living." *Saturday Night,* December 24, 1910, 21-22.

"Practical Political Economy VIII. The International Movement of Money and the Foreign Exchanges." *Saturday Night,* December 31, 1910, 10.

"The Devil and the Deep Sea: A Discussion of Modern Morality." *University Magazine* [McGill], 9 (December 1910), 616-26.

1911

The Great Victory in Canada. London [1911].

Nonsense Novels. London: John Lane; New York: John Lane, 1911.

"Practical Political Economy IX. The Theory of Free Trade." *Saturday Night,* January 7, 1911, 13.

"Practical Political Economy X. Free Trade in Great Britain." *Saturday Night,* January 14, 1911, 10, 21.

"Practical Political Economy XI. The Economic Basis of Protection." *Saturday Night,* January 21, 1911, 10.

"Practical Political Economy XII. The Tariff Policy of the German Empire." *Saturday Night,* January 28, 1911, 21.

"Practical Political Economy XIII. Free Trade in Great Britain and Protection in Germany; a comparison." *Saturday Night*, February 4, 1911, 10.

"Practical Political Economy XIV. The Tariff System of the United States." *Saturday Night*, February 11, 1911, 10.

"Practical Political Economy XV. The Theory of Banking and the Bank of England." *Saturday Night*, February 18, 1911, 23.

"Practical Political Economy XVI. The National Banking System of the United States." *Saturday Night*, February 25, 1911, 21.

"Practical Political Economy XVII. The Theory of Wages." *Saturday Night*, March 4, 1911, 21.

"Practical Political Economy XVIII. Industrial Legislation: Factory Acts." *Saturday Night*, March 11, 1911, 10.

"Practical Political Economy XIX. State Insurance and Old Age Pensions." *Saturday Night*, March 18, 1911, 5, 23.

"Practical Political Economy XX. State Arbitration of Industrial Disputes." *Saturday Night*, March 25, 1911, 5, 10.

"Practical Political Economy XXI. The General Theory of Taxation." *Saturday Night*, April 1, 1911, 9, 14.

"Practical Political Economy XXII. Taxation in Great Britain." *Saturday Night*, April 8, 1911, 10.

"Practical Political Economy XXIII. Taxation in the United States." *Saturday Night*, April 15, 1911, 9-10.

"Practical Political Economy XXIV. The Theory of Socialism." *Saturday Night*, April 22, 1911, 15, 20.

"Practical Political Economy XXV. Socialism as a Political Force." *Saturday Night*, April 29, 1911, 5, 23.

"Canada and the Immigration Problem." *National Review*, 57 (April 1911), 316-27.

"The Political Rights of Women—The Case Against the Suffrage." *Toronto Star Weekly*, May 13, 1911.

"The Great Victory in Canada." *National Review*, 58 (November 1911), 381-92.

"What Shall We Do About the Navy?" *University Magazine* [McGill], 10 (December 1911), 535-53.

1912

Sunshine Sketches of a Little Town. London: John Lane, The Bodley Head; New York: John Lane; Toronto: Bell and Cockburn, 1912.

"Mariposa and Its People." *Montreal Star*, February 17, 1912, 21.

"The Glorious Victory of Mr. Smith." *Montreal Star*, February 24, 1912, 12.

"Speculations of Jefferson Thorpe." *Montreal Star*, March 2, 1912, 23.

"The Marine Excursion of the Knights of Pythias." *Montreal Star*, March 16, 1912, 23.

"The Ministrations of Canon Drone." *Montreal Star*, March 23, 1912, 23.

"Mariposa's Whirlwind Campaign." *Montreal Star*, March 30, 1912, 23.
"The Engagement of Mr. Pupkin." *Montreal Star*, April 13, 1912, 29.
"The Fore-Ordained Attachment of Zena McGaw and Peter Pupkin." *Montreal Star*, April 20, 1912, 21.
"The Great Mariposa Bank Mystery." *Montreal Star*, May 4, 1912, 23.
"The Great Election in Missinaba County." *Montreal Star*, May 25, 1912, 22.
"The Candidacy of Mr. Smith." *Montreal Star*, June 8, 1912, 21.
"L'Envoi: The Train to Mariposa." *Montreal Star*, June 22, 1912, 22.
"My College Days: A Retrospect." *Old McGill*, 15 (1912), 28.
"A Retrospect. My College Days." *Old McGill*, 15 (1912), 28.

1913

Behind the Beyond, and Other Contributions to Human Knowledge. London: John Lane, 1913.
"The Canadian Senate and the Naval Bill." *National Review*, 61 (July 1913), 986-98.
"The Dentist and the Gas." *American Magazine*, 76 (July 1913), 71-72.
"Behind the Beyond: in Three Acts and Two Drinks." *American Magazine*, 76 (August 1913), 46-52.
"Familiar Incidents: With the Photographer." *American Magazine*, 76 (September 1913), 82-84.
"An Academic Discussion: Homer and Humbug." *Century Magazine*, 86 (October 1913), 952-55.
"Under the Barber's Knife." *American Magazine*, 76 (October 1913), 84, 86.
"My Unknown Friend. Familiar Incidents." *American Magazine*, 76 (November 1913), 71-72.
"Making a Magazine: The Dream of a Contributor." *American Magazine*, 76 (December 1913), 69-70, 72.

1914

Adventures of the Far North, a chronicle of the frozen seas. Toronto, Glasgow: Brook and Company, 1914.
Arcadian Adventures with the Idle Rich. London: John Lane, 1914.
The Dawn of Canadian History: A Chronicle of Aboriginal Canada and The Coming of The White Man. Toronto, Glasgow: Brook and Company, 1914.
The Mariner of St. Malo: A Chronicle of the Voyages of Jacques Cartier. Toronto, Glasgow: Brook and Company, 1914.
The Methods of Mr. Sellyer; A Book Store Study. New York: John Lane, 1914.
My Financial Career and How to Make a Million Dollars. New York: Winthrop Press, c1914.

Number Fifty-six. New York: Winthrop Press, 1914.

"Aristocratic Anecdotes; or, Little Stories of Great People." *Century,* 87 (March 1914), 803-805.

"Education Made Agreeable; or, The Diversions of a Professor." *American Magazine,* 77 (March 1914), 55-56.

"The Perils and Pitfalls of College Journalism." *The McGilliad,* 1 (March 1914), 3.

"An Everyday Experience." *Century Magazine,* 87 (April 1914), 968.

"The First Newspaper: A Sort of Allegory." *University Magazine* [McGill], 13 (April 1914), 220-29.

"Who is Also Who: A Companion Volume to Who's Who." *American Magazine,* 77 (May 1914), 64-65.

"Arcadian Adventures With the Idle Rich." *American Magazine,* 77 (July 1914), 29-34; (September 1914), 34-38; (October 1914), 49-54; (November 1914), 50-54.

"The European War." *The Orillia News Letter,* August 12, 1914, 1, 4.

"American Humour." *Nineteenth Century,* 76 (August 1914), 444-57.

"Familiar Incidents: My Unknown Friend." *American Magazine,* 76 (November 1914), 71-72.

"Novels Read to Order: First Aid for the Busy Millionaire." *Century Magazine,* 89 (November 1914), 156-60.

"The American Attitude." *University Magazine* [McGill], 13 (December 1914), 595-97.

1915

Marionettes' Calendar 1916. London: John Lane, 1915.

Marionettes' Engagement Book. London: John Lane, 1915.

Moonbeams from the Larger Lunacy. New York: John Lane, 1915.

"Q"; A Farce in One Act, By Stephen Leacock and Basil Macdonald Hastings. New York: S. French, c1915.

The Truth About Prohibition from the Viewpoint of an Eminent Professor. New York: Allied Printing Trades Council [1915?].

"Why People Should Own and Read Books." *North American Book Page,* March 20, 1915.

"Sidelights on the Superman: An Interview With General Bernhardi." *McGill Daily,* March 1915 [Special War Contingent], 10, 40.

"Dickens Fireside Fantasy." *Bookman,* 41 (April 1915), 169-78.

"Speeding Up Business." *Puck,* 77 (July 17, 1915), 9, 21.

"The Lot of the Schoolmaster." *Maclean's Magazine,* 28 (September 1915), 11-13, 101-102.

"The Woman Question." *Maclean's Magazine,* 28 (October 1915), 7-9.

"Two Little Boys: An Allegory." *Collier's,* 56 (November 27, 1915), 50.

"Madeline of the Movies: A Photoplay Done Back into Words." *Puck,* 78 (December 4, 1915), 22, 30, 32, 34, 44.

"The Peace-makers." *Maclean's Magazine,* 29 (December 1915), 7-9, 104-108.

1916

Essays and Literary Studies. New York: John Lane; London: John Lane, The Bodley Head; Toronto: S.B. Gundy, 1916.

Further Foolishness: Sketches and Satires on the Follies of the Day. New York: John Lane; London: John Lane, The Bodley Head; Toronto: S.B. Gundy, 1916.

"After the War—Ruin or Prosperity?" *Maclean's Magazine*, 29 (January 1916), 11-13, 107-108.

"The Call of the Carburetor; or, Mr. Blinks and His Friends." *Puck*, 78 (January 1, 1916), 17, 23-24.

"Simple Stories of Success." *Maclean's Magazine*, 29 (February 1916), 9-12.

"English As She Is Taught at College." *Harper's Weekly*, 62 (February 1916), 203.

"Germany From Within." *Maclean's Magazine*, 29 (March 1916), 13-16.

"More Than Twice-Told Tales." *Maclean's Magazine*, 29 (April 1916), 39-41, 56.

"The Old, Old Trouble." *Puck*, 79 (April 15, 1916), 10.

"Humour As I See It and Something About Humour in Canada." *Maclean's Magazine*, 29 (May 1916), 11-13, 111-113.

"Our Shorter Still Stories." *Century Magazine*, 92 (June 1916), 318-19.

"My Delusions." *Puck*, 80 (July 29, 1916), 10.

"Our Perplexity Column." *Puck*, 80 (August 19, 1916), 10.

"Is Permanent Peace Possible?" *Maclean's Magazine*, 29 (August 1916), 7-8, 77-79; (October 1916), 12-13, 92-93.

"Study in Still Life, My Tailor." *Century Magazine*, 92 (August 1916), 637-38.

"Let Us Learn Russian." *Star* (Toronto), September 23, 1916.

"The Errors of Santa Claus." *Puck*, 81 (December 2, 1916), 17.

"O. Henry and His Critics." *New Republic*, 9 (December 2, 1916), 120-22.

"Abdul Aziz Has His." *Maclean's Magazine*, 30 (December 1916), 19-22, 77-81.

1917

Merry Christmas. Two hundred copies printed in the shop of William Edwin Rudge for his friends, Christmas, 1917.

National Organization for War. Ottawa: National Service Board of Canada, 1917.

"Lost in New York." *Puck*, 81 (January 20, 1917), 9, 24.

"In Dry Toronto." *Maclean's Magazine*, 30 (January 1917), 13-15.

"In Merry Mexico." *Maclean's Magazine*, 30 (February 1917), 16-18, 76-79.

"Ten Million Dollars for the Asking." *Maclean's Magazine*, 30 (March 1917), 9-12.

"Forty Years Ago." *Puck*, 81 (April 14, 1917), 10.

"Sunshine in Mariposa: A Play in Four Acts." *Maclean's Magazine*, 30 (May 1917), 18-21, 75-82; (June) 23-26, 83-89; (July) 51-53, 95-102.

"Frenzied Fiction for the Dog Days." *Maclean's Magazine*, 30 (August 1917), 33-35.

"The Old, Old Story of How Five Men Went Fishing." *Maclean's Magazine*, 30 (September 1917), 21-23.

"Back to the City!" *Maclean's Magazine*, 30 (October 1917), 39-42.

"Politics From Within." *Maclean's Magazine*, 31 (December 1917), 23-25.

1918

Frenzied Fiction. London: John Lane, The Bodley Head; New York: John Lane, 1918.

Wet or Dry? Privately printed, 1918.

"My New Year's Resolutions." *Puck*, 82 (January 20, 1918), 9.

"Inside the Tank." *Maclean's Magazine*, 31 (January 1918), 38-40.

"May Time in Mariposa." *Maclean's Magazine*, 31 (May 1918), 13-15.

"Edwin Drood Is Alive." *Bellman*, 24 (June 15, 1918), 655-62.

"The Boarder's War Pledge." *Puck*, 83 (August 1918), 21.

"Better Dead." *Maclean's Magazine*, 31 (November 1918), 24-26.

1919

The Hohenzollerns in America; With the Bolsheviks in Berlin and Other Impossibilities. London: John Lane, The Bodley Head; New York: John Lane, 1919.

"The Book Agent: or, Why Do People Buy Books?" *Canadian Bookman*, 1 (January 1919), 17-19.

"More About Germany From Within." *Maclean's Magazine*, 32 (February 1919), 10-11, 65-67.

"Reconstruction in Turkey." *Maclean's Magazine*, 32 (April 1919), 20-21, 66.

"The Warning of Prohibition in America." *National Review*, 73 (July 1919), 680-87.

"Tyranny of Prohibition." *Living Age*, 302 (August 2, 1919), 301-306.

"Social Unrest After the War." *New York Times*, August 31, 1919, sec. 4, 1.

"Lecturer at Large." *Maclean's Magazine*, 32 (August 1919), 13-14, 61-62.

"The Road of Freedom." *New York Times*, September 7, 1919, sec. 4, 7.

"Man's Work and His Wage." *New York Times*, September 14, 1919, sec. 4, 7.

"Work and Wages and the Peril of the Industrial Balance of Power." *New York Times*, September 21, 1919, sec. 3, 4.

"Social Control for Equal Opportunity." *New York Times*, October 2, 1919, sec. 9, 2.

"Socialism in Operation: a Prison." *New York Times*, October 5, 1919, v. 69, no. 22, 534; sec. 10, 3.

"My Memories and Miseries." *Maclean's Magazine*, 32 (November 1919), 18-19.
"The Passing of the Christmas Ghost Story." *Bookman* (N.Y.), 50 (November 1919), 257-61.

1920

How Mr. Bellamy Looked Backward..., Milwaukee, Wis., American Constitutional League of Wisconsin [c1920].
The Unsolved Riddle of Social Justice. New York: John Lane; London: John Lane, The Bodley Head; Toronto: S.B. Gundy, 1920.
Winsome Winnie, and Other New Nonsense Novels. Toronto: S.B. Gundy; London: John Lane, The Bodley Head; New York: John Lane, 1920.
"Teaching of French in Ontario." *Canadian Bookman*, 2 (January 1920), n.s., 6-9.
"Little Glimpses of the Future in America." *Vanity Fair*, June 1920, 53.
"John and I; or, How I Nearly Lost My Husband." *Bystander* (London), 67 (July 21, 1920), 191-92, 194.
"New Nonsense Novels." *Harper's Magazine*, 141 (July-October 1920), 187-95, 305-11, 545-49, 599-610.
"What I Read As A Child." *Toronto Public Library Book Bulletin*, 10, n.s., no. 7-9 (July-September 1920), 1-2.
"Winsome Winnie: or, Trial and Temptation." *Bystander* (London), 67 (July 7-14, 1920), 47-48, 50, 52, 117-18, 121-22.
"Who Do You Think Did It? or, the Mixed-up Murder Mystery." *Bystander* (London), 67 (August 11-September 1, 1920), 389-90, 451-52, 454, 513-14, 516, 559-60, 562.
"Split in the Cabinet; or, The Fate of England." *Bystander* (London), 67 (September 1920), 621-22, 624, 697-98, 700, 704.
"Broken Barriers; or, Red Love on a Blue Island." *Bystander* (London), 68 (October 1920), 125-26, 130, 132, 217-18, 220, 222.
"What the Colleges Really Need." *New York Times*, November 14, 1920, sec. 3, 16.
"Personal Experiments With the Black Bass." *Bystander* (London), 68 (December 1, 1920), 645-46, 648.
"The Graduates and the Campaign." *McGill News*, 2 (1920-21), 10.
"A Tale of the New Time. The Kidnapped Plumber." *Bystander* (London), 68 (1920), 65-68, 70, 94, 98.

1921

The Case Against Prohibition. London: The Freedom Association, 1921.
The Need For Dormitories at McGill. [Montreal: McGill Centennial Endowment, 1921].
"That Vampire Woman." *The Standard* (Montreal), January 15, 1921.

"A Sermon on College Humour." *Goblin*, 1 (February 1921), 3-4.

"The Approach of the Comet." *The* (Montreal) *Standard*, March 5, 1921. (Syndicated, 1921).

"On the Art of Taking a Vacation." *Outlook* (N.Y.), May 25, 1921, 160-62.

"Painless Tax." *Collier's*, 67 (June 18, 1921), 56.

"Tom Lachford, Promoter." *Life*, 78 (September 8, 1921), 17, 26.

"How I Succeeded in My Business." *Vanity Fair*, September, 1921, 46.

"Disarmament and Common Sense." *Collier's*, 118 (October 8, 1921), 5-6.

"My Impressions of England: As Exported to America." *Illustrated Sunday Herald*, October 16, 1921, 3.

"Does Euclid Make Good Wives?" *Sunday Pictorial*, November 20, 1921, 7.

"Inflation and Deflation." *The Morning Post* (London), December 12, 1921, 7.

"Stephen Leacock Interviews Himself." *Detroit Athletics Club News*, 6 (December 1921), 33, ill.

"Stephen Interviews Leacock." *Maclean's Magazine*, 34 (December 1, 1921), 9.

"Preface." *The Letters of Si Whiffletree—Freshman*. Frank D. Genest, ed. Montreal, 1921.

"Are Moving Pictures Punk?" (Syndicated, 1921).*

"The Crime Wave." (Syndicated, 1921).*

"Crossing the Frontier." (Syndicated, 1921).*

"The Drama As It Was and Is." (Syndicated, 1921).*

"Easy Marks." (Syndicated, 1921).*

"Is Dancing Immoral?" (Syndicated, 1921).*

"The Moral Wave of the New Year." (Syndicated, 1921).*

"Should Bachelors be Taxed to Extinction?" (Syndicated, 1921).*

"This Blue Law Business." (Syndicated, 1921).*

"Tight Money." (Syndicated, 1921).*

"Whose Move Is It?" (Syndicated, 1921).*

"Why I Murdered My Landlord." (Syndicated, 1921).*

"Why I Refuse to Play Golf." (Syndicated, 1921).*

1922

My Discovery of England. London: John Lane, 1922.

"Introduction." *Of All Things*. Robert Benchley. London: John Lane, 1922.

"Prohibition Comes to London." *Maclean's Magazine*, 35 (January 1, 1922), 16.

"Co-Education Roasted." *McGill Daily*, January 31, 1922, 2.

"Stories and Storytellers." *Outlook*, 130 (February 1, 1922), 183-84.

"Exporting Humour to England." *Harper's Magazine*, 144 (March 1922), 435-40.

"Is Prohibition Coming to England?" *Collier's*, 69 (April 15, 1922), 9-10.

"My Discovery of England." *Harper's Magazine*, 144 (April 1922), 560.

"Why I Like Bad Music." *The Fellowcrafter*, 4 (April 1922), 10-11.
"As I Saw Politics in England." *Maclean's Magazine*, 35 (May 1, 1922), 20, 46-48.
"Wanted: More Profiteers." *Collier's*, 69 (May 6, 1922), 3-4.
"Oxford As I See It." *Harper's Magazine*, 144 (May 1922), 738-45.
"Horrors of Oxford." *Living Age*, 313 (June 24, 1922), 779-81.
"British and the American Press." *Harper's Magazine*, 145 (June 1922), 1-9.
"The Faded Actor." *Goblin*, 3 (June-July, 1922), 7-10.
"Roughing it in the Bush." *Maclean's Magazine*, 36 (October 1, 1922), 18.
"My Plans for Moose Hunting." *Detroit Athletic Club News*, 7 (October 1922), 7, 21.
"We Are Teaching Women All Wrong." *Collier's*, 68 (December 31, 1922), 15.
"The Oldest Living Graduate." *McGill Yearbook*, 1 (1922), 60.

1923

College Days. New York: Dodd, Mead, 1923.
Over The Footlights. Toronto: S.B. Gundy, 1923.
"The Drama As I See It. I. Cast Up By the Sea." *Maclean's Magazine*, 36 (February 1, 1923), 15-16, 46-51.
"The Drama As I See It. II. The Soul Call." *Maclean's Magazine*, 36 (March 1, 1923), 14-15, 65-67.
"The Drama As I See It. III. Dead Men's Gold." *Maclean's Magazine*, 36 (April 1, 1923), 18-19, 57-58.
"On My Objections to Golf." *St. Martin-in-the-Fields Review*, 386 (April 1923), 163-67.
"The Drama As I See It. IV. The Greek Drama." *Maclean's Magazine*, 36 (May 1, 1923), 22-23, 73-74.
"The Drama As I See It. V. Masterpieces of Other Nations." *Maclean's Magazine*, 36 (June 1, 1923), 22-23, 48-50.
"The Drama As I See It. VI. Historical Drama." *Maclean's Magazine*, 36 (July 15, 1923), 14-15, 40-44.
"My Interviewer." *Harper's Magazine*, 147 (August 1923), 425-27.
"My Unposted Correspondence." *London Magazine* (December 1923), 751-53.
"Then and Now: The College News of Forty Years Ago and the College News of Today." *McGill News*, 5 (December 1923), 2-3.
"McGill in 2000 A.D.: A Fragment From A Future History...." *Old McGill*, 25 (1923), 201.

1924

The Garden Of Folly. Toronto: S.B. Gundy, 1924.

A Book of Ridiculous Stories. Little Blue Book No. 1115. Girard, Kansas: Haldeman-Julius, 1924.

A Book of Funny Dramatics. Little Blue Book No. 1116. Girard, Kansas: Haldeman-Julius, 1924.

The Human Animal and Its Folly. Little Blue Book No. 1117. Girard, Kansas: Haldeman-Julius, 1924.

Life As I See It. Little Blue Book No. 1118. Girard, Kansas: Haldeman-Julius, 1924.

Follies in Fiction. Little Blue Book No. 1119. Girard, Kansas: Haldeman-Julius, 1924.

Essays of Serious Spoofing. Little Blue Book No. 1120. Girard, Kansas: Haldeman-Julius, 1924.

The Gold Standard. An address delivered before the 1924 Life Insurance Educational Congress held at Toronto, Ont. [n.p., 1924].

The Proper Limitations of State Interference. Toronto, 1924.

"Introduction of the Horseless Cab." *Library Digest,* 80 (January 26, 1924), 36.

"The Secrets of Success." *Harper's Magazine,* 148 (February 1924), 334-42.

"Manual of the New Mentality." *Harper's Magazine,* 148 (March 1924), 471-80.

"The Human Body, Its Care and Prevention." *Harper's Magazine,* 148 (April 1924), 593-602.

"Business As I See It." *Harper's Magazine,* 148 (May 1924), 815-25.

"Personal Habits and Sayings of the Emperor Napoleon." *Harper's Magazine,* 149 (June 1924), 126-27.

"State Salary." *Collier's,* 74 (August 30, 1924), 19.

"Such Fine Murders We're Having!" *Collier's,* 74 (November 1, 1924), 16, 37.

"Randolph Ketchum Jones." *Financial Post,* November 21, 1924, 10.

"The Old College and the New University." *Old McGill,* 26 (1924), 21-22.

1925

"Preface." *The Transportation of Canadian Wheat to the Sea.* L.M. Fair. University Economic Studies; National Problems of Canada, No. 1. Montreal: McGill University, 1925.

"Preface." *Reciprocal and Preferential Tariffs.* The 1925 Graduating Class in Commerce. Toronto: Macmillan, for the Dept. of Economics and Political Science, McGill University, Montreal [1925].

"Preface." *Ocean and Inland Water Transport.* The 1925 Graduating Class in Commerce. McGill University Economic Studies; National Problems of Canada, No. 2. Montreal: McGill University [1925].

"Bygone Education and Radio." *Radio, the Wireless Quarterly*, 1 (New Year, 1925), 6-7.
"How My Wife and I Built Our Home for $4.90." *Maclean's Magazine*, 38 (January 15, 1925), 7, 55.
"Americans and Humours of War." *Collier's*, 75 (May 30, 1925), 11.
"Bed-Time Stories for Grown-Up People." *Forum*, 79 (May 30, 1925), 11.
"Humor and Humors of War." *Collier's*, 75 (May 30, 1925), 11.
"The Twenty-Second General Strike in England." *Orillia Newsletter*, July 14, 1925, 11.
"Slams Across the Sea." *Collier's*, 76 (July 18, 1925), 16, 34.
"As the Cat Jumps." *Collier's*, 76 (August 29, 1925), 23.
"New Light From Light Minds." *Collier's*, 76 (September 12, 1925), 15.
"The Mother of Parliaments." *Harper's Magazine*, 151 (September 1925), 418-19.
"Vehicle for Literary Expression Is Needed at McGill." *McGill Daily*, 15 (October 28, 1925), 1.
"The Flight of College Time." *McGill Fortnightly Review*, 1 (November 21, 1925), 3.
"On the Continued Progress of McGill University." *Old McGill*, 27 (1925), 56, 322.
"Things Wanting at McGill: A Message to the Annual." *Old McGill*, 27 (1925), 30.

1926

Winnowed Wisdom; A New Book of Humour. New York: Dodd, Mead, 1926.
"Preface." *The Port of Montreal*. Laurence Chalmers Tombs. Toronto: Macmillan, for the Dept. of Economics and Political Science, McGill University, Montreal [1926].
"Throwing Down the Uplift." *Collier's*, 77 (January 9, 1926), 22, 45.
"The Transit of Venus." *Good Housekeeping Magazine*, 82 (January 1926), 78-81.
"On Debates at College." *McGill Fortnightly Review*, 1 (February 6, 1926), 47-48.
"The Work of the Universities." *Institute Bulletin*, 6 (March 1926), 2-8.
"How I Made Myself Young at Seventy." *Metropolitan Newspaper Service*, May 30, 1926.*
"The Return of the Graduate." *Metropolitan Newspaper Service*, June 6, 1926.*
"My Fellow Club Men." *Orillia Newsletter*, June 23, 1926.
"A Diary of the League of Nations." *Saturday Evening Post*, 198 (June 26, 1926), 11.
"What the Duce!" *Collier's*, 78 (July 3, 1926), 15.
"Old Junk and New Bunk." *Collier's*, 78 (October 30, 1926), 20.
"Quebec Liquor Law." *Review of Reviews*, 74 (October 1926), 370.
"The Value of Criticism." *Bookman* (London), 71 (November 1926), 105.

1927

"Preface." *Assisted Emigration and Land Settlement With Special Reference to Western Canada.* John Thomas Culliton. Montreal: Dept. of Economics and Political Science, McGill University [1927], 79.

"Social Justice and the Revolution." *Proceedings of the Professional Institute of Civil Service,* March 28, 1927, 32.

"The Colleges and Humour." *McGill Martlet,* 1 (March 1927), 7-8, 32-33.

"A Call to Youth. (The Environment of Letters: Culture of the Mind)." *The Times* (London), July 1, 1927, xxi-g.

"On Literature." *The Times* (London), July 1, 1927, 21.

"Roughing It." *Collier's,* 80 (July 9, 1927), 27.

"Children's Poetry Revised." *Harper's Magazine,* 155 (July 1927), 252-53.

"Scenery and Signboards." *Harper's Magazine,* 155 (August 1927), 382-83.

"Save Me From the Man Who Has a Speech to Make." *Harper's Magazine,* 155 (September 1927), 516-17.

"My Friend the Reporter." *Harper's Magazine,* 155 (October 1927), 647-48.

1928

Short Circuits. Toronto: Macmillan [1928].

"Mother Goose-Step For Children." *Forum,* 79 (March 1928), 365-69.

"See the Conquering Aero Come!" *Goblin,* 8 (March 1928), 9.

"Mathematics for Golfers." *Harper's Magazine,* 156 (April 1928), 647-49.

"The Economic Aspect of Aviation." *Royal Society of Canada, Proceedings and Transactions,* 22, series 3 (May 1928), 213-32.

"Elegy Written Near a City Freight Yard." *Forum,* 79 (May 1928), 690-93.

"Heroines." *Forum,* 80 (July 1928), 45-48.

"The Future of American Humour." *St. Louis Post-Dispatch,* December 9, 1928, Fiftieth Anniversary Supplement: American Sec., 4-5.

"The National Literature Problem in Canada." *The Canadian Mercury,* 1 (December 1928), 8-9.

1929

The Iron Man & The Tin Woman, With Other Such Futurities; A Book of Little Sketches of To-Day and To-Morrow. New York: Dodd, Mead, 1929.

"Preface." *The Foreign Trade of Canada.* Henry Laureys. Toronto: Macmillan, 1929.

"The Memoirs of a Night-Watchman." *Metropolitan Newspaper Service,* March 10, 1929.*

"This Heart-to-Heart Stuff." *The Standard* (Montreal), March 16, 1929, 50.

"Mr. Chairman, I Beg to Move—." *The Standard* (Montreal), March 23, 1929, 52.

"Long After Bedtime." *The Standard* (Montreal), March 30, 1929, 48. *Toronto Star Weekly*, March 30, 1929, 12.
"Overhauling the Encyclopedia." *The Standard* (Montreal), April 6, 1929, 50.
"Portents of the Future." *The Standard* (Montreal), April 13, 1929, 50.
"Legislative Language." *Metropolitan Newspaper Service*, May 5, 1929.*
"Tennis at the Smiths'." *Metropolitan Newspaper Service*, August 4, 1929.*

1930

Economic Prosperity in The British Empire. Toronto: Macmillan, 1930.
"A Medieval Hole in One." *Harper's Magazine*, 160 (January 1930), 249-52.
"On Empire Trade." *The Times* (London), April 12, 1930, 11.
"In Praise of Brook Trout." *Holiday* (October 1930), 31, 67.
"What Next?" *Spectator*, 145 (November 22, 1930), 776-77.
"Once to Everyman." *The Sportsman Pilot* (December 1930), 17, 46.

1931

Wet Wit and Dry Humour, Distilled from the Pages of Stephen Leacock. New York: Dodd, Mead, 1931.
"Charles Thompson Noble." *McGill News*, 12 (March 1931), 53-55.
"Americans Are Queer." *Forum*, 85 (April 1931), 224-25.
"The Fall of the Pound Sterling." *Montreal Daily Star*, October 10, 1931, 1, 21; October 13, 1931, 1, 21.
"If the Gandhi Habit Spreads." The Rogues' Gallery. Bell Syndicate, November 8, 1931.*
"Let There be Peace in Saskatchewan." *The Sheaf*, November 12, 1931, 1.
"The Income Tax: Its Fallacy and its Failure." *The Spectator*, 147 (November 21, 1931), 697-98.
"Beating Back to Prosperity." *Mail and Empire* (Toronto), November 28, 1931, 3.
"Correspondence, The Tangent and the Ten Cent Plug." *McGill Daily*, November 28, 1931, 2.
"Needed—A Happy New Year." *New York Herald Tribune Magazine*, December 27, 1931, 1-2.
"Be Honest With Yourself in Choosing Your Reading." *Ontario Library Review*, 16 (1931), 15-16.
"A Convenient Calendar for Future Years." *Old McGill*, 34 (1931), 62.
"Our Class, Advice and Warning from 1891 to 1931." *The Cornell Widow* (1931), 20.

1932

Afternoons in Utopia; tales of the new time. Toronto: Macmillan, 1932.
Back to Prosperity; The Great Opportunity of the Empire Conference. Toronto: Macmillan, 1932.
The Dry Pickwick and Other Incongruities. London: John Lane, The Bodley Head, 1932.
Lahontan's Voyages. Edited with introduction and notes by Stephen Leacock. Ottawa: Graphic Publishers, 1932.
Mark Twain. London: Peter Davies, 1932.
"Preface." *The Story of Money.* Mary (Duncan) Carter. New York: Farrar and Rinehart, [c1932].
"Colonies for War Debts." *New York Herald Tribune,* January 17, 1932, 1-2.
"Novel Idea Proposed Recommending a Weekly Literary Issue." *McGill Daily,* January 22, 1932, 1; January 23, 1932, 2; January 25, 1932, 1; January 28, 1932, 2.
"War Stuff." *Rotarian,* 42 (January 1932), 9-10, 49.
"Leacock Outlines Recovery Plan in Cincinnati Speech." *The Montreal Daily Star,* February 5, 1932.
"Brook Trout as a National Asset." *Rod and Gun in Canada,* 33 (March 1932), 5-7.
"Baron Lahontan, Explorer." *Canadian Geographical Journal,* 4 (May 1932), 281-94.
"An Irreducible Detective Story." *Golden Book,* 15 (May 1932), 419.
"If Gold Should Cease To Be Gold." *Canadian Mining and Metal Bulletin,* 244 (August, 1932), 430-36.
"Christmas Fiction and National Friction: 1. Story of the Repentant Earl; 2. Story of the Christmas Ghost." *Spectator,* 149 (November 18, 1932), 730-32.
"Mr. Gandhi and Uncle Sam." *Spectator,* 149 (December 23, 1932), 888-89.
"Mythical Men." (Syndicated, 1932).*
"Ominous News." (Syndicated, 1932).*
"Why Graduate? A Last Appeal of the Class of 1932." *Old McGill,* 35 (1932), 60.

1933

Charles Dickens, His Life and Work. London: P. Davies, 1933.
The Economic Analysis of Industrial Depression. n.p., 1933.
Stephen Leacock's Plan to Relieve the Depression in 6 Days, To Remove It in 6 Months, To Eradicate It in 6 Years. Toronto: Macmillan, 1933.
"Happy New Year, Mars!" *New York Herald Tribune Magazine,* January 1, 1933, 1-2.
"Ourselves and Communists." *Ottawa Journal,* January 2, 1933.

"Canadians Hopeful But Not Predicting." *New York Times*, January 8, 1933, 4, 8.

"Ills of the Present System of Education Deplored." *McGill Daily*, February 10, 1933, 1.

"Finding a Formula." *Harper's Magazine*, 166 (March 1933), 490-92.

"Dr. Leacock's Protest." *London* (Ont.) *Advertiser*, June 2, 1933.

"The Plain Man at the Play." *Rotarian*, 43 (October 1933), 20-21, 55-56.

"General Currie." *Herald* (Montreal), December 6, 1933.

"Who's Who in Humour." *New York Herald Tribune*, December 10, 1933, 9-10.

"Lahontan in Minnesota." *Minnesota History*, 14 (December 1933), 367-77.

"Rare Traveller's Account." *Canadian Historical Review*, 14 (December 1933), 409-11.

1934

The Greatest Pages of Charles Dickens; a Biographical Reader and a Chronological Selection from the Works of Dickens With a Commentary on His Life and Art. Garden City, N.Y.: Doubleday, Doran, 1934.

Lincoln Frees The Slaves. New York: G.P. Putnam's Sons, 1934.

The Perfect Salesman. Edited by E.V. Knox. New York: Robert M. McBride, [1934].

The Pursuit of Knowledge; A Discussion of Freedom and Compulsion in Education. New York: Liveright Publishing Corporation [c1934].

"Preface." *La liberté d'opinion.* George R.W. Owen. Montreal: Guy Drummond, 1934, 5-6.

"Preface." *A Christmas Carol, in prose; being a ghost story of Christmas.* Charles Dickens. Boston: Printed for the members of the Limited Editions club at the Merrymount Press, 1934. xi, 100 pp.

"The Advancement of Learning: A Talk to Graduate Students." *McGill Daily*, 23 (March 16, 1934), 2.

"Why Do We Laugh?" *Christian Science Monitor Magazine*, April 18, 1934, 1-2.

"The Humorist Who Made Lincoln Laugh." *New York Times Book Review*, April 22, 1934, 8-9.

"The Last Five Years in Canada: How the Country Reacted in a Period of Depression." *The World Today: Encyclopaedia Britannica*, 1 (April 1934), 22-25.

"My Revelations As a Spy." *Golden Book Magazine*, 19 (April 1934), no. 112, 417-21.

"Stirring Pageant of Canadian History (Jacques Cartier)." *New York Times Magazine*, August 19, 1934, 6-7, 17.

"Two Humorists: Charles Dickens and Mark Twain." *Yale Review*, 24 (September 1934), n.s., 118-29.

"Is Canada Breaking Up?" *Montreal Daily Star*, December 15, 1934, 19.

"Our Lost Anatomist." (Montreal), December 17, 1934.

"Colleges and the Public." *McGill News*, 16 (1934-35), 48-49.

"The Revision of Democracy." [Presidential Address]. *Canadian Political Science Association Papers and Proceedings*, 6 (1934), 5-16.

1935

Humor: Its Theory and Technique, With Examples and Samples; A Book of Discovery. Toronto: Dodd, Mead, [c1935].

The Restoration of the Finances of McGill University; Suggestions Submitted to the Consideration of My Fellow Members of the University. 1. To Diminish the Deficit. 2. To Carry the Deficit. 3. To Remove the Deficit. Montreal. Privately printed, 1935.

Suggestions for Economy at McGill. Privately printed, January 1935.

"Preface." *Le nationalisme économique français*. Harrison Clark. Montreal: Guy Drummond, [1935].

"Preface." *Mark Twain Wit and Wisdom*. Cyril Clemens. New York: Fred A. Stokes, 1935.

"Bankers Are Farmers at Heart." *New York Herald Tribune*, February 11, 1935, 1, 13.

"Recovery After Graduation: or, Looking Back Upon College." *Golden Book Magazine*, 21 (February 1935), 114-16.

"What Is Left of Adam Smith?" *Canadian Journal of Economics and Political Science*, 1 (February 1935), 41-51.

"How Bankers Talk." *Banker's Magazine*, 130 (April 1935), 512-13.

"Mark Twain and Canada." *Queen's Quarterly*, 42 (Spring 1935), 68-81.

"Mr. Bennett's National Policy." *McGill News*, 91 (Spring 1935), 7.

"Crisis Held Rising on the Rhine Zone." *New York Times*, May 21, 1935, 9.

"Our Ignoramus Club." *Star* (Washington, D.C.), June 2, 1935.

"Good Times Can Come Again." *Current History*, 42 (June 1935), 233-39.

"Everlasting Woman Question." *Rotarian*, 47 (August 1935), 13-14.

"The Ignoramus Club." *Column Review*, 1 (August 1935), 73-75.

"The Lake Simcoe Country." *Canadian Geographic Journal*, 11 (September 1935), 109-16.

"The Spiritual Outlook of Mr. Doomer." *Golden Book Magazine*, 22 (September 1935), 285-87.

"Canada's Crossroads." *This Week* (Herald Tribune), October 13, 1935, 2, 24-25.

"Mark Twain." *The Evening Standard*, November 18, 1935, 7, 11.

"Sex, Sex, Sex—I'm Sick of It." (Syndicated, 1935). *The Chattanooga Times*, May 5, 1935, 6.

1936

Funny Pieces: A Book of Random Sketches. New York: Dodd, Mead, 1936.

The Gathering Financial Crisis in Canada: A Survey of the Present Critical Situation. Toronto: Macmillan, 1936.

The Greatest Pages of American Humor, Selected and Discussed by Stephen Leacock: A Study of the Rise and Development of Humorous Writings in America With Selections from The Most Notable of the Humorists. Garden City, N.Y.: Doubleday, Doran, 1936.

Hellements of Hickonomics in Hiccoughs of Verse Done in Our Social Planning Mill. New York: Dodd, Mead, 1936.

The Leacock Laughter Book: Containing Short Circuits, Afternoons in Utopia. London: John Lane [1936].

"Prefaces." *The French Franc and the Gold Standard.* 1926-1936. Philip F. Vienberg. Montreal: Printed at the Witness Press, [1936?].

"Academic Freedom." *Maclean's Magazine,* 49 (February 1, 1936), 14-15, 38-39.

"The Tide Turns in Canada: The Recent Election and What It Means." *The World Today: Encyclopaedia Britannica,* 3 (February 1936), 7-10.

"Diplomatic Detours." *This Week,* March 8, 1936, 7.

"I'll Stay in Canada." *This Week,* March 8, 1936, 6, 21.

"The Past Quarter Century." *Maclean's Magazine,* 49 (March 15, 1936), 36, 38.

"Senility Gang Execution." *Montreal Daily Star,* 68 (March 25, 1936), 35.

"Edward VIII and Canada." *Review of Reviews,* 93 (March 1936), 29-30.

"This International Stuff." *Rotarian,* 49 (July 1936), 6-8.

"What the Reviewers Missed." *American Mercury,* 38 (July 1936), 368-71.

"Through a Glass Darkly." *Atlantic Monthly,* 158 (July 1936), 94-98.

"Canada Won't Go Yankee." *Post Dispatch* (St. Louis), September 8, 1936.

"Too Much Alphabet." *Parade,* 1 (September 1936), 113-15.

"Imaginary Persons." *Atlantic Monthly,* 158 (October 1936), 490-93.

"The New Deal: Canada's View of It." *Cleveland News,* November 10, 1936.

"Social and Other Credit in Alberta." *Fortnightly Review,* 146 (November 1936), 525-35.

"The Social Credit Warning." *This Week,* December 13, 1936, 4, 29.

"How Soon Can We Start the Next War?" *Amherst Alumni Council News,* 10 (December 1936), Suppl. 2, 51-56.

"My Fishpond." *Atlantic Monthly,* 158 (December 1936), no. 6, 720-22.

"Reflections on the North." *Beaver,* 267 (December 1936), 9-12.

1937

Here Are My Lectures and Stories. New York: Dodd, Mead, 1937.

Humour and Humanity: An Introduction to the Study of Humour. London: Thornton Butterworth, [1937].

A Memorandum on Social Research at McGill University. [n.p.], 1937.

My Discovery of the West: A Discussion of East and West in Canada. Toronto: Thomas Allen, 1937.

What Nickel Means To the World. Toronto: Prepared expressly for Johnson, Ring and Company, c1937.

"Social Credit." *Review of Reviews,* 95 (January 1937), 65-66.

"Initial Complaint." *Scholastic*, 30 (February 6, 1937), 7-8.

"My Discovery of the West 1." *Globe and Mail*, March 6, 1937, 1, 10.

"My Discovery of the West 2." *Globe and Mail*, March 8, 1937, 1, 11.

"My Discovery of the West 3." *Globe and Mail*, March 13, 1937, 1, 9.

"My Discovery of the West 4." *Globe and Mail*, March 15, 1937, 1, 12.

"My Discovery of the West 5." *Globe and Mail*, March 16, 1937, 1, 5.

"My Discovery of the West 6." *Globe and Mail*, March 20, 1937, 1, 10.

"My Discovery of the West 7." *Globe and Mail*, March 22, 1937, 1, 11.

"My Discovery of the West 8." *Globe and Mail*, March 27, 1937, 1, 11.

"My Discovery of the West 9." *Globe and Mail*, March 29, 1937, 1, 13.

"McGill in the West: Notes on a Personally Conducted Tour." *McGill Graduates' Bulletin*, 1 (March 1937), 3-6.

"My Discovery of the West 10." *Globe and Mail*, April 3, 1937, 1, 8.

"My Discovery of the West 11." *Globe and Mail*, April 5, 1937, 1, 10.

"My Discovery of the West 12." *Globe and Mail*, April 9, 1937, 1, 5.

"My Discovery of the West 13." *Globe and Mail*, April 12, 1937, 2, 12.

"My Discovery of the West 14." *Globe and Mail*, April 13, 1937, 5.

"My Discovery of the West 15." *Globe and Mail*, April 17, 1937, 11.

"My Discovery of the West 16." *Globe and Mail*, April 19, 1937, 3.

"My Discovery of the West 17." *Globe and Mail*, April 24, 1937, 5.

"My Discovery of the West 18." *Globe and Mail*, April 26, 1937, 9.

"Labor and Law in Canada: An Interpretation of the Oshawa Strike." *Standard* (Montreal), May 1, 1937, 1.

"Labor Should Organize But Do It the Right Way or Suffer Stiff Set Back." *Telegram* (Toronto), May 1, 1937.

"My Discovery of the West 19." *Globe and Mail*, May 1, 1937, 11.

"My Discovery of the West 20." *Globe and Mail*, May 3, 1937, 11.

"My Discovery of the West 21." *Globe and Mail*, May 8, 1937, 11.

"My Discovery of the West 22." *Globe and Mail*, May 10, 1937, 10.

"My Discovery of the West 23." *Globe and Mail*, May 11, 1937, 9.

"My Discovery of the West 24." *Globe and Mail*, May 15, 1937, 5.

"My Discovery of the West 25." *Globe and Mail*, May 17, 1937, 13.

"My Discovery of the West 26." *Globe and Mail*, May 22, 1937, 5.

"My Discovery of the West 27." *Globe and Mail*, May 24, 1937, 10.

"The Blow of Thunder; or, The Two Milords." *Atlantic Monthly*, 159 (May 1937), 597-99.

"Disown Your Own Home? Expert Advice on Knocking Your House into Shape." *Commentator*, 1 (May 1937), 14-16.

"Gold Mines As Investments." *Barron's*, 18 (June 14, 1937), 3-4.

"Alberta's Fairy Story." *Commentator*, 1 (June 1937), 67-72.

"Alberta's Financial Experiments: The Story of the Social Dividend of $25.00 a Month for Adults." *The World Today: Encyclopaedia Britannica*, 4 (June 1937), 17-18.

"Farewell to Farms." *Commentator*, 2 (August 1937), 9-11.

"How to Borrow Money." *Lilliput*, 1 (August 1937), 3-8.

"Free, But a Bit Forlorn." *Commentator*, 2 (September 1937), 19-22.

"The Average Man." *Lilliput*, 1 (October 1937), 7-8.

"Stephen Leacock Writes of One-Man Rule." *Barron's*, 17 (November 8, 1937), 11.

"Why I Am Leaving My Farm: I Can't Live Up to It." *John O'London's Weekly*, 38 (1937), 300.

"What's Next in Alberta?" *Barron's*, 17 (November 22, 1937), 11, 12.

"The Art of Opening a Conversation." *Reader's Digest*, 31 (November 1937), 90-91.

"Foggy Finance: Be a Fiscal Expert and Learn Less Than You Know." *Commentator*, 2 (November 1937), 17-21.

"History Revised: 1. Columbus and the Egg; 2. Wolfe and Gray's Elegy; 3. King Alfred and the Cakes." *Lilliput*, 1 (November 1937), 40-44.

"The Nine Sovereignties of Canada." *Barron's*, 17 (December 13, 1937), 12.

"Another Year." *Atlantic Monthly*, 160 (December 1937), 799-800.

"Can Professors Teach Bankers?" *Banking*, 30 (December 1937), 20-21.

"I Am Photographed." *Lilliput*, 1 (1937), 63-64, 66.

1938

Model Memoirs And Other Sketches From Simple to Serious. New York: Dodd, Mead, 1938.

"The Economic Analysis of Industrial Depression." *Papers and Proceedings of the Canadian Political Science Association*, 5 (1938), 5-24.

"Happy Horoscope of 1938." *Barron's*, 18 (January 10, 1938), 11-12.

"Leacock Reviews the Canadian Scene as Set for 1938: King, Rowell, Hepburn, and Aberhart in Leading Roles." *Montreal Daily Star*, January 22, 1938, 11.

"Leacock Views Dominion as Beautiful Stage Setting With Sound Asleep." *Evening Telegram* (Toronto), January 22, 1938.

"Anglo-American Trade Pact—So Far." *Barron's*, 18 (January 31, 1938), 11.

"Maddened by Mystery; or, The Defective Detective." *Lilliput*, 2 (January 1938), 73-76, 78-79.

"The World's Muddle over Gold." *Nation's Business*, 26 (January 1938), 18-20, 103.

"John McCrae (Letter on the Death of)." *McGill Daily*, 27 (February 2, 1938), 1.

"I Want to Build a College." *Commentator*, 3 (February 1938), 78-82.

"Mr. Peabody's Portrait Gallery: What He Thinks of His Fellow Men." *Lilliput*, 2 (February 1938), 193-97.

"My Ladders." *Atlantic Monthly*, 161 (March 1938), 410.

"Emigration in English Literature." *Quarterly Review*, 270 (April 1938), 204-220.

"Hoe! Hoe! Spring is Here." *Commentator*, 3 (April 1938), 41-45.

"The Man Who Lived To Do Good." *Lilliput*, 2 (April 1938), 369-72, 374.

"What Happened Next? The Sequel to Some World-Famous Stories." *Lilliput*, 2 (June 1938), no. 6, 605-608.

"All Is Not Lost! A Recollection." *New York Times Magazine*, August 7, 1938, 1-2, 14.

"Who? When? Where? What?—The Questions Fly." *New York Times Magazine*, September 11, 1938, 3, 26.

"Is Education Eating Up Life?" *New York Times Magazine*, October 23, 1938, 1-2, 19.

"How to Keep Education From Eating Up Life." *New York Times Magazine*, October 31, 1938, 3, 20.

"What's Next in Europe?" *Barron's*, 18 (November 7, 1938), 3, 17.

"Model Memoirs: My Victorian Girlhood, by Lady Nearleigh Slopover." *Saturday Evening Post*, 211 (November 12, 1938), 32, 129-30, 132.

"Thrown Out." *Miller Services Ltd.*, November 19, 1938.*

"Auto Waves Magic Wand." *New York Times Magazine*, November 13, 1938, 1, 10.

"Under the Barber's Knife." *Miller Services Ltd.*, November 19, 1938.*

"How Teachers Swim." *Miller Services Ltd.*, November 26, 1938.*

"Andrew Macphail." *Queen's Quarterly*, 45 (November 1938), 445-52.

"I'm Leaving My Farm." *Miller Services Ltd.*, December 3, 1938.*

"My Resurrected Friends." *Miller Services Ltd.*, December 10, 1938.*

"Feeding Time." *Miller Services Ltd.*, December 17, 1938.*

"All Nice People." *Miller Services Ltd.*, December 24, 1938.*

"Dickens: A Self-Portrait." *Saturday Review of Literature*, 19 (December 24, 1938), 3-4, 16.

"A Christmas Star Shines Through the Mists." *New York Times Magazine*, December 25, 1938, 3, 12.

"Attention Psychologists." *Miller Services Ltd.*, December 31, 1938.*

"A Capsule for the Utopians." *Banking*, 31 (December 1938), 22-23.

"How I Read My Newspaper." *Rotarian*, 53 (December 1938), 16-17.

1939

All Right, Mr. Roosevelt (Canada and the United States). New York: Farrar and Rinehart, 1939.

Too Much College; or, Education Eating Up Life, With Kindred Essays in Education and Humour. New York: Dodd, Mead, 1939.

"Introduction." *Unsolved Mysteries of the Arctic*. Vilhjalmur Stefanssen. New York: G.G. Harrap, 1939.

"The Art of Carving, or Hints for the Hapless." *New York Times Magazine*, January 1, 1939, 7, 11.

"Truck Problem Solved." *Miller Services Ltd.*, January 7, 1939.*

"Canada's Horoscope for 1939." *Barron's*, 19 (January 9, 1939), 12-13.

"Quality Does It." *Miller Services Ltd.*, January 14, 1939.*

"How Much Does Language Change?" *John O'London's Weekly*, 40 (January 20, 1939), 621-22, 630, 632.

"The Way of the Professor." *Miller Services Ltd.*, January 21, 1939.*

"For Puzzle Men Only." *Miller Services Ltd.*, January 28, 1939.*

"Go to Mother." *Miller Services Ltd.*, February 4, 1939.*

"A Laugh of the Law Books." *Miller Services Ltd.*, February 4, 1939.*

"Meet the College President." *Miller Services Ltd.*, February 11, 1939.*

"Five Dollars Right Now." *Miller Services Ltd.*, February 18, 1939.*

"Are College Professors Absent-Minded?" *Miller Services Ltd.*, February 25, 1939.*

"Our Living Language: A Defence." *New York Times Magazine*, February 26, 1939, 9, 14.

"Charles Dickens and Canada." *Queen's Quarterly*, 46 (February 1939), 28-37.

"A Note on Latin." *The Classical Outlook*, 16 (February 1939), 45.

"Wanted: A Goldfish." *Miller Services Ltd.*, March 4, 1939.*

"Couldn't Sleep a Wink." *Miller Services Ltd.*, March 11, 1939.*

"Three on Each." *Miller Services Ltd.*, March 18, 1939.*

"Nothing Missing." *Miller Services Ltd.*, March 25, 1939.*

"Canada and National Unity." *Journal of Canadian Dental Association*, 5 (March 1939), 147-49.

"Our Dinner Club and How it Died." *Rotarian*, 54 (March 1939), 11-13.

"Thinking of Tomorrow." *Miller Services Ltd.*, April 1, 1939.*

"Information While You Drink." *Miller Services Ltd.*, April 8, 1939.*

"No Place for Gentlemen." *Miller Services Ltd.*, April 15, 1939.*

"We Have With Us Tonight." *Miller Services Ltd.*, April 22, 1939.*

"Oh, Sleep! Oh, Gentle Sleep!" *Miller Services Ltd.*, April 29, 1939.*

"A Humble Lover." *Miller Services Ltd.*, May 6, 1939.*

"A Golfer Tells All." *New York Times Magazine*, May 12, 1939, 9, 21.

"The Magic of Finance." *Miller Services Ltd.*, May 13, 1939.*

"Come Out to Canada." *The Times*, May 15, 1939, xvii.

"Writers of Quebec." (Review of Ian Forbes' *Spirit of French Canada*). *Saturday Review of Literature*, 20 (June 3, 1939), 10.

"Canada and the Monarchy." *Atlantic Monthly*, 163 (June 1939), 735-43.

"Twenty Cents' Worth of Murder." *Saturday Review of Literature*, 20 (July 8, 1939), 10-11.

"Investing in Canada." *Barron's*, 19 (July 17, 1939), 7.

"Lost in The Jungle of Economics." *New York Times Magazine*, August 20, 1939, 1, 16, 18.

"We Are What We Joke About." *New York Times Magazine*, September 3, 1939, 4-5, 14.

"With Women or Without." *Rotarian*, 55 (August 1939), 28-30.

"Buggam Grange: A Good Old Ghost Story." *Picture Post*, 4 (September 9, 1939), 69, 71, 73-74.

"Can I Learn to Be a Writer?" *The Gregg Writer*, 42 (September 1939), 11-14.

"Come Into the Kitchen." *Canadian Home Journal*, 36 (September 1939), 46-47.

"Leacock Sees Good Times Ahead." *Barron's*, 19 (December 4, 1939), 9.

"We Need a Santa Claus." *New York Times Magazine*, December 24, 1939, 5, 15.

1940

Laugh Parade: A New Collection of The Wit and Humor of Stephen Leacock. New York: Dodd, Mead, 1940.

Our British Empire: Its Structure, Its History, Its Strength. London: John Lane, 1940.

"Three Score and Ten." *Spectator,* 164 (January 19, 1940), 72-73.

"Napoleon at St. Helena." *Men Only,* 13 (January 1940), 57-60.

"Other People's Money: An Outside View of Trusts and Investments." *Trusts and Estates,* 79 (January 1940), 11-16.

"Of Georgina Township and Its First Church." *Gazette* (Montreal), February 10, 1940, 5.

"This Business of Growing Old." *Reader's Digest,* 36 (March 1940), 78-80.

"School and Real Learning for Oldsters." *New York Times Magazine,* May 19, 1940, sec. 7, 8.

"Perfect Index." *Saturday Review of Literature,* 22 (May 25, 1940), 9.

"Cricket for Americans." *Atlantic Monthly,* 165 (June 1940), 766-69.

"On Growing Old." *New World Illustrated,* August 1940, 41-43, 52.

"Bath Through the Ages." *Canadian Home Journal,* 37 (September 1940), 54-55.

"Babes in the Wood." *Saturday Night,* 56 (October 12, 1940), 12.

"Courage: An Interlude on the South Coast of England." *Standard* (Montreal), October 26, 1940, 11.

"Soft Stuff for Children." *Rotarian,* 57 (October 1940), 16-17.

1941

Canada, The Foundations of Its Future. Montreal: Privately printed for the House of Seagram by the Gazette Printing Company, 1941.

"The Whole Duty of a Citizen." *Canadian Spokesman,* 1 (January 1941), 1-4.

"First Call for Spring." *Reader's Digest,* 38 (March 1941), 80.

"How to Swear in Print." *Saturday Review of Literature,* 23 (April 5, 1941), 7-8.

"Our American Visitors." *Montreal Daily Star,* April 23, 1941.

"Canada Depicted As an Eager Host." *New York Times,* April 27, 1941, 3.

"Minority Report." *Reader's Digest,* 38 (April 1941), 143.

"The Difference of Degree." *Reader's Digest,* 38 (May 1941), 70.

"America." *New World Illustrated,* 2 (July 1941), 5.

"The Most Unforgettable Character I've Met." *Reader's Digest,* 39 (July 1941), 18-22.

"Questions Nobody Answers." *Canadian Banker,* 48 (July 1941), 459-65.

"Who Canonizes the Classics?" *Answers* (July [?] 1941), 2-4.

"Come On Up." *McGill News,* 22 (Summer 1941), 20.

"My Uncle Was a Quaint Character." *Winnipeg Free Press*, October 18, 1941, Mag. Sec., 5.

"The Ceiling's the Limit." *Banking*, 34 (December 1941), 19-22.

"In Memory of René du Roure." *Old McGill*, 44 (1941), 11-13.

1942

Montreal, Seaport and City. Garden City, N.Y.: Doubleday, Doran, 1942.

My Remarkable Uncle, and Other Sketches. New York: Dodd, Mead, 1942.

Our Heritage of Liberty, Its Origin, Its Achievement, Its Crisis: A Book For War Time. London: John Lane, 1942.

"Christmas, 1941." *New World*, 2 (January 1942), 122, 169.

"We Canadians." *Rotarian*, 60 (January 1942), 21-24.

"Was Hochelaga a Myth?" *Standard* (Montreal), February 28, 1942, Mag. Sec., 10.

"I Squirm to Recall." *Saturday Review of Literature*, 25 (May 30, 1942), 13.

"Common Sense and the Universe." *Atlantic Monthly*, 169 (May 1942), 627-34.

"The England I Remember." *New World Illustrated* (October 1942), 6-9.

"New Program for Canada." *Saturday Night*, 58 (November 28, 1942), 14.

"Sleeve Trick." *Reader's Digest*, 41 (November 1942), 37-38.

"Rebuilding the Cities: A Broad View of Reconstruction." *Royal Architect Institute of Canada Journal*, 19 (December 1942), 229-30.

1943

"Gold." *Canadian Banker*, 50 (1943), 39-51.

Happy Stories, Just to Laugh At. New York: Dodd, Mead, 1943.

How to Write. New York: Dodd, Mead, 1943.

Memories of Christmas. Toronto: Private printing, Charles Bush, 1943.

My Old College, 1843-1943. [Montreal] Private printing, 1943.

"Optimism in War-Time: 1. The Dentist." *Saturday Night*, 58 (January 30, 1943), 8.

"Come Up the Mountain With Stephen Leacock." *Maclean's Magazine*, 56 (February 1, 1943), 19-20, 24-25.

"Wartime Optimism: Cooking for Victory." *Saturday Night*, 58 (February 13, 1943), 10.

"Wartime Optimism: The Jones's Enchanted Castle." *Saturday Night*, 58 (February 27, 1943), 17.

"Plea for Geographical Science." *Queen's Quarterly*, 50 (February 1943), 1-13.

"To Many Women Knitting (poem)." *Good Housekeeping*, 116 (February 1943), 48.

"Tale of Two Cities." *Maclean's Magazine*, 56 (March 1, 1943), 7-8, 40-42.

"Wartime Optimism: Mr. Alcorn Improves Himself." *Saturday Night*, 58 (March 6, 1943), 10-11.

"Optimism for Wartime: Good News! A New Party!" *Saturday Night*, 58 (March 20, 1943), 16-17.

"This Business of Prophecy." *New York Times Magazine*, March 21, 1943, sec. 6, 12.

"Wartime Optimism: The Life of Lea and Perrins." *Saturday Night*, 58 (March 27, 1943), 16.

"Clouds That Rolled By: Mr. Alldone's Awful Day." *Saturday Night*, 58 (April 3, 1943), 16.

"Angel Pond, Lure of the North." *Saturday Night*, 58 (April 17, 1943), 18-19.

"Dickens Distilled." *Saturday Review of Literature*, 26 (April 17, 1943), 16-18.

"Why Study English?" *Montreal Daily Star*, 75 (April 20, 1943), 10.

"Leacock Tells How Sultan Abdul Raised Loans by Head-chopping." *Gazette* (Montreal), April 29, 1943, 13.

"The Case of Boob Smith." *Canadian Publishers War Finance Publicity Committee*, April 30, 1943.

"Will It Bust the Country?" *Canadian Publishers War Finance Publicity Committee*, May 1, 1943.

"Leacock Writes Off Boob Smith; He's Made All the Sacrifices He Can." *Gazette* (Montreal), April 30, 1943, 13.

"Leacock Finds Loan Won't Bust Us: Call to Ilsley Found Unnecessary." *Gazette* (Montreal), May 1, 1943, 13.

"Mushroom Days." *Saturday Review of Literature*, 26 (May 1, 1943), 13.

"Piscatorial Perspicacities Make War Loan Publicity Substitute." *Gazette* (Montreal), May 3, 1943, 17.

"Barber shop Psychology Lesson Aids War Loan Certificate Sale." *Gazette* (Montreal), May 4, 1943, 15.

"Fiery Scot to Wreck Mariposa if Leacock's Town Fails in Loan." *Gazette* (Montreal), May 6, 1943, 15, 16.

"Case of Whisky Too Sacrificial, Mariposa Loan Head Gets Cane." *Gazette* (Montreal), May 7, 1943, 13, 14.

"Economic Paradise Is Uncovered In Wake of Farm Auction Sale." *Gazette* (Montreal), May 8, 1943, 21.

"National Debt National Blessing." *The Sarnia* (Ont.) *Canadian Observer*, May 10, 1943, 8.

"Have You Got Even One Cent?" *The Sarnia* (Ont.) *Canadian Observer*, May 11, 1943, 9.

"Leacock's Mariposa Out of Joint As Loan Drive Cuts Social Lines." *Gazette* (Montreal), May 15, 1943, 23.

"Britain and America." *Thought*, 18 (June 1943), 204-207.

"Statement on the Four Freedoms." *Biosophical Review*, 6 (June 1943).

"George Drew." *High Park Riding Elect George Drew*. Progressive Conservative Pamphlet, July 1943, 3.

"Some Anecdotes of McGill." *McGill News*, 24 (Summer 1943), no. 4, 31-32.

"Woman's Level." *Chatelaine*, 16 (October 1943), 9, 45-46, 50-51.

"Leacock Likes Aldington's Book on the Life of Duke of Wellington." *Gazette* (Montreal), November 13, 1943, 7.

"What's Ahead for Canada?" *Financial Post*, 37 (December 4, 1943), 9-16; (December 11), 11, 19; (December 18), 11-17; (December 25), 3; 38 (January 1, 1944), 3; (January 8), 9; (January 22), 12; (January 29), 22; (February 5), 11, 15; (January 15), 1, 8.

1944

Canada and the Sea. Montreal: Alvah M. Beatty, 1944.

1945

Last Leaves. Toronto: McClelland and Stewart, [c1945].

While There is Time; The Case Against Social Catastrophe. Toronto: McClelland and Stewart, [c1945].

1946

The Boy I Left Behind Me. Garden City, New York: Doubleday, 1946.

1947

Other People's Money: An Outside View of Trusts and Investments. Montreal: Royal Trust Company [1947].

"Introduction." *Unusual Facts of Canadian History.* W.A.L. Styles, M.D. Toronto: McClelland and Stewart, c1947. pp. 5-6.

*These syndicated pieces have no proof of publication, although there are references to them in Leacock's correspondence; Leacock was paid for publication on these dates.

NOTES

CURRY Leacock and the Media

1. Cf. "Jazzled Journalism," *The Iron Man and the Tin Woman* (London: John Lane, 1929), pp. 250-56; or "How I Read My Newspaper," *Rotarian*, 53 (Dec. 1938), 16-17.

2. "Radio. A New Form of Trouble," *Over the Footlights* (New York: Dodd, Mead, 1923), pp. 226-27.

3. "If We Had Only Had the Radio Sooner," *Short Circuits* (Toronto: McClelland and Stewart, 1967), p. 96. Used by permission of McClelland and Stewart Limited.

4. Richard Morris to Leacock, 16 Nov. 1931. All correspondence is in the archives of the Stephen Leacock Memorial Home, Orillia, Ontario.

5. W. N. DeFoe to Leacock, 18 Feb. [1932]. A typographical error has this 1931 on the original.

6. Leacock to W. N. DeFoe, 22 Feb. 1932.

7. J. E. McDougall to Leacock, 15 Feb. 1934.

8. J. E. McDougall to Leacock, 29 Mar. 1934.

9. V. C. Clinton-Baddeley to Leacock, 3 Mar. [1935].

10. Hans Christian Rude to Leacock, 4 Aug. 1936.

11. William Gladstone Murray to Leacock, 5 June 1937.

12. "Miss Rush Leaps at Leap Year," Stephen Leacock Memorial Home Archives.

13. Leacock to Paul Reynolds, 8 Sept. 1938.

14. T. W. Tweed to Leacock, 3 July 1940, and 6 Nov. 1940.

15. Howard Reinheimer to Leacock, 30 Apr. 1941.

16. Jacques Chambrun to Leacock, 7 May 1943.

17. V. C. Clinton-Baddeley to Leacock, 7 Oct. [1937].

18. John Lane to Leacock, 24 Mar. 1938.

19. John Lane to Leacock, 9 Sept. 1915.

20. "Madeline of the Movies," *Further Foolishness* (Toronto: McClelland and Stewart, 1968), pp. 48-50. Used by permission of McClelland and Stewart Limited.

21. "The Discovery of America," *The Hohenzollerns in America* (Toronto: S. B. Grundy, 1919), pp. 217-19.

22. Gerhard Lomer, comp., *Stephen Leacock: A Check-List and Index of His Writings* (Ottawa: National Library of Canada, 1954), p. 27.

23. "F. S.," "Professor Stephen Leacock," (Vancouver) *Daily Province*, 17 Jan. 1920.

24. Leacock to Jefferson Jones, [Jan. 1923].

25. "Dead Men's Gold," pp. 72-91.

26. "People We Meet in the Movies," p. 174.

27. "One Crowded Quarter Second," *Short Circuits*, pp. 105-106.

28. "Done Into Movies," *Short Circuits*, pp. 109-10.

29. "McGill University, Session 1930-31, Graduate School in Economics and Political Science," Stephen Leacock Memorial Home Archives.

30. Stephen Leacock Memorial Home Archives.

31. Paul Reynolds to Leacock, 27 July 1939.

32. Charles Clement to Leacock, 28 Jan. 1941; and Leacock to Charles Clement, 6 Feb. [1941].

33. Richard Mealand to Leacock, 15 Jan. 1942.

34. Dorothy Purdell to Leacock, 20 Jan. 1942.

35. Leacock to Richard Mealand, 6 Feb. [1942].

36. Dorothy Purdell to Leacock, 24 Mar. 1942.

37. Dorothy Purdell to Leacock, 5 May 1942.

38. Dorothy Purdell to Leacock, 18 May 1943.

39. "Boom Times," *Happy Stories* (New York: Dodd, Mead, 1943), p. 154.

40. Leacock to Frank Dodd, 7 June 1943.

ROBERTSON The Historical Leacock

1.   Douglas Bush, "Stephen Leacock," in David Staines, ed., *The Canadian Imagination: Dimensions of a Literary Culture* (Cambridge, Mass.: Harvard University Press, 1977), p. 126.
2.   See *Canadian Journal of Economics and Political Science*, 10 (May 1944), 216-30. It might be noted, however, that Leacock was cross-appointed in history and political science during the 1901-1902 session; see Stanley B. Frost, *McGill University: For the Advancement of Learning, Volume II, 1895-1971* (Kingston and Montreal: McGill-Queen's University Press, 1984), pp. 28-29.
3.   Ralph L. Curry, *Stephen Leacock: Humorist and Humanist* (Garden City, N.Y.: Doubleday, 1959), p. 71.
4.   See W.P.M. Kennedy, Editor's Preface to Stephen Leacock, *Mackenzie, Baldwin, LaFontaine, Hincks* (London and Toronto: Oxford University Press, 1926), p. vii; W. L. Grant, General Introduction to N. E. Dionne, *Champlain* (London and Toronto: Oxford University Press, 1926).
5.   *Review of Historical Publications Relating to Canada*, 19 (1915), 15. A former professor of Canadian history at McGill recalls from his acquaintance with Leacock in the late 1930s and the 1940s that "Leacock had one historical hobby — the Canadian Arctic. He was fond of talking about it to me and he had a considerable collection of books on the subject. He was greatly interested in the discovery of uranium, gold, and so on along Great Slave Lake. He had the books of . . . one of the pioneers of the Mackenzie valley exploitation" (J. I. Cooper to author, 5 January 1985).
6.   Stephen Leacock, *Canada: The Foundations of Its Future* (Montreal: privately printed for the House of Seagram, 1941), Author's Foreword, p. xxx.
7.   See *Canadian Historical Review*, 24 (March and September 1943), 56 and 306-308.
8.   See J.M.S. Careless, "Frontierism, Metropolitanism, and Canadian History," *ibid.*, 35 (March 1954), 1-21.
9.   See J. M. Bumsted, "Historical Writing in English," in William Toye, ed., *The Oxford Companion to Canadian Literature* (Toronto: Oxford University Press, 1983), pp. 350-56.
10.   See Jacques Monet, "Sir Louis-Hippolyte LaFontaine," *Dictionary of Canadian Biography*, 9 (Toronto: University of Toronto Press, 1976), p. 451; William G. Ormsby, "Sir Francis Hincks," *ibid.*, 11 (Toronto: University of Toronto Press, 1982), p. 416; Michael S. Cross and Robert L. Fraser, "Robert Baldwin," *ibid.*, 8 (Toronto: University of Toronto Press, 1985), p. 59.
11.   See Kenneth N. Windsor, "Historical Writing in Canada to 1920," in Carl F. Klinck *et al.*, eds., *Literary History of Canada: Canadian Literature in English* (Toronto: University of Toronto Press, 1965), pp. 215, 229-32; Carl Berger, *The Writing of Canadian History: Aspects of English-Canadian Historical Writing, 1900-1970* (Toronto: Oxford University Press, 1976), p. 218.
12.   J. K. Johnson, "Upper Canada," in D. A. Muise, ed., *A Reader's Guide to Canadian History, I: Beginnings to Confederation* (Toronto: University of Toronto Press, 1982), p. 154. Also see A. B. McKillop, ed., *A Critical Spirit: The Thought of William Dawson LeSueur* (Toronto: McClelland and Stewart, 1977), Part IV; A. B. McKillop, Introduction to William D. LeSueur, *William Lyon Mackenzie: A Reinterpretation* (Toronto: Macmillan, 1979).
13.   See G.G.S. Lindsey, *William Lyon Mackenzie* (Toronto: Morang, 1908). This book was not included in the revised version of the series published in 1926; material on Mackenzie was incorporated into Kennedy's revision of Leacock's volume.
14.   Stephen Leacock, *Baldwin, LaFontaine, Hincks: Responsible Government* (Toronto: Morang, 1907), p. 9.
15.   Michiel Horn, "Academics and Canadian Social and Economic Policy in the Depression and War Years," *Journal of Canadian Studies*, 13 (Winter 1978-79), 3. Also see Berger, *The Writing of Canadian History*, p. 31.
16.   Inside cover of *The University Magazine*, 6 (February 1907). Concerning Macphail's breadth and its importance for understanding him as a writer, see Ian Ross Robertson, "Andrew Macphail: A Holistic Approach," *Canadian Literature*, 107 (Winter 1985), 179-86.
17.   Desmond Morton, *A Short History of Canada* (Edmonton: Hurtig, 1983), p. 158.
18.   Frank Watt, "Critic or Entertainer: Stephen Leacock and the Growth of Materialism," *Canadian Literature*, 5 (Summer 1960), 33.

19. *Ibid.*, p. 34.
20. *Ibid.*, p. 36.
21. *Ibid.*, p. 42.
22. Ramsay Cook, "Stephen Leacock and the Age of Plutocracy, 1903-1921," in John S. Moir, ed., *Character and Circumstance: Essays in Honour of Donald Grant Creighton* (Toronto: Macmillan, 1970), p. 164.
23. *Ibid.*, p. 167.
24. *Ibid.*
25. Alan Bowker, ed., *The Social Criticism of Stephen Leacock: The Unsolved Riddle of Social Justice and Other Essays* (Toronto: University of Toronto Press, 1973), p. 4.
26. *Ibid.*, p. 6.
27. Andrew Macphail, "The Navy and Politics," *The University Magazine*, 12 (February 1913), 7.
28. Cook, "Stephen Leacock and the Age of Plutocracy, 1903-1921," in Moir, ed., *Character and Circumstance*, p. 176. Cook gave relatively little attention to *Arcadian Adventures*, presumably because its critical thrust is so undisguised.
29. *Ibid.*, p. 167. The respected *Review of Historical Publications Relating to Canada* recommended *Sunshine Sketches* to its readers for its realism concerning politics in the small towns of Ontario; see 17 (1913), 111-12.
30. Cook, "Stephen Leacock and the Age of Plutocracy, 1903-1921," p. 177.
31. See Bowker, ed., *The Social Criticism of Stephen Leacock*, p. 135.
32. See Cook, "Stephen Leacock and the Age of Plutocracy, 1903-1921," p. 178.
33. Carl Berger, *The Sense of Power: Studies in the Ideas of Canadian Imperialism, 1867-1914* (Toronto: University of Toronto Press, 1970), p. 43.
34. Richard Wilbur, *The Bennett Administration 1930-1935*, Canadian Historical Association booklet No. 24 (Ottawa, 1969), p. 20; also see Berger, *The Sense of Power*, p. 196.
35. Carl Berger, "The Other Mr. Leacock," *Canadian Literature*, 55 (Winter 1973), 28; also see 23.
36. Leacock, Preface to *Baldwin, LaFontaine, Hincks*, p. ix.
37. Berger, "The Other Mr. Leacock," 31.
38. *Ibid.*, p. 24; also see Stephen Leacock, Preface to *Hellements of Hickonomics in Hiccoughs of Verse Done in Our Social Planning Mill* (New York: Dodd, Mead, 1936), p. vi. An economist, Craufurd D. W. Goodwin, has described *Hellements of Hickonomics* as "a choleric little work . . . [which] turned out to be a crude ridicule in extremely poor taste"; see *Canadian Economic Thought: The Political Economy of a Developing Nation 1814-1914* (Durham, N.C.: Duke University Press, 1961), p. 191.
39. Goodwin, who did not mention *The Unsolved Riddle of Social Justice*, went further: "Leacock was a humorist first and an economist only in name" (*ibid.*, p. 196). He also believed Leacock to have been a better historian than economist; see *ibid.*, p. 193, but also Bush, "Stephen Leacock," p. 127. Surviving evidence suggests strongly that Leacock's colleagues and students perceived him as a much better political scientist than economist, and one former student has expressed the opinion that Leacock used his economics classes to try out humorous material. See Robertson Davies, "Stephen Leacock," in Claude Bissell, ed., *Our Living Tradition*, first series (Toronto: University of Toronto Press, 1957), pp. 131-32; David M. Legate, *Stephen Leacock: A Biography* (Toronto: Doubleday, 1970), pp. 53-54; H. Carl Goldenberg in Edgar A. Collard, ed., *The McGill You Knew: An Anthology of Memories 1920-1960* (Don Mills, Ont.: Longman Canada, 1975), p. 49; Allan Anderson, comp., *Remembering Leacock: An Oral History* (Ottawa: Deneau, 1983), pp. 57-58.
40. Berger, "The Other Mr. Leacock," 34.
41. Bowker, Introduction to *The Social Criticism of Stephen Leacock*, p. xxxix. Evidence emerging in a recent oral history suggests a motive for Leacock to adopt a writing strategy calculated to maximize financial returns: to leave an estate sufficient to provide for his son Stephen Jr. (d. 1974), a dwarf who had serious personal and behavioural problems which resulted in, for example, his being banned from the University Club; see Anderson, comp., *Remembering Leacock*, pp. 28-32. Also see H. Carl Goldenberg to author, 12 April 1985.
42. Bowker, Introduction to *The Social Criticism of Stephen Leacock*, p. xviii.
43. See *ibid.*, pp. xxxiv, x-xi; Stephen Leacock, *Elements of Political Science* (Boston: Houghton Mifflin, 1906), pp. 361-63, 369, 378, 403, 406.

44. Bowker, Introduction to *The Social Criticism of Stephen Leacock*, p. xxxv.

45. *Ibid.*, p. xxxii.

46. Watt, "Critic or Entertainer: Stephen Leacock and the Growth of Materialism," 40.

47. Bowker, ed., *The Social Criticism of Stephen Leacock*, p. 80.

48. For evidence of recognition by Leacock that imperialism was in decline, see *Elements of Political Science* (Boston: Houghton Mifflin, 1921), pp. 279-81.

49. Bowker, ed., *The Social Criticism of Stephen Leacock*, p. 6.

50. *Ibid.*, p. 25.

51. *Ibid.*, p. 26.

52. Stephen Leacock, "Andrew Macphail," *Queen's Quarterly*, 45 (Winter 1938), 449-50.

53. See Ian Ross Robertson, "Sir Andrew Macphail as a Social Critic," (unpublished Ph.D. thesis, University of Toronto, 1974), pp. 102, 104, 145, 193, 199.

54. Archibald MacMechan, *Head-waters of Canadian Literature* (Toronto: McClelland and Stewart, 1924), p. 202.

55. See Terry Copp, *The Anatomy of Poverty: The Condition of the Working Class in Montreal 1897-1929* (Toronto: McClelland and Stewart, 1974), p. 32.

56. Dalhousie University Archives, Archibald MacMechan Papers, Macphail to Mac-Mechan, 2 April 1907.

57. See Sir Andrew Macphail Papers, in private possession, Macphail to James Mavor, 17 September 1913.

58. University of Toronto Library, Rare Book Department, Sir Edmund Walker Papers, Macphail to Walker, 1 February 1907.

59. See Sonia Leathes, "Votes for Women," *The University Magazine*, 13 (February 1914), 68-78; Andrew Macphail, "On Certain Aspects of Feminism," *ibid.*, 79-91.

60. Stephen Leacock, "The Psychology of American Humour," *ibid.*, 6 (February 1907), 75.

61. Stephen Leacock, "The University and Business," *ibid.*, 12 (December 1913), 544.

62. *Ibid.*, 547.

63. Stephen Leacock, "Canada and the Monroe Doctrine," *ibid.*, 8 (October 1909), 352.

64. Stephen Leacock, "What Shall We Do About The Navy?" *ibid.*, 10 (December 1911), 535.

65. Leo Cox, *Fifty Years of Brush and Pen: A Historical Sketch of the Pen and Pencil Club of Montreal* (n.p., 1939), p. 3.

66. Andrew Macphail, "John McCrae: An Essay in Character," in John McCrae, *In Flanders Fields and Other Poems* (Toronto: The Ryerson Press, 1919), pp. 127-28.

67. Leacock, "Andrew Macphail," 447; also see Stephen Leacock, *Montreal: Seaport and City* (Garden City, N.Y.: Doubleday Doran, 1942), p. 311.

68. Macphail Papers, Andrew Macphail, untitled address to the University Club, Montreal, n.d. [after 1908].

69. T. B. Bottomore, *Social Criticism in North America* (Toronto: Canadian Broadcasting Corporation, 1966), p. 58. *Cf.* Claude Bissell, "Haliburton, Leacock and the American Humourous Tradition," *Canadian Literature*, 39 (Winter 1969), 19, where Leacock's position is described as "individualistic and uncommitted."

70. See Cook, "Stephen Leacock and the Age of Plutocracy, 1903-1921," p. 181; Berger, "The Other Mr. Leacock," 38; Bowker, Introduction to *The Social Criticism of Stephen Leacock*, p. xix. Other commentators on Leacock have also noted his inconsistency. See Legate, *Stephen Leacock*, pp. 105-106; Donald Cameron, *Faces of Leacock: An Appreciation* (Toronto: The Ryerson Press, 1967), pp. 17, 63.

71. Leacock, "Andrew Macphail," 451-52.

72. B. C. Parekh writes that "A philosophical understanding of an activity . . . points to its essential and permanent features, and offers criteria for evaluating relevant practical proposals and actions—not, of course, in their specificity but in their general assumptions and orientation"; Parekh, "The Nature of Political Philosophy," in Preston King and B. C. Parekh, eds., *Politics and Experience: Essays Presented to Professor Michael Oakeshott on the Occasion of His Retirement* (Cambridge, U.K.: Cambridge University Press, 1968), p. 181.

73. Bowker, ed., *The Social Criticism of Stephen Leacock*, p. 142; also see pp. 140, 145.

74. *Ibid.*, p. 139.

75. *Ibid.*, p. 143. Also see J. Kushner and R. D. MacDonald, "Leacock: Economist/Satirist in *Arcadian Adventures* and *Sunshine Sketches*," *Dalhousie Review*, 56 (Autumn 1976), 494-95.

76. Leacock, *Elements of Political Science*, 1921 ed., p. 398.

77. See *e.g.* the writings of Gad Horowitz: "Conservatism, Liberalism, and Socialism in Canada: An Interpretation," *Canadian Journal of Economics and Political Science*, 32 (May 1966), 143-71; "Tories, Socialists and the Demise of Canada," *Canadian Dimension*, 2 (May-June 1965), 12-15.

78. See William Lyon Mackenzie King, *Industry and Humanity: A Study in the Principles Underlying Industrial Reconstruction* (Toronto: University of Toronto Press, 1973 ed.); H. S. Ferns, "The Ideas of Mackenzie King," *Manitoba Arts Review*, 6 (Winter 1948-49), 11.

79. The proposed titles were "The Political Ideas of Stephen Leacock" and "The Public Mind of Stephen Leacock" (source: *Register of Post-Graduate Dissertations in Progress in History and Related Subjects*, an annual publication of the Canadian Historical Association).

80. Leacock to LeSueur, 11 October 1906, cited in McKillop, ed., *A Critical Spirit*, p. 250; also see pp. 251, 272, and n. 27 on p. 266.

81. See Bush, "Stephen Leacock," p. 126.

82. See Zailig Pollock, "Stephen Leacock" and "*Sunshine Sketches of a Little Town*," in Toye, ed., *The Oxford Companion to Canadian Literature*, pp. 438-40, 777. Some early commentators recognized that *The Unsolved Riddle* was an important revelation of Leacock. See Peter McArthur, *Stephen Leacock* (Toronto: The Ryerson Press, 1923), pp. 146-47, 149; Desmond Pacey, "Leacock as a Satirist," *Queen's Quarterly*, 58 (Summer 1951), 212-13. At the other end of the spectrum among literary critics is Davies with his repeated assertion that "Leacock's importance to Canada rests solely upon the body of his work as a humorist"; see *e.g.* his "Stephen Leacock" in Bissell, ed., *Our Living Tradition*, first series, p. 132. Albert and Theresa Moritz, *Leacock: A Biography* (Toronto: Stoddart, 1985) was received too late for consideration in this article.

83. J. L. Granatstein *et al.*, *Twentieth Century Canada* (Toronto: McGraw-Hill Ryerson, 1983), pp. 243-44. A reading of the volume reveals a second reference to him, which credits him with insight into the relationship between Canada and Britain between the world wars; see p. 322.

FRANKMAN Stephen Leacock, Economist

1. Harold Innis, "Stephen Butler Leacock 1869-1944," *Canadian Journal of Economics and Political Science (CJEPS)*, 10 (May 1944), 216-26. Innis' lecture was one in a series marking the fiftieth anniversary of the Department of Political Economy of the University of Toronto in 1938. The lectures in the series devoted to William James Ashley and Adam Shortt were published in 1938 in the *CJEPS* and *The Commerce Journal*.

2. *Ibid.*, p. 226.

3. *Ibid.* See also p. 219 ("In 1907 an ominous storm of imperialism broke over him and carried him from his moorings"), p. 221 ("thrown off his stride by imperialism"), and p. 225 ("the difficulties under which he laboured in the face of the demands of imperialism").

4. *Ibid.*, p. 221. Craufurd D. W. Goodwin is far more severe than Innis in his judgement of Leacock the economist: "It was unfortunate for both Leacock and for Canadian economics that he was forced to earn a living from a subject which he disliked, was unable to comprehend, and took time away from areas where he made best use of his talents." Goodwin, *Canadian Economic Thought: The Political Economy of a Developing Nation 1814-1914* (Durham, N.C.: Duke University Press, 1961), p. 193. See also pp. 190-93.

5. Innis, p. 226.

6. "What is Left of Adam Smith?", *CJEPS*, I (February 1935), 41-51.

7. Innis, p. 226.

8. Alan Bowker, *The Social Criticism of Stephen Leacock: The Unsolved Riddle of Social Justice and Other Essays* (Toronto: University of Toronto Press, 1973), pp. xix. See also p. xxxviii.

9. McGill University Archives, Sir Arthur Currie Papers, file C63, Leacock to Currie, May 26, 1930.

10. *Ibid.*, Currie to F. I. Kerr [Ker], May 13, 1933.

11. Innis, p. 225.

12. W. A. Mackintosh, "Adam Shortt, 1859-1931," *CJEPS*, IV (May 1938), 164-76.

13. *Our Heritage of Liberty: Its Origin, Its Achievement, Its Crisis; A Book for War Time* (London: John Lane, The Bodley Head, 1942), p. 48.

14. "The Economic Analysis of Industrial Depression," *Papers and Proceedings of the Canadian Political Science Association,* V (1933), p. 8.
15. *Economic Prosperity in the British Empire* (Toronto: Macmillan, 1930), p. 165.
16. *Our Heritage,* p. 48.
17. John Stuart Mill, *Principles of Political Economy,* 5th ed. (New York: D. Appleton, 1865), vol. II, p. 338.
18. McGill University Library, Rare Books Department, Stephen Leacock Collection, Mss, Box 12. There are only twenty-seven pages of this manuscript; page 28 indicates that material from an Ottawa lecture was to follow at that point. The text covers the chapter outline, preface and Chapter I dealing with Adam Smith and the *Wealth of Nations.*
19. *My Discovery of the West* (Toronto: Thomas Allen, 1937), pp. 136-38.
20. *Ibid.,* p. 137. See also Carl Berger, "The Other Mr. Leacock," *Canadian Literature,* 55 (Winter 1973), 32-33.
21. *The Quarterly Journal of Economics,* XII (July 1898).
22. "The Cultural Incidence . . ." appeared as Chapter IX of Veblen's *The Theory of Business Enterprise* (1904).
23. *The Vested Interests and the Common Man: ("The Modern Point of View and the New Order")* (New York: B. W. Huebsch, 1919).
24. *My Discovery,* p. 137.
25. C. E. Ayres, review of *The Unsolved Riddle of Social Justice* by Stephen Leacock, *Journal of Political Economy,* 28 (May 1920), 439-40. For Claude T. Bissell, the influence on Leacock's humour of Thorstein Veblen (and Mark Twain) is unmistakable: "*Arcadian Adventures with the Idle Rich* was almost a fictional companion piece to *The Theory of the Leisure Class.*" "Haliburton, Leacock and the American Humorous Tradition," *Canadian Literature,* 39 (Winter 1969), 14.
26. *The Unsolved Riddle of Social Justice* (London: John Lane, The Bodley Head, 1920) and "The Proper Limitations of State Interference," an address before the Empire Club of Canada, Toronto (March 6, 1924), 14 pp.
27. *The Unsolved Riddle,* p. 133.
28. *Ibid.,* pp. 119-20.
29. *Ibid.,* pp. 131-32.
30. *Ibid.,* p. 130.
31. *Ibid.,* p. 129.
32. *Ibid.*
33. Paul Streeten, *et al., First Things First: Meeting Basic Human Needs in Developing Countries* (New York: Oxford University Press, 1981).
34. *Ibid.,* p. 219.
35. "The Gold Standard," an address before the 1924 Life Insurance Educational Congress, Toronto, p. 8.
36. *Economic Prosperity,* p. 166.
37. *Ibid.,* p. 231. For a discussion of the movement in Canada for imperial unity and Leacock's relation to it see Carl Berger, *The Sense of Power: Studies in the Ideas of Canadian Imperialism 1867-1914* (Toronto: University of Toronto Press, 1970).
38. "Economic Separatism in the British Empire," *The Quarterly Review,* no. 525 (July 1935), p. 9.
39. *Economic Prosperity,* pp. 177-79.
40. *Ibid.,* pp. 163-64.
41. *Hellements of Hickonomics in Hiccoughs of Verse Done in Our Social Planning Mill* (New York: Dodd, Mead, 1936), p. 84.
42. *Ibid.,* p. vi.
43. *Stephen Leacock's Plan to Relieve the Depression in 6 Days, To Remove It in 6 Months, To Eradicate It in 6 Years* (Toronto: Macmillan, 1933), p. 1.
44. J. M. Keynes, *The General Theory of Employment Interest and Money* (New York: Harcourt, Brace, 1936), p. 98.
45. *Stephen Leacock's Plan,* p. 6.
46. Keynes, p. 129.
47. McGill Library, Leacock Mss, Box 4.
48. Keynes, p. 126, n. 2. Keynes did not hold a chair, but rather was a Fellow and Bursar of King's College, Cambridge.

49. "The Invasion of Human Thought."
50. *Ibid.*
51. W. H. Dawson, review of *Economic Prosperity in the British Empire*, by Stephen Leacock, *The Economic Journal* (June 1931), pp. 295-97.
52. *The Unsolved Riddle*, pp. 137-38.
53. *Ibid.*, p. 99.

STEELE Imperial Cosmopolitanism

1. *Sunshine Sketches of a Little Town* (Toronto: McClelland and Stewart, 1960), p. 1.
2. *My Discovery of England* (New York: Dodd, Mead, 1922), pp. vi-vii.
3. *My Remarkable Uncle, and Other Sketches* (Toronto: McClelland and Stewart, 1965), p. 32.
4. *The Boy I Left Behind Me* (London: John Lane, 1947), pp. 57-58.
5. Vishnu R. K. Chopra, "Stephen Leacock: An Edition of Selected Letters," Diss. McGill, 1975.
6. Ralph L. Curry, *Stephen Leacock: Humorist and Humanist* (New York: Doubleday, 1959), p. 71.
7. Curry, p. 127.
8. *Elements of Political Science* (Boston: Houghton Mifflin, 1906), p. 15.
9. *Ibid.*, p. 17.
10. *Ibid.*, p. 18.
11. *Ibid.*
12. *Ibid.*, p. 20.
13. Stephen Leacock, *Economic Prosperity in the British Empire* (Toronto: Macmillan, 1930), Ch. 1. See also *The British Empire: Its Structure, Its Unity, Its Strength* (New York: Dodd, Mead, 1940), Ch. 3.
14. "Canada and the Monroe Doctrine," *University Magazine*, 8 (October 1909), 369-70.
15. *Elements*, p. 259.
16. For a strong statement of this point, see Leacock's *Our Heritage of Liberty: Its Origin, Its Achievement, Its Crisis* (London: John Lane, 1942), *passim*. In *Sunshine Sketches*, Jefferson Thorpe's ill-fated investments in the New York–based Cuban Land Development Company represent one comic aspect of this imperial development.
17. Stephen Leacock, "The White House from Without In," *Further Foolishness* (London: John Lane, 1919), *passim*. See also "Father Knickerbocker: A Fantasy," *Frenzied Fiction* (Toronto: McClelland and Stewart, 1965), pp. 33-34.
18. *Further Foolishness, passim.*
19. "Canada and the Monarchy," *Atlantic Monthly*, 163, No. 6 (June 1939), 738.
20. *While There is Time: The Case Against Social Catastrophe* (Toronto: McClelland and Stewart, 1945), p. 39. For illuminating comments on the doctrine of vitalism in American social thought, see Michael Roe, *Nine Australian Progressives: Vitalism in Bourgeois Social Thought 1890-1960* (St. Lucia, Australia: University of Queensland Press, 1984), pp. 1-20.
21. *Canada: The Foundations of Its Future* (Montreal: privately printed, 1941), p. 244.
22. *Canada: The Foundations of Its Future*, pp. 244-45.
23. See *While There is Time* . . . , p. 29, for a more mildly worded formulation of the aims of this alliance.
24. "Canada and the Monarchy," p. 740.
25. *Canada: The Foundations of Its Future*, p. 225.
26. "Education and Empire Unity," *Empire Club Speeches*, ed. J. Castell Hopkins (Toronto: William Briggs, 1907), pp. 285-86.
27. "Empire and Education," p. 288.
28. *While There is Time*, p. 44.
29. *Elements*, Ch. 6.
30. *The British Empire: Its Structure, Its Unity, Its Strength*, p. 234.
31. "Canada and the Monarchy," pp. 742-43.
32. *Canada: The Foundations of Its Future*, p. 216.
33. *The British Empire: Its Structure, Its Unity, Its Strength*, Ch. 7.
34. *Humor: Its Theory and Technique* (Toronto: Dodd, Mead, 1935), p. 199.

35. *My Remarkable Uncle*, pp. 92-99.
36. "Germany From Within Out," *Further Foolishness*, pp. 121-34.
37. *The Canadian Mercury* (December 1928), p. 9.

RASPORICH **Stephen Leacock, Humorist**

1.   Stephen Leacock, *The Greatest Pages of American Humour* (London: Methuen & Co., 1937), p. 25.
2.   Stephen Leacock, "Literature and Education in America," *Essays and Literary Studies* (London: John Lane, Bodley Head, 1917), p. 55.
3.   Stephen Leacock, "American Humour," *Essays and Literary Studies*, p. 85.
4.   Ralph L. Curry, *Stephen Leacock: Humorist and Humanist* (New York: Doubleday, 1959), p. 7.
5.   Stephen Leacock, "Canada Won't Go Yankee," *American Mercury*, 39 (September 1936), 40.
6.   Claude Bissell, "Haliburton, Leacock and the American Humorous Tradition," *Canadian Literature*, 39 (Winter 1969), 5.
7.   Stephen Leacock, *The Boy I Left Behind Me* (London: Bodley Head, 1947), p. 58.
8.   Stephen Leacock, *The Greatest Pages of American Humour*, pp. 126-27.
9.   Stephen Leacock, *The Greatest Pages of American Humour*, p. 107.
10. Constance Rourke, *American Humor* (New York: Harcourt, Brace, 1931), p. 209.
11. Stephen Leacock, *Happy Stories* (New York: Dodd, Mead, 1943), p. 155.
12. Stephen Leacock, *My Remarkable Uncle* (New York: Dodd, Mead, 1942), p. 5.
13. Stephen Leacock, *Happy Stories*, p. 155.
14. Constance Rourke, *American Humor*, p. 131.
15. See R. E. Watters, Introduction to James de Mille, *A Strange Manuscript Found in a Copper Cylinder* (Toronto: McClelland and Stewart, rpt. 1969), p. x.
16. Stephen Leacock, *Humor: Its Theory and Technique* (Toronto: Dodd, Mead, 1935), p. 104.
17. Constance Rourke, *American Humor*, p. 11.
18. Stephen Leacock, *The Greatest Pages of American Humour*, p. 98.
19. Constance Rourke explains that in Twain's humorous stories, manner was everything. She quotes him as saying, "The humorous story is American, the comic story is English, the witty story is French. The humorous story depends for its effect upon the *manner* of telling; the comic story and the witty story upon the matter." *American Humor*, p. 211. A good example of the puritan manner in Twain is "Abelard and Heloise."
20. Stephen Leacock, *Literary Lapses* (Toronto: McClelland and Stewart, 1910, rpt. 1971), p. 100.
21. Stephen Leacock, *Winnowed Wisdom* (Toronto: McClelland and Stewart, 1971), Author's Preface.
22. See Beverly Rasporich, "The Leacock Persona and the Canadian Character," *Mosaic*, 14, No. 2 (Spring 1981), 77-92.
23. James Austin, *Artemus Ward* (New Haven: Twayne, 1964), p. 115.
24. Silver Donald Cameron, *Faces of Leacock* (Toronto: The Ryerson Press, 1967), p. 93.
25. Stephen Leacock, *My Discovery of England* (New York: Dodd, Mead, 1922), p. 3.
26. Stephen Leacock, *The Greatest Pages of American Humour*, p. 71.
27. Stephen Leacock, *Essays and Literary Studies*, p. 104.
28. Stephen Leacock, *Literary Lapses*, p. 15.
29. Gordon Roper, S. Ross Beharriell, and Rupert Schieder, "Writers of Fiction (1880-1920)," in *Literary History of Canada* (Toronto: University of Toronto Press, 1965), p. 335.
30. Bill Nye, cited in Stephen Leacock, *The Greatest Pages of American Humour*, p. 156.
31. Stephen Leacock, *Nonsense Novels* (New York: Dodd, Mead, 1963), p. 56.
32. Dwight G. Macdonald, *Parodies: An Anthology from Chaucer to Beerbohm and After* (New York: 1960), p. xiii.
33. Stephen Leacock, *The Greatest Pages of American Humour*, p. 108.

34. Stephen Leacock, *Winsome Winnie* (New York: Dodd, Mead, 1923), p. 70.
35. Stephen Leacock, *Humor: Its Theory and Technique*, pp. 123, 141.
36. Artemus Ward, cited in *The Wit and Humor of America*, Vol. I, ed. Marshall P. Wilder (New York: Funk and Wagnalls, 1907), p. iii.
37. *The Wit and Humor of America*, Vol. III, p. 508.
38. Stephen Leacock, *Further Foolishness* (London: John Lane, 1919), pp. 83-84.
39. Stephen Leacock, *How to Write* (New York: Dodd, Mead, 1943), p. 123.
40. Leacock wrote an interesting essay on Lewis Carroll in which he admires Carroll's talent for nonsense—i.e., *The Hunting of the Snark*—and the queer process of his (Carroll's) brain: "something, half-suggested, a peculiar power to write half an idea, which the reader half-gets" but he worries about the writer's equally queer fondness for little girls. See "Alice Walks in Wonderland" in *Last Leaves* (Toronto: McClelland and Stewart, 1945).
41. Stephen Leacock, *Nonsense Novels*, p. 59.
42. George Ade, cited in Stephen Leacock, *Laugh With Leacock* (Toronto: McClelland and Stewart, 1931), p. v.
43. Stephen Leacock, *My Discovery of England*, p. vii.

LYNCH   Religion and Romance in Mariposa

1. See Douglas Spettigue, "A Partisan Reading of Leacock," *The Literary Half-Yearly*, 13 (July 1972), 171-80, who does discuss a few of the organizational similarities between *Sunshine Sketches* and *Arcadian Adventures with the Idle Rich*.
2. See "*Sunshine Sketches*: Mariposa Versus Mr. Smith," *Studies in Canadian Literature*, 9, No. 2 (1984), 169-205.
3. See the following for positive appraisals of Smith's role in the *Sketches*: Desmond Pacey, "Leacock as a Satirist," *Queen's Quarterly*, 58 (Summer 1951), 213; Donald Cameron, *Faces of Leacock* (Toronto: Ryerson, 1967), p. 127; J. Kushner and R. D. Macdonald, "Leacock: Economist/Satirist in *Arcadian Adventures* and *Sunshine Sketches*," *Dalhousie Review*, 56 (Autumn 1976), 506; and William H. Magee, "Genial Humour in Stephen Leacock," *Dalhousie Review*, 56 (Summer 1976), 277-78.
4. *Sunshine Sketches of a Little Town* (Toronto: Bell & Cockburn; London: John Lane, 1912), p. 34. References hereafter cited in text.
5. "A Strange Aesthetic Ferment," *Canadian Literature*, 68-69 (Spring-Summer 1976), 17.
6. *Last Leaves* (New York: Dodd, Mead, 1945), p. 106.
7. See Desmond Bowen, *The Idea of the Victorian Church* (Montreal: McGill University Press, 1968), pp. 55-67.
8. *How To Write* (New York: Dodd, Mead, 1943), p. 106.
9. Preface, *Humour and Humanity* (London: Thornton Butterworth, 1937), n.p.
10. *My Remarkable Uncle* (New York: Dodd, Mead, 1942), pp. 206-207.
11. *The Victorian Temper* (London: Frank Cass, 1952), p. 234.

THOMAS   The Roads Back

1. Stephen Leacock, *Sunshine Sketches of a Little Town* (Toronto: McClelland and Stewart, 1960).
2. George Elliott, *The Kissing Man* (Toronto: Macmillan, 1962).
3. William L. Riordan, *Plunkitt of Tammany Hall: A Series of Very Plain Talks on Very Practical Politics*, Introduction by Arthur Mann (New York: Dutton, 1963). I am indebted to John Thomas, Dept. of History, York University, for bringing to my attention Riordan's *Plunkitt*.
4. *Plunkitt*, p. 3.
5. Sherwood Anderson, *Winesburg, Ohio* (New York: Penguin, 1976), pp. 23-24.

JEWINSKI   **Untestable Inferences**

1.   D. J. Dooley, *Moral Vision in the Canadian Novel* (Toronto: Clarke, Irwin, 1979), p. 5.
2.   Stephen Leacock, *Sunshine Sketches of a Little Town* (Toronto: McClelland and Stewart, 1960), hereafter cited as *Sketches*. The suicide of Fizzlechip (*Sketches*, p. 29), the death of the child Willie Yodel (*Sketches*, p. 57), and the death in war of Neil Pepperleigh (*Sketches*, p. 91) are three examples of the darkness brooding in the shadows of the "sunshine" of these sketches.
3.   The notion of "differance" as used here is most concisely clarified by Jacques Derrida in his chapter entitled "Differance" in *Margins of Philosophy*, trans. Alan Bass (Chicago: The University of Chicago Press, 1982), pp. 1-28.
4.   Paul de Man, *Allegories of Reading: Figural Language in Rousseau, Nietzsche, Rilke, and Proust* (New Haven, Conn.: Yale University Press, 1979), p. 9.
5.   Jacques Derrida discusses the matter of "problematics" in "Structure, Sign and Play" in *The Structuralist Controversy*, ed. R. Mackesey and E. Donato (Baltimore: The Johns Hopkins University Press, 1972), pp. 247-64. I refer to this book because it has been the most influential of the works introducing Derrida and "deconstruction" to North American readers.

CONTRIBUTORS

GLENN CLEVER — Department of English
University of Ottawa

RALPH L. CURRY — Department of English
Georgetown College
Georgetown, Kentucky

TIMOTHY FINDLEY — Novelist and playwright
Cannington, Ontario

MYRON J. FRANKMAN — Department of Economics
McGill University

ED JEWINSKI — Department of English
Wilfrid Laurier University

ALEC LUCAS — Department of English
McGill University

GERALD LYNCH — Department of English
University of Ottawa

R. L. MCDOUGALL — Department of English
Carleton University

BEVERLY RASPORICH — Faculty of General Studies
University of Calgary

ERIKA RITTER — Essayist and playwright
Toronto, Ontario

IAN ROSS ROBERTSON — Department of History
Scarborough College
University of Toronto

MALCOLM ROSS — Department of English
Dalhousie University

DAVID STAINES — Department of English
University of Ottawa

JAMES STEELE — Department of English
Carleton University

CLARA THOMAS — Department of English
York University

GUY VANDERHAEGHE — Novelist
Saskatoon, Saskatchewan

REAPPRAISALS: Canadian Writers

This series is the outcome of symposia on Canadian writers presented by the Department of English, University of Ottawa. The object is to make permanently available the criticism and evaluation of writers as presented by scholars and literary figures at the symposia. Where considered significant by the editor, additional critical articles and bibliographical material are included.

Lorraine McMullen
General Editor

Other titles in the series:

THE GROVE SYMPOSIUM, edited and with an introduction by John Nause

THE A.M. KLEIN SYMPOSIUM, edited and with an introduction by Seymour Mayne

THE LAMPMAN SYMPOSIUM, edited and with an introduction by Lorraine McMullen

THE E.J. PRATT SYMPOSIUM, edited and with an introduction by Glenn Clever

THE ISABELLA VALANCY CRAWFORD SYMPOSIUM, edited and with an introduction by Frank M. Tierney

THE DUNCAN CAMPBELL SCOTT SYMPOSIUM, edited and with an introduction by K. P. Stich

THE ETHEL WILSON SYMPOSIUM, edited and with an introduction by Lorraine McMullen

THE CALLAGHAN SYMPOSIUM, edited and with an introduction by David Staines

TRANSLATION IN CANADIAN LITERATURE, edited and with an introduction by Camille La Bossière

THE CHARLES G.D. ROBERTS SYMPOSIUM, edited and with an introduction by Glenn Clever

THE THOMAS CHANDLER HALIBURTON SYMPOSIUM, edited and with an introduction by Frank M. Tierney

DUE DATE

FEB 2 2 1993			
FEB 2 0 1996			
MAR 4 1996			
MAR 1 7			
APR 1 1997			
FEB 2 1999			
NOV 2 7 2002			
			Printed in USA